International Debt Report 2023

International Debt Report 2023

Contents

Foreword

The *International Debt Report 2023* arrives at a time of rising fears about unsustainable debt in developing countries. As these countries grapple with an array of destabilizing economic forces, the poorest among them are at increasing risk of tumbling into a debt crisis.

Today, one of every four developing countries is effectively priced out of international capital markets. In the past three years alone, the number of sovereign debt defaults in these countries has surged to 18, outstripping the total of the previous two decades. For the poorest countries, debt has become a nearly paralyzing burden: 28 countries eligible to borrow from the World Bank's International Development Association (IDA) are now at high risk of debt distress. Eleven are in distress.

These developments constitute a grave danger to prospects for progress on global development goals. Developing countries today also confront higher energy prices, steeper interest rates, and geopolitical turmoil in key regions of the world. It is a combustible mix—not unlike the conditions 50 years ago that prompted the World Bank to take a crucial step to advance debt transparency across the world.

In 1973, having established the Debtor Reporting System (DRS) two decades earlier to monitor the debt of our borrowers, we decided the time had come to use it as a public force for good—to guide sustainable financing to advance development in developing countries. Debt crises tend to recur. The surest way to prevent them is to adopt preemptive policies. But that requires accurate, timely, and comprehensive data. So we began to publish an annual report outlining key trends in the debt of all World Bank borrowers.

Today, our International Debt Statistics database has become the most comprehensive publicly available source of comparable cross-country data on the external debt of developing countries. This year marks the debt report's 50th consecutive year of publication. With this edition, we have expanded its analytical scope. The report now goes beyond strict reporting of the latest debt data. It also features analysis of emerging trends in debt management and debt transparency.

International Debt Report 2023 sounds an alarm about the danger confronting low- and middle-income countries—particularly the poorest. In 2022, the latest year for which data are available, low- and middle-income countries paid a record US$443.5 billion to service their external public and publicly guaranteed debt. In a time of pinched government budgets, these payments diverted spending away from health, education, and other critical needs.

Debt servicing costs on public and publicly guaranteed debt are projected to grow by 10 percent for all developing countries over the 2023–24 period—and by nearly 40 percent for low-income countries. Countries eligible to borrow from IDA are likely to face a rough ride in the coming years: interest payments on their total external debt stock have quadrupled since 2012, to an all-time high of US$23.6 billion. These payments are consuming an ever-larger share of export revenues, putting some countries just one shock away from a debt crisis. More than a third of this debt involves variable interest rates that could rise suddenly.

Besides the steeper interest rates that all countries are paying on their debt, the poorest face an additional burden: the accumulated principal, interest, and fees they incurred for the privilege of debt service suspension under the Group of Twenty's Debt Service Suspension Initiative. The exact costs of that privilege will not be known until the data are reported in 2024. But it is safe to say the costs will not be small—and poor countries will need more global help to ease their debt than they are receiving now.

This report makes it clear who has—and who has not—thrown a lifeline to countries struggling to meet key development objectives. As interest rates climbed in advanced economies, private creditors followed the money in 2022: they largely withdrew from developing countries, pulling out US$185 billion more in principal repayments than they disbursed in loans. That marked the first time since 2015 that they have withdrawn more funds than they put into developing countries.

The World Bank, along with other multilateral development banks, stepped in to help close the gap. Multilateral creditors provided a record US$115 billion in new financing for developing countries in 2022, nearly half of which came from the World Bank. For many countries—particularly the poorest—multilateral creditors were the primary source of new financing in 2022. Through IDA, the World Bank provided US$16.9 billion more in new financing for these countries than it received in principal repayments—nearly three times the comparable number a decade ago. In addition, the World Bank disbursed US$6.1 billion in grants to these countries, three times the amount in 2012.

Over the remainder of this decade, full disclosure of public debt data will remain as critical to sustainable borrowing and rules-based lending practices as it was 50 years ago. Ensuring such transparency is seldom straightforward. It is painstaking work. It demands steady engagement with borrowers, creditors, and academia to identity and close gaps. It calls for building and maintaining debt reporting systems that can stay abreast of the rapidly changing landscape of domestic and international creditors. We hope that reports like this will lead to greater transparency in reporting and will facilitate sharper analytics and improved debt sustainability.

Indermit S. Gill
Senior Vice President and Chief Economist
The World Bank Group

Acknowledgments

This volume was prepared by the World Bank's Debt Statistics Team of the Development Data Group, led by Evis Rucaj and comprising Parul Agarwal, Ogma Dessirama Bale, Arzu Aytekin Balibek, Kifaye Didem Bayar, Matthew Benjamin, Sylvie Kabaziga Bishweka, Wendy Huang, Chineze Olive Okafor, Malvina Pollock, Rubena Sukaj, Tin Yu To, Rasiel Vellos, and Bedri Zymeri. The work was carried out under the management of Nada Hamadeh and the direction of Haishan Fu. The team was assisted by Nancy Kebe.

The overview was prepared by the Debt Statistics Team, with contributions from Sebastian Andreas Horn from the Development Economics Vice Presidency; David Mihalyi and Diego Rivetti with guidance from Frederico Gil Sander from the Macroeconomics, Trade and Investment Global Practice; Xubei Luo from the Development Finance Vice Presidency; and Hayley Marie Pallan and Naotaka Sugawara with guidance from M. Ayhan Kose and Carlos Arteta from the Development Economics Prospects Group.

Valuable guidance was provided by Indermit S. Gill, senior vice president and chief economist of the World Bank Group, and Haishan Fu, chief statistician of the World Bank and director of the Development Data Group. Valuable feedback was provided by Brian R. Pinto, former senior advisor at the World Bank. The Development Economics Vice Presidency; Macroeconomics, Trade and Investment Global Practice; Development Finance Vice Presidency; and Development Economics Prospects Group of the World Bank provided helpful feedback on the overview section. The final statistics were reviewed by country economists from the Macroeconomics, Trade and Investment Global Practice.

The cover was designed by Parul Agarwal and Bill Pragluski. Mark McClure, Jewel McFadden, and Orlando Mota coordinated the publication and dissemination of this volume. Kristin Milhollin, Joseph Rebello, and Shane Kimo Romig managed the communications surrounding the release.

The accompanying International Debt Statistics electronic products were prepared with support from a team led by Sebastian Ariel Dolber, Ramgopal Erabelly, and Kunal Patel, and comprising Yuliyan Nikolaev Bogdanov, Rajesh Kumar Danda, Svetoslava Georgieva Dimitrova, Debora Manandhar, Vijayakumar Juttu Mohan, Gangadhar Simhani, and Tsvetelina Nikolova Stefanova.

Introduction: International Debt Statistics at 50—Past, Present, and Future

The *International Debt Report 2023* is the 50th edition of the World Bank's annual publication on external debt along with the International Debt Statistics (IDS) database,[1] the most comprehensive and transparent source of verifiable, cross-country comparable external debt data of low- and middle-income countries (LMICs).

Much has changed over 50 years. Yet there are many similarities between 1973, the first year the World Bank publicly disseminated the data it collected through its Debtor Reporting System (DRS) on the external debt obligations of its borrowers, and now. Much like this year, 1973 was marked by a challenging global economy with multiple destabilizing forces. The Bretton Woods international monetary system had recently been abandoned. An oil crisis began that generated inflation through higher energy and commodity prices and threw the world economy into recession.

Total World Bank lending reached US$3.6 billion that year—higher than any previous year. It achieved a goal set by World Bank President Robert McNamara to double World Bank–provided assistance in 1969–73 over the previous five-year period.

Today the world is emerging from a pandemic that shook economies, disrupted international trade, and ignited global inflation. LMICs in particular are struggling with the effects of an ongoing war in Europe, rising energy prices, sharply higher interest rates, and slowing growth. World Bank Group loans, grants, and guarantees have grown to more than US$128 billion and are as critical as ever to the World Bank's central mission of ending extreme poverty on a livable planet. Fifty years on, however, one challenge remains the same: debt levels and debt servicing costs are rising in many LMICs—fueling fears of impending debt crises.

In 1973, the World Bank stood out as an early champion of debt transparency by recognizing that public debt should be publicly disclosed and that debt statistics drawn from the DRS constituted an important public good. The World Bank committed to an annual publication on debt, accompanied by the dissemination of a database that provides comprehensive and timely information on the external debt stocks and flows of LMICs.

The World Bank remains steadfast in that commitment today. In fact, the World Bank is now better equipped to disseminate accurate, verifiable, and transparent data about external debt held by LMICs. Over the past 50 years, its annual publication on debt has undergone numerous improvements and name changes. Multiple expansions of DRS reporting requirements have ensured that data collected have kept pace with the ever-changing landscape of international finance for LMICs and continue to meet the evolving needs of policy makers and the broader international community.

History of the DRS

To understand how the *International Debt Report* arrived at its current form, it is worth reviewing the history of the World Bank's collection and dissemination of external debt data and how those processes have changed through the years.

The World Bank began collecting data on the external debt obligations of its borrowers in the 1950s. Instituted in 1951, the DRS made the provision of detailed, loan-by-loan information of all public and publicly guaranteed long-term external debt a condition of borrowing from the International Bank for Reconstruction and Development. This information was seen as both essential input to the Bank's macroeconomic analyses and an assurance to its bondholders that the creditworthiness of the countries to which it lent was being closely monitored. The requirement was extended to borrowing from the International Development Association (IDA) when it was established in 1960. By the mid-1960s, the Economics Department of the World Bank was drawing on DRS data to produce regular debt reports and support a burgeoning body of research on debt-related issues.

The first major expansion of the DRS reporting requirement came in 1970, when reporting of private nonguaranteed external debt was initiated. This development reflected the emergence in some of the World Bank's more advanced borrowers of private sector entities that were sufficiently creditworthy to borrow externally without the need for a guarantee from the sovereign or other public entity.

The new directive required aggregate reporting of private nonguaranteed debt stocks and flows, grouped by type of financing. Initially, many countries resisted the new requirements on the grounds that these data could not be obtained without the introduction of formal exchange controls, would raise private sector concerns about government interference, and could incentivize misreporting. Nevertheless, private nonguaranteed debt currently constitutes about 45 percent of the total long-term external debt of LMICs, and these data are routinely reported to the DRS.

A Sea Change

Initially, the World Bank used the debt data it collected solely for internal purposes. A sea change came in 1973 with the publication of *World Debt Tables,* which marked the first in an unbroken 50-year series of external debt data publications.

Mexico's announcement in 1982 that it would default on its external debt sparked a debt crisis that swept the globe. Over the ensuing decade, two-thirds of DRS reporting countries were forced to reschedule their external debt, most on multiple occasions. The DRS had begun to collect information on restructured debt service payments in the late 1970s, but the reporting requirement around debt restructuring expanded significantly in the 1980s and thereafter. The additional DRS reporting requirements paralleled the multiplicity of innovations that emerged from the debt restructuring process, including discounted buybacks, collateralized bonds, debt reduction measured in terms of present value, and a range of debt swap mechanisms. The overview section of the World Bank's annual publication on debt also expanded to include detailed analyses and quantification of each debt restructuring arrangement concluded with official and private creditors, in the process becoming the international community's recognized reference point for comprehensive and accurate information on debt restructuring.

The fall of the Berlin wall in 1989 and collapse of the Soviet bloc in 1991 had important ramifications for the world and for the World Bank. In the three-year period 1990–92, 24 East European and former Soviet republics joined the World Bank. Most became borrowers and had to be absorbed into the DRS. During this period, LMICs also began to shift from manual debt recording and reporting systems to computerized debt management platforms. In 1985, only 10 countries reported to the DRS electronically. By 2000, this number had swelled to over half of DRS reporting countries. World Bank staff managing the DRS played a major role both in facilitating the new reporting norms and in ensuring that standards, definitions, and recording principles in the debt management software accorded with international standards and reporting requirements.

The 2000s was a decade marked by the delivery of widespread debt reduction for the world's poorest countries. Endorsement of the enhanced Heavily Indebted Poor Countries (HIPC) Initiative by the boards of the World Bank and the International Monetary Fund in the fall of 1999 accelerated the process launched in 1996 to reduce the debt of the poorest countries to sustainable levels. Since then, 36 eligible countries have reached the HIPC Completion Point and received substantive debt relief through the HIPC Initiative and the Multilateral Debt Relief Initiative established in 2005. Measuring the level of debt relief required, and its impact, was challenged by weak debt management capacity in almost all HIPC-eligible countries and poor or nonexistent recording of prior restructuring arrangements. Meeting the widespread demand both internally and from the international community for an accurate and comprehensive database for all HIPC-eligible countries, reflecting external debt stock and debt service before and after debt relief, was a core priority for the DRS.

The decade following the global financial crisis of 2008 was marked by a surge in borrowing by LMICs, fueled by unprecedented low interest rates and the emergence of nontraditional creditors. This surge was accompanied by an array of more complex lending instruments; a sharp increase in contingent debt liabilities associated with nonguaranteed borrowing by state-owned enterprises, public-private partnerships, and special purpose vehicles; and the rising importance of borrowing in domestic debt markets.

The focus of the DRS was twofold: first, validation of data reported by borrowers on which the accuracy and comprehensiveness of IDS depend, in order to eliminate data discrepancies and gaps; and second, expansion in the scope of the data set to provide a comprehensive breakdown by sector of borrower. To this end, the DRS drew extensively on the data reported by borrowers to the joint International Monetary Fund–World Bank Quarterly External Debt Statistics and Quarterly Public Sector Debt, managed in parallel with the DRS. It also now maintains a regular dialogue with national debt managers and draws on all available borrower and creditor publications to identify potential data gaps.

As a result of these changes and improvements, the debt data the World Bank now disseminates are granular to an extent that earlier users would find unrecognizable. The IDS database stands as the most extensive and transparent source of verifiable, cross-country comparable external debt data of LMICs.

Yet much more still needs to be done.

Moving Forward

The total debt stock in LMICs has been on an upward trajectory since 2016 and surged in the wake of the COVID-19 pandemic. Over the past decade, debt accumulation in LMICs has also outpaced economic growth, raising serious concerns about the ability to service that debt. The situation is more acute in the poorest countries eligible for IDA resources; those countries have accumulated debt at a faster pace than other LMICs.

Today, debt servicing burdens remain sizeable in LMICs and are poised to grow. The cost of servicing external debt in 2023–24 is expected to rise significantly from that in the previous two years, and the cost for low-income countries is projected to be much higher still. These projected increases in debt service take place against a backdrop of rising global interest rates and largely unfavorable exchange rate movements. Servicing external debt could, therefore, become increasingly burdensome for many countries in coming years and could crowd out spending on other priorities.

As a result, disclosure of public debt data is as critical to sustainable borrowing and lending practices today as it was when the first World Bank report on external debt was published 50 years ago. And, although the DRS and the *International Debt Report* have improved immeasurably over the years, plans are already laid to make further enhancements.

DRS priorities to be implemented over the next two to three years center on reformulating the DRS to fully reflect current borrowing patterns in LMICs and the plethora of new lending instruments, in addition to expanding the reporting requirement to support current data needs. The most important and far-reaching element will be responding to calls to extend the coverage of the DRS reporting requirement to the domestic component of public debt to reflect its increasing importance in LMICs' overall debt portfolios. Efforts to close data gaps to enhance data quality and coverage remain an ongoing imperative, with a particular emphasis on achieving loan-by-loan coverage of the external obligations of state-owned enterprises in which the government holds a share of 50 percent or more. These obligations may not have an explicit guarantee from the sovereign government, but they nevertheless constitute an implicit contingent liability for the central government.

The platform that has long been used to record and disseminate data captured through the DRS is now being replaced with a state-of-the-art cloud-based system to accommodate all the new data requirements, allow for faster and easier electronic transfer of DRS reports from national debt systems, and provide users of the IDS database expanded access and the capability to extract customized reports to support policy making, research, and analysis.

Despite the many changes in international borrowing and lending over the past five decades, the priorities and objectives of the DRS remain constant. First and foremost, they are to assist DRS reporters in compiling and disclosing comprehensive, accurate, and timely public debt data. Second, they aim to ensure that the information the World Bank collects and disseminates in the IDS database reflects the current needs of policy makers and the broader international community. Finally, they spearhead the agenda for debt transparency that the World Bank has long recognized as the key to sustainable public borrowing and accountable rules-based lending practices.

Note

1. For more about the IDS database, see https://www.worldbank.org/en/programs/debt-statistics.

Key Takeaways

Over the past decade, the rise in the external debt stock of low- and middle-income countries (LMICs) has outpaced economic growth, raising concerns about these countries' ability to service their debt. The situation is especially worrisome in the poorest countries that are eligible for International Development Association (IDA) resources, where external debt stocks have risen at an even faster pace than other LMICs. This decade-long asymmetry between economic growth and debt accumulation has created or exacerbated debt vulnerabilities in many LMICs, and actions to address these vulnerabilities have become increasingly more urgent. Currently, about 60 percent of IDA-eligible countries are assessed at high risk of debt distress or are already in debt distress.

Key takeaways from the 2022 data include the following:

- External debt stock of LMICs fell in 2022 for the first time since 2015, decreasing by 3.4 percent, to US$9.0 trillion in 2022 from US$9.3 trillion in 2021. The decrease was due to negative debt flows (disbursements minus principal repayments) and the appreciation of the US dollar against other major currencies in which external debt of LMICs is denominated. Long-term and short-term debt stocks fell at much the same pace, with the decline in long-term external debt stocks due primarily to the 5.0 percent decrease in obligations to private creditors. The combined external debt stock of IDA-eligible countries rose 2.7 percent in 2022 to an all-time high of US$1.1 trillion, more than double the 2012 level.
- Total net debt flows (loan disbursements minus principal repayments) to LMICs turned negative in 2022 for the first time since 2015 to outflows of US$185 billion, a stark contrast to inflows of US$556 billion recorded in 2021. Both short- and long-term debt flows were negative in 2022—US$90.6 billion and US$94.5 billion, respectively—with long-term debt flows at a record low and negative for the first time since the beginning of the millennium. The fall in net long-term debt inflows was due entirely to the US$189 billion outflow from private creditors, reflecting a sharp retrenchment in bond issuance by sovereigns and other public and private sector borrowers. Tighter monetary policy in advanced economies to curb inflation raised borrowing costs, pricing some LMICs out of the markets, and offered investors attractive returns in the US and European bond markets. As a result, there was a net outflow of US$127.1 billion from LMICs to bondholders in 2022, compared to an average annual inflow of $202 billion in 2019–21.
- The ratio of total external debt stock to gross national income (GNI) for LMICs declined by 2 percentage points in 2022, to 24 percent. This decline resulted from an increase in the US dollar value of LMICs' combined GNI, which rose 5.8 percent in 2022, to US$37.4 trillion, a rebound in economic growth and a 3.4 percent fall in external debt stock.
- Over the past decade, low-income countries accumulated external debt at a faster rate than middle-income countries. The debt stock of low-income countries increased by 109 percent from 2012 to 2022, whereas GNI rose 33 percent. In contrast, in middle-income countries external debt stock rose 58 percent, only moderately more than GNI, which increased by 51 percent. In IDA-eligible countries, external debt stock accumulation significantly

outpaced GNI growth from 2012–22, increasing 134 percent compared to a 53 percent rise in GNI over the same period.

- New external loan commitments plummeted in 2022 and recorded the largest decline in a decade. New commitments to public and publicly guaranteed sector entities fell in 2022 for a second consecutive year, decreasing 23 percent to US$372 billion to their lowest level since 2011. The principal driver was the 33 percent fall in new commitments from private creditors to US$218 billion, their lowest level since 2011, with the decline from bondholders the most drastic. New bonds issuance by LMICs in international markets dropped to US$114 billion, less than half the level of issuance in 2021, and new bond issuance by IDA-eligible countries fell by more than three-quarters to US$3.1 billion.

- An important exception was new commitments by multilateral creditors, which rose 1.5 percent in 2022 to US$115.6 billion. Multilateral creditors continued to step up and partly offset the decline in lending from private creditors. New commitments from the World Bank (International Bank for Reconstruction and Development and IDA) rose a further 1.3 percent in 2022, to US$53.5 billion, equivalent to 46 percent of new commitments by all multilateral institutions and an all-time high. For many countries, including most of the world's poorest, multilateral lenders were the primary source of new external financing in 2022.

- Public and publicly guaranteed (PPG) debt service payments by LMICs (including the International Monetary Fund) totaled US$443.5 billion in 2022, the highest level in history, and are forecast to continue to grow. Debt service on PPG external debt alone is expected to rise 10 percent in 2023–24 from the previous two years. This increase takes place during a time of rising interest rates and largely unfavorable exchange rate movements, which exacerbated the fiscal burden of external debt service payments.

- As a result, servicing external debt could become increasingly burdensome for many LMICs and could crowd out spending on other priorities.

In addition to the release of the 2022 external debt data in the newly updated online International Debt Statistics database, this edition of the *International Debt Report*

- Provides analysis of the debt situation of LMICs and rising debt vulnerabilities against the backdrop of global monetary and fiscal tightening;
- Presents forward-looking analyses of the debt-related challenges LMICs face and the public and external debt burdens that may evolve in the context of prospects for growth in 2023 and beyond;
- Draws on outcomes of the IDA Sustainable Development Finance Policy to show how it is catalyzing greater debt transparency and enhancing comprehensive and timely reporting to the Debtor Reporting System;
- Discusses the need for innovative approaches to debt management in LMICs and the value that World Bank debt data can bring to this process; and
- Explores how the wealth of information in the International Debt Statistics database could help create an early warning system for debt distress in LMICs.

Abbreviations

AfDB	African Development Bank
AFESD	Arab Fund for Economic and Social Development
BADEA	Arab Bank for Economic Development in Africa
BCIE	Central American Bank for Economic Integration
BDEAC	Development Bank of the Central African States
CIBM	China Interbank Bond Market
DRS	Debtor Reporting System
DSEP	Debt Sustainability Enhancement Program
EIB	European Investment Bank
FDI	foreign direct investment
FTSE	Financial Times Stock Exchange
FY	fiscal year
GDP	gross domestic product
GNI	gross national income
HIPC	Heavily Indebted Poor Countries
IBRD	International Bank for Reconstruction and Development
IDA	International Development Association
IDB	Inter-American Development Bank
IDS	International Debt Statistics
IMF	International Monetary Fund
LIC DSF	Debt Sustainability Framework for Low-Income Countries
LMICs	low- and middle-income countries
MPA	multipronged approach
NPV	net present value
OPEC	Organization of the Petroleum Exporting Countries
PCO	Program of Creditor Outreach
PPA	Performance and Policy Action
PPG	public and publicly guaranteed debt
SDFP	Sustainable Development Finance Policy
SDRs	special drawing rights
SOE	state-owned enterprise
SSA	Sub-Saharan Africa

All dollar amounts are in US dollars unless otherwise indicated.

PART 1
Overview

1. Analyses of External Debt Stocks and Debt Flows as of End-2022

Trends in External Debt Stock, 2012–22

The external debt stock of low- and middle-income countries (LMICs) decreased by 3.4 percent, from US$9.3 trillion in 2021 to US$9.0 trillion in 2022 (figure 1.1). This decrease marked the first deviation from the upward debt trajectory that has characterized this group of countries since 2015. The external debt stock of countries eligible for International Development Association (IDA) resources, however, increased by 2.7 percent in 2022, to an all-time high of US$1.1 trillion.

Despite the slight decrease in 2022, the external debt stock of LMICs remained at unprecedented high levels following more than a decade of rapid debt accumulation. The main contributors to the 2022 decline were net debt outflows in combination with adjustments in the exchange rates between the currencies in which external debt is denominated and an appreciating US dollar.

The decrease in the external debt stock of LMICs expressed in US dollar terms was also the result of appreciation of the US dollar against many major currencies in 2022. As the US dollar climbed against the Chinese yuan, euro, Japanese yen, British pound, and many other currencies, debt stock denominated in these currencies shrank in 2022 when converted into US dollars. The US dollar climbed more than 14 percent against the yen, 9 percent against the yuan, 6 percent against the euro, and 5 percent against special drawing rights, because these four currencies made up the largest portions of IDA debt stock not denominated in US dollars. Although the appreciation of the US dollar translated into a fall in debt stock expressed in US dollar terms for IDA-eligible countries, it does not relieve the fiscal burden of external debt payments for borrowing countries. Debt service comes at a higher cost for a country if the national currency has depreciated against the denomination currency of the country's external debt obligations.

China, which accounted for more than a quarter (26.6 percent) of the combined end-2022 external debt stock of LMICs,

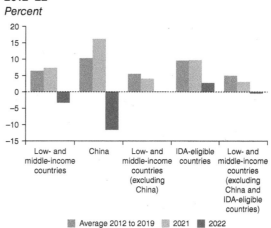

Figure 1.1 **Percent Change in External Debt Stocks of Low- and Middle-Income Countries, 2012–22**

Percent

Legend: Average 2012 to 2019 | 2021 | 2022

Source: World Bank International Debt Statistics database.
Note: IDA = International Development Association.

drove the trend (figure 1.2). In 2022, China's external debt stock declined 11.6 percent, to US$2.4 trillion. When China is excluded, the total external debt stock of LMICs remained broadly unchanged in 2022, reaching a record level of US$6.6 trillion, marginally above the end-2021 level and representing a much slower 0.04 percent accumulation. The external debt of LMICs continued to be heavily concentrated in 10 middle-income countries (not including China),[1] whose combined debt stock as of end-2022 accounted for 43 percent of the total external debt of LMICs. The total debt stock of these 10 borrowing countries declined 1.8 percent in 2022. This overall decline masked a wide divergence in external debt stock trends at the country level during 2022, ranging from a 7 percent increase for Colombia to a 20.3 percent decline for the Russian Federation.

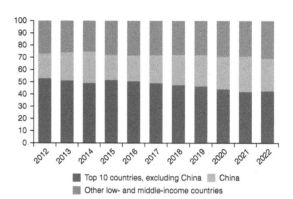

Figure 1.2 Share of External Debt Stocks of Low- and Middle-Income Countries, 2012–22
Percent

Legend: ■ Top 10 countries, excluding China ■ China ■ Other low- and middle-income countries

Source: World Bank International Debt Statistics database.
Note: The 10 largest borrowers are based on total external debt stock at end-2022. Excluding China, they are Argentina, Brazil, Colombia, India, Indonesia, Mexico, the Russian Federation, South Africa, Thailand, and Türkiye.

Excluding China, long-term public and publicly guaranteed (PPG) external debt stock—including use of International Monetary Fund credit and special drawing rights allocation (box 1.1)—of LMICs decreased marginally by 1 percent to US$3.3 trillion in 2022, equivalent to 51 percent of total external debt stock (figure 1.3). Long-term private nonguaranteed (PNG) external debt declined 2.6 percent to US$2.1 trillion, equivalent to 33 percent of total external debt stock. Both PPG and PNG debt stock were affected by a tightening of global financial conditions. During the last decade, the ratio of PPG external debt to total debt stock has

---

Box 1.1 Allocation of the IMF's Special Drawing Rights in 2022

In August 2021, the International Monetary Fund (IMF) made a general allocation of special drawing rights (SDRs) equivalent to US$650 billion. The newly created SDRs were credited to IMF members in proportion to their existing quotas in the Fund. The allocation's main purpose was to help mitigate the economic crisis created by the COVID-19 pandemic and to meet the long-term need to supplement members' existing reserve assets in a manner that avoided economic stagnation and deflation as well as excess demand and inflation (IMF 2021).

SDR allocations do not change a country's net wealth but do create an increase in long-term debt liabilities and a corresponding increase in gross international reserves (holdings of SDRs). Both transactions are reflected in balance-of-payments statistics and international investment positions (IMF 2009). In government finance statistics, SDR allocations are recorded as a long-term debt liability within public sector gross debt, with a corresponding entry for SDR holdings as a part of the public sector's financial assets (IMF 2014). Following these guidelines, the International Debt Statistics database records SDR allocations as part of long-term gross external public debt and identifies them separately.

SDR liabilities are not subject to debt limits in IMF programs because they do not fall within the definition of "debt" for program purposes under the Fund's Guidelines on Public Debt Conditionality in Fund Arrangements. SDR allocations are generally considered to have limited impact on debt sustainability, but that may depend on how they are used. New guidance issued in August 2021

(Box continues on next page)

Box 1.1 **Allocation of the IMF's Special Drawing Rights in 2022** (*continued*)

on incorporating SDR allocations into debt sustainability analyses addresses this issue and aims to better reflect the use of SDRs and the impact on debt sustainability (IMF 2021). In line with that guidance, the external debt stock figures in *International Debt Report 2023* (and related ratios to exports and gross national income) include SDR allocations. However, the measure of debt flows does not take SDR allocations into account. This approach differs from *International Debt Report 2022*, in which analyses of both external debt stocks and debt flows excluded SDR allocations.

Total outstanding SDR allocations of the 121 low- and middle-income countries included in *International Debt Report 2023* were US$260 billion at end-2022, equivalent on average to 10 percent of general government external debt stocks and 4 percent of international reserves, but with sharp divergences at the regional level (figure B1.1.1).

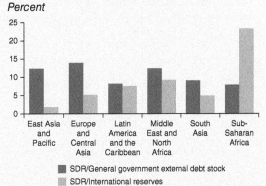

Figure B1.1.1 **SDR Allocations as a Share of General Government External Debt and International Reserves, by Region, 2022**
Percent

■ SDR/General government external debt stock
■ SDR/International reserves

Sources: World Bank Debtor Reporting System and International Monetary Fund.
Note: SDR = special drawing rights.

increased from 42 percent as of end-2012 to 51 percent at end-2022, whereas the share of PNG debt—affected by rising global uncertainty—decreased from 40 percent to 33 percent in 2022. Short-term debt increased by 9.7 percent in 2022, to US$1.1 trillion. See box 1.2 for a discussion of debt concepts, coverage, and the data sources used for this report.

The slight decrease in the long-term PPG external debt stock of LMICs, not including China, was partially offset by the resilience of multilateral creditors, whose debt stock position as of end-2022 increased 4 percent to US$1.2 trillion. Multilateral creditors played an even steadier role for IDA-eligible countries.

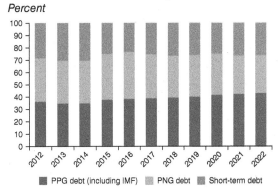

Figure 1.3 **Composition of Debt Stock in Low- and Middle-Income Countries, 2012–22**
Percent

■ PPG debt (including IMF) ■ PNG debt ■ Short-term debt

Source: World Bank International Debt Statistics database.
Note: IMF = International Monetary Fund; PNG = private nonguaranteed; PPG = public and publicly guaranteed.

Trends in External Debt Stock of IDA-Eligible Countries, 2012–22

In 2022, the external debt stock of IDA-eligible countries increased 2.7 percent to a record US$1.1 trillion, more than double the 2012 level (table 1.1). PPG debt stock, including the International Monetary Fund (IMF), increased 1.7 percent in 2022 to US$728 billion,

Table 1.1 External Debt Stock of IDA-Eligible Countries, 2012–22
US$ (billion)

	2012	2013	2014	2015	2016	2017	2018	2019	2020	2021	2022
Debt stock	457.9	512.1	556.1	597.0	634.4	735.0	786.3	857.0	949.8	1,042.1	1,070.5
Long-term	401.8	450.2	494.4	534.6	572.1	652.9	706.2	762.9	856.7	932.3	953.1
Official creditors	275.5	288.9	298.6	313.5	331.0	374.0	401.0	438.6	507.9	559.5	575.8
Bilateral creditors	102.6	109.9	118.6	128.0	137.8	154.6	170.6	185.4	203.8	214.0	213.2
Multilateral creditors	172.9	179.0	180.0	185.5	193.2	219.5	230.4	253.2	304.1	345.5	362.5
World Bank (IBRD and IDA)	72.5	78.0	80.0	83.3	87.3	100.4	107.2	118.4	136.9	143.7	152.3
IMF (Use of credit and SDR allocations)	33.5	31.3	29.2	29.5	29.7	31.9	31.4	32.9	50.0	79.7	79.4
Private creditors	126.3	161.3	195.8	221.1	241.1	278.9	305.3	324.3	348.8	372.8	377.4
Bonds	11.5	18.2	33.8	41.1	46.0	60.0	73.3	80.7	84.8	99.8	98.3
Banks and other private	114.8	143.1	162.0	180.0	195.0	218.9	232.0	243.7	264.0	273.0	279.1
Short-term	56.1	61.9	61.7	62.4	62.3	82.1	80.0	94.1	93.1	109.8	117.4
Memorandum item											
Long-term public and publicly guaranteed	306.3	331.5	356.9	382.4	405.2	470.1	515.3	564.6	646.8	716.2	728.1
Long-term private nonguaranteed	95.5	118.6	137.5	152.2	166.9	182.8	190.9	198.3	209.9	216.1	225.0

Source: World Bank International Debt Statistics database.
Note: IBRD = International Bank for Reconstruction and Development; IDA = International Development Association; IMF = International Monetary Fund; SDR = special drawing rights.

whereas PNG debt rose at a much faster pace, increasing 4.1 percent to US$225 billion. Viewed from a creditor perspective, the composition of long-term PPG debt stock of IDA-eligible countries was 50 percent owed to multilateral creditors, 29 percent to bilateral creditors, and 21 percent to private creditors. This mix has shifted somewhat since 2012, when these creditor groups accounted for 56 percent, 33 percent, and 10 percent, respectively.

Multilateral creditors' share of the total PPG debt stock of IDA-eligible countries declined from 56 percent in 2012 to 45 percent in 2019, before rising again during the COVID-19 pandemic (figure 1.4). Debt stock owed to the World Bank accounted for 42 percent of debt owed to multilateral creditors in 2022. Multilateral creditors have played an increasingly important role as lenders of last resort during the uncertain global economic environment of the last few years, whereas lending by other types of creditors remained steady or declined. PPG debt stock owed to multilateral creditors increased 4.9 percent to US$362.5 billion in 2022, and debt stock owed to bilateral creditors declined marginally by 0.4 percent to US$213 billion. The total debt stock owed to private creditors by public and private sector borrowers remained steady for the IDA-eligible countries, with a 1.2 percent increase to US$377.4 billion in 2022. The increase was driven by lending from commercial banks and other private creditors, which increased by 2.2 percent to US$279.1 billion in 2022, whereas the debt stock owed to bondholders fell 1.5 percent to US$98.3 billion.

Figure 1.4 Creditor Composition of Long-Term Public and Publicly Guaranteed External Debt for IDA-Eligible Countries, 2012–22
US$ (billion)

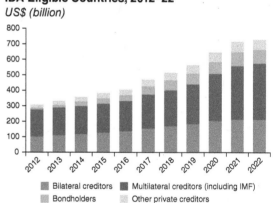

Source: World Bank International Debt Statistics database.
Note: IDA = International Development Association; IMF = International Monetary Fund.

Escalating debt vulnerabilities in many LMICs and overlapping crises—the COVID-19 pandemic, the war in Ukraine, devastating climate events, and the daunting global macroeconomic environment—are forcing an increasing number of countries to seek debt restructuring from external creditors. In 2022, multiple countries requested or concluded debt restructuring agreements in the context of the Group of Twenty Common Framework or the Paris Club, or with bondholders. Like the Paris Club, the Common Framework involves a case-by-case approach to reaching sovereign debt resolutions—with the support of and coordination by all bilateral creditors with claims on the country, and comparable treatment from private creditors.

Box 1.2 **External Debt Data: Concepts, Sources, and Coverage**

This report presents data and analysis on external debt for 121 low- and middle-income countries and Guyana. The primary source for these data is reports to the World Bank's Debtor Reporting System (DRS) from member countries that have received either International Bank for Reconstruction and Development loans or International Development Association credits and have outstanding obligations to the World Bank. The DRS, instituted in 1951, has its origins in the World Bank's need to monitor and assess the financial position of its borrowers. Comprehensive information on data sources and the methodology used to compile the statistics presented in this report can be found in the appendix under "Data Sources." The following describes the key concepts and data sources.

- The DRS follows international standards and defines *external debt* as the outstanding amount of actual current liabilities in both domestic and foreign currency that require payment(s) of principal and/or interest by the debtor at some point(s) in the future and that are owed to nonresidents by residents of an economy. The sum of principal and interest payments is defined as *debt service*.

- The *total external debt* of a country is the sum of public and publicly guaranteed (PPG) debt, private nonguaranteed (PNG) debt, and short-term debt.

- *PPG external debt* comprises long-term external obligations (maturities of over one year) of all public debtors, including debt held by the central government and state-owned enterprises. Data are collected on a loan-by-loan basis through the DRS. Reporting countries submit quarterly reports on new loan commitments and annual reports on loan status and transactions (new commitments, gross disbursements, principal, and interest payments).

- *PNG debt* comprises long-term external obligations of private debtors that are not guaranteed by a public entity. The DRS has covered private nonguaranteed debt since 1973; however, for this category of debt data, the annual status and transactions (gross disbursements, principal, and interest payments) are reported in aggregate.

- *Short-term debt* is defined as debt with an original maturity of one year or less and is not covered under DRS reporting requirements. However, most DRS reporters provide an annual report on outstanding short-term debt stocks on a voluntary basis. For countries that do not provide these data, information on their short-term debt is drawn from the Quarterly External Debt Statistics database, a joint World Bank–International Monetary Fund initiative, wherein data are compiled and reported by countries' central banks, along with data compiled by the Bank for International Settlements.

All debt data reported to the DRS are validated against—and, when appropriate, supplemented by—data from other sources. These additional data include the Balance of Payments and International Investment position statistics, Quarterly External Debt Statistics, information published on official government websites, reports from the International Monetary Fund, regional development banks, the Organisation for Economic Co-operation and Development, the Bank for International Settlements, and websites and annual publications of lending agencies.

Since the establishment of the Common Framework in 2020, four countries have applied for debt treatment under it: Chad, Ethiopia, Ghana, and Zambia. Chad was the first to conclude an agreement with its bilateral creditors in October 2022, and with private creditors, including Glencore PLC, shortly thereafter. The agreement with private creditors rescheduled US$1 billion over 12 years, including a two-year grace period at a reduced interest rate. Ghana's and Zambia's requests for debt relief followed default on their external debt obligations to bondholders. In 2023, Zambia reached a milestone agreement with bilateral creditors, including China, to restructure US$6.3 billion, paving the way for formal negotiations on restructuring of US$3 billion owed to bondholders.

In the Paris Club, Argentina and Suriname reached debt restructuring agreements in October and June 2022, respectively, and Sri Lanka is in the process of negotiating with creditors. Regarding Argentina, US$2 billion of arrears related to the 2014 agreement were restructured over a six-year period at a reduced interest rate. The agreement with Suriname restructured US$58 million in arrears and debt service payments due in 2023–24 over an extended 17- to 20-year period, with the provision for a stock rescheduling in 2025 subject to outcomes of the IMF program. Suriname also reached agreement with its bondholders in 2022 to reschedule US$600 million owed on its two outstanding dollar-denominated bonds to a new 10-year amortizing bond. Sri Lanka's economic collapse led to default on external debt obligations to both official and private creditors. Negotiations are ongoing with the two major bilateral creditors, China and India, and with bondholders.[2] In July 2023 the Sri Lankan government approved a domestic debt restructuring plan that will convert Treasury bills into longer-maturity Treasury bonds.

LMICs continue to be disproportionally affected by multiple shocks in an environment of elevated debt vulnerabilities. Timely, accurate, and transparent external debt data in the wake of the COVID-19 pandemic are of utmost importance. Comprehensive and systematic reconciliation of debtor and creditor records is an essential element of good debt management and the most effective and reliable way to validate debt data, resolve discrepancies, and close data gaps. To this end, in 2020, the World Bank took the lead in disseminating data that provide the creditor composition of LMICs' external debt. And, in 2022, calls for greater debt transparency continued under the Japanese presidency of the Group of Seven. The World Bank's Debtor Reporting System and Group of Seven member countries conducted an extensive data-sharing exercise, which was then extended on a voluntary basis to members of the Paris Club (IDA 2023).

Debt Indicators, 2012–22

Rebounding economic growth, along with robust export earnings—which reached an all-time high of US$10.1 trillion in 2022—have improved the debt indicators of LMICs. Nevertheless, over the last decade, the accumulation of external debt has outpaced LMICs' gross national income (GNI) growth and global trade, despite the recent rebound from the COVID-19 pandemic.

Economic growth continued to rebound for a second consecutive year after the contraction caused by the COVID-19 pandemic, despite the effects on countries of multiple crises that included unfavorable global financial conditions, the war in Ukraine, persistent inflationary pressures, high interest rates, and increasing debt servicing costs. The GNI of LMICs rose 5.8 percent in 2022, to US$37.4 trillion; GNI growth for these countries was 17.8 percent in the first year of recovery that followed the pandemic. See box 1.3 for a more detailed discussion of debt-to-GDP (gross domestic product) versus debt-to-GNI ratios. Consequently, as debt stock levels of LMICs decreased and growth rebounded, the ratio of external debt to GNI for all LMICs fell by 2 percentage points, to 24 percent, in 2022 (figure 1.5).

Box 1.3 Debt-to-GDP versus Debt-to-GNI Ratios

Gross domestic product (GDP) and gross national income (GNI) both measure a country's income, but GDP counts only income received from domestic sources, whereas GNI includes net income received from abroad. The World Bank favors the use of GNI for operational purposes. Member countries' relative poverty is measured in relation to GNI per capita, and this measure underpins the annual income classification published by the International Bank for Reconstruction and Development (IBRD) and the International Development Association (IDA) operational cutoff (US$1,315 per capita for FY24) and the IBRD and IDA lending terms (interest rate and maturity) for specified borrowers. The International Debt Statistics database follows this convention and provides users with GNI data for each reporting country and the relevant external ratios of debt stock and debt service to GNI ratios. The International Monetary Fund (IMF) uses the concept of GDP in Article IV consultation reports and IMF programs to measure macroeconomic outcomes. The practice is carried forward to the joint World Bank–IMF Debt Sustainability Analysis, with debt stocks and debt service measured in relation to GDP. Conceptually, GDP may be regarded as a more accurate measure of a national government's capacity to raise domestic resources from which debt-related obligations must be serviced. For most countries, the difference between GDP and GNI is minimal. For example, the World Bank calculates US GNI to be only 1.5 percent higher than GDP in 2022. GNI may be lower than GDP if nonresidents control a sizable proportion of a country's production or higher than GDP if, for example, a country receives a large amount of foreign aid. For most low- and middle-income countries, the difference between end-2022 GDP and GNI was small, but there were some outliers; aid-dependent Pacific islands such as Kiribati and Tuvalu had a GNI significantly higher than their GDP. Conversely, in countries such as Kazakhstan and Mongolia, GDP surpassed GNI by 12 percent.

Excluding China, LMICs' debt-to-GNI ratio decreased by 3.6 percentage points, to 33.5 percent. For this smaller group, the decline in 2022 was solely the outcome of an increase in the US dollar value of their combined GNI, which rose 10.9 percent in 2022, to US$19.6 trillion from US$17.7 trillion, because the combined external debt stock when China is excluded remained virtually unchanged at US$6.6 trillion.

Despite the increase in economic activity since 2020, the rise in external debt stock has outpaced economic growth during the past decade in LMICs excluding China. The GNI of this group, in US dollars, rose on average 21 percent between 2012 and 2022, and the combined external debt stock rose 46 percent. This decade-long asymmetry between economic growth and debt accumulation has created or exacerbated debt vulnerabilities in many LMICs, making actions to address these vulnerabilities increasingly more urgent. Currently, about 60 percent of countries that are eligible for IDA resources are assessed at high risk of debt distress or are already in debt distress.

When countries are grouped according to World Bank income classifications (box 1.4), those classified as low-income have accumulated external debt stocks at a faster rate than middle-income countries. Between 2012 and 2022, the external debt stock of low-income

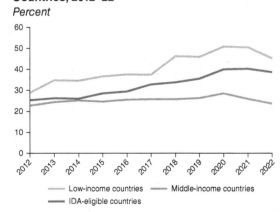

Figure 1.5 **External Debt-to-GNI Ratios for Low- and Middle-Income Countries and IDA-Eligible Countries, 2012–22**

Percent

Source: World Bank International Debt Statistics database.
Note: GNI = gross national income; IDA = International Development Association.

Box 1.4 **World Bank Income and Lending Classifications Used in *International Debt Report 2023***

The World Bank classifies economies by income level for analytical purposes (to broadly group countries by level of development) and operational purposes (to determine their Financial Terms and Conditions of Bank Financing). This report presents data for 122 countries, 121 low- and middle-income countries and Guyana, which is the only high-income country eligible for International Development Association (IDA) resources, reporting to the World Bank Debtor Reporting System. Of these, 24 countries are classified as low-income, with per capita income of US$1,135 or less; 97 countries are classified as middle-income, with per capita income of US$1,136 to US$13,845; and one country, Guyana, is classified as high-income, with per capita income of US$13,846 or more.[a] Income classifications are updated annually at the start of the World Bank fiscal year (July 1) on the basis of gross national income per capita for the previous year. This year Guinea and Zambia were reclassified from low-income to middle-income; Guyana was reclassified from middle-income to high-

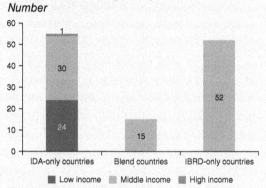

Figure B1.4.1 **Number of Low- and Middle-Income Countries and Guyana Covered in *International Debt Report 2023*, by FY2024 Income and Lending Groups**
Number

Sources: World Bank Country and Lending Groups (https://datahelpdesk.worldbank.org/knowledgebase/articles/906519-world-bank-country-and-lending-groups) and World Bank IDA (https://ida.worldbank.org/en/home).
Note: IBRD = International Bank for Reconstruction and Development; IDA = International Development Association.

income following a doubling of its oil and gas production in 2022. Gross national income is expressed in US dollars and determined by conversion factors derived according to the Atlas methodology.[b] Fifty-two of the middle-income countries covered in this report are eligible only for nonconcessional loans from the International Bank for Reconstruction and Development (IBRD), and are referred to as IBRD-only countries. The remaining 24 low-income, 45 middle-income countries, and Guyana reporting to the Debtor Reporting System are either (a) eligible only for concessional lending from IDA and referred to as IDA-only countries; or (b) eligible for a mix of IBRD and IDA lending and referred to as "blend" countries. Together, IDA-only and IBRD-IDA blend countries are referred to as IDA-eligible countries. Figure B1.4.1 shows the distribution of the 121 low- and middle-income countries and Guyana included in *International Debt Report 2023* by income and lending groups. A comprehensive list of each country's income and lending classifications is given in the appendix of this report under "Country Groups."

a. The country grouping is held fixed when data are compared over time in the International Debt Report. For example, the aggregate for low-income countries from 2010 to 2022 consists of the same group of countries that are classified as low-income countries according to the latest World Bank income classification as of end-2022.

b. For more information on the Atlas methodology, see https://datahelpdesk.worldbank.org/knowledgebase/articles/378832-what-is-the-world-bank-atlas-method.

countries increased 109 percent, while GNI increased 33 percent (figure 1.6). There was a divergence for countries classified as middle-income: among lower-middle-income countries, the external debt stock increased 89 percent between 2012 and 2022 and GNI increased 48 percent; among upper-middle-income countries, excluding China, the external debt stock increased by 28 percent and GNI increased by 7 percent over the same period.

From a lending classification perspective, in IDA-eligible countries, external debt stock accumulation outpaced GNI for the 2012–22 period, increasing 134 percent, compared to a

53 percent rise in GNI. This rapid increase in external debt stocks, exacerbated by borrowing to mitigate the economic and social impact of the COVID-19 pandemic, further strained these countries' debt sustainability capacity and already limited fiscal space. The pace at which external debt stocks accumulated was much slower in the group of countries borrowing only from the International Bank for Reconstruction and Development (the IBRD-only group). Excluding China, external debt stock of IBRD-only countries increased 36 percent during the 2012–22 period, while GNI increased 17 percent.

The situation varied at the regional level. Europe and Central Asia and South Asia were the only two regions where GNI growth outpaced the accumulation of external debt (figure 1.7). In Europe and Central Asia, the debt stock increased 1 percent during the last decade while GNI increased 6 percent. In the South Asia region, GNI increased 88 percent during the decade while external debt increased 73 percent. External debt growth outpaced GNI growth in the Middle East and North Africa region by 99 percentage points, in Sub-Saharan Africa by 72 percentage points, and in Latin America and the Caribbean by 55 percentage points during the decade.

External debt stock accumulation over the past decade in Latin America and the Caribbean and in the Middle East and North Africa has been accompanied by negative economic growth, raising concerns about debt vulnerabilities in an environment of rising interest rates. The aggregate regional figures, however, mask large disparities between countries affected by economic crises, conflict, climate change, and natural disasters. Regional figures for Latin America and the Caribbean are dominated by Brazil, which accounted for an average 32 percent share of total debt stock of the region and a 42 percent share of regional GNI during the past decade. Over this period, Brazil's debt stock increased by 31 percent whereas its GNI declined by 23 percent. Ecuador and Suriname experienced the greatest divergence between the accumulation of debt and GNI growth. In Ecuador, debt grew by 273 percent while GNI increased by 31 percent; in Suriname,

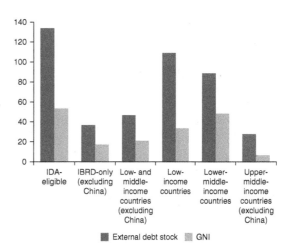

Figure 1.6 **Change in External Debt Stock and GNI, by Income and Lending Group, 2012–22**
Percent

Sources: World Bank International Debt Statistics and World Development Indicators databases.
Note: GNI = gross national income; IBRD = International Bank for Reconstruction and Development; IDA = International Development Association.

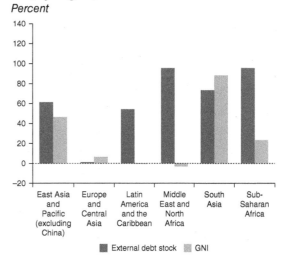

Figure 1.7 **Change in External Debt Stock and GNI, by Region, 2012–22**
Percent

Sources: World Bank International Debt Statistics and World Development Indicators databases.
Note: GNI = gross national income.

debt increased by 331 percent while GNI decreased by 31 percent. More than half of countries in the Middle East and North Africa region experienced zero or negative GNI growth over the decade, whereas debt rose 28 percent. In the Arab Republic of Egypt, debt increased by 307 percent and GNI rose 69 percent. Iraq was the only country in the region where GNI growth outpaced debt accumulation, by 11 percent.

The ratio of external debt to export earnings showed a similar pattern for LMICs in 2022. Export earnings from goods, services, and primary income increased 9.9 percent in 2022, reaching an all-time high of US$10.1 trillion. Excluding China, the increase in export earnings was even more pronounced at 16.7 percent, to US$6.2 trillion, as debt stock levels remained unchanged at US$6.6 trillion. Consequently, the ratio of external debt-to-export earnings decreased for a second consecutive year in 2022, to 107 percent. These ratios should be interpreted with care, however, because they mask increased debt service costs arising from the appreciation of the US dollar as well as significant disparities among both country groups and individual countries. IDA-eligible countries saw the debt-to-export earnings ratio decrease on average by 26 percentage points in 2022 to 186 percent. However, over the past decade, that ratio *increased* by 78 percentage points, putting additional pressure on debt sustainability. During the 2012–22 period, external debt stock of IDA-eligible countries increased 134 percent, outpacing export earnings that increased 36 percent. For IBRD-only countries (excluding China), the average ratio of external debt to export earnings at the start of the decade stood at 99 percent, only 10 percentage points below the comparable ratio of the IDA-eligible countries. In contrast to the IDA-eligible countries group, IBRD-only countries' debt-to-export ratio remained unchanged at the end of the decade, largely because of the slower pace of debt accumulation among these countries during the period. For the IBRD-only group, excluding China, external debt stock and export earnings increased at the same pace of 37 percent during the past decade (figure 1.8).

By income-group classification, low-income countries had the biggest gap, 59 percentage points, between the pace of debt accumulation and export earnings growth during the 2012–22 period. The group's debt-to-export ratio stood at 210 percent in 2022, well above the 151 percent ratio of 2012, with 80 percent of countries having a debt-to-export earnings ratio above this threshold. Over the decade, the number of low-income countries with an external debt-to-export earnings ratio that exceeded 300 percent rose from two to eight in 2022 (Burundi, The Gambia, Guinea-Bissau, Mozambique, Niger, Rwanda, Sudan, and Uganda). The lower-middle-income group's debt-to-export earnings ratio stood at 105 percent in 2022, 24 percentage points above the 2012 level. Lebanon and Senegal experienced the biggest increases for this group, with their ratios more than doubling over the last decade and standing at 514 percent and 467 percent, respectively. The upper-middle-income group excluding China had a debt-to-export earnings ratio of 105 percent in 2022 and was the only income group in which robust export earnings

Figure 1.8 **Change in External Debt Stock and Exports, by Income and Lending Group, 2012–22**
Percent

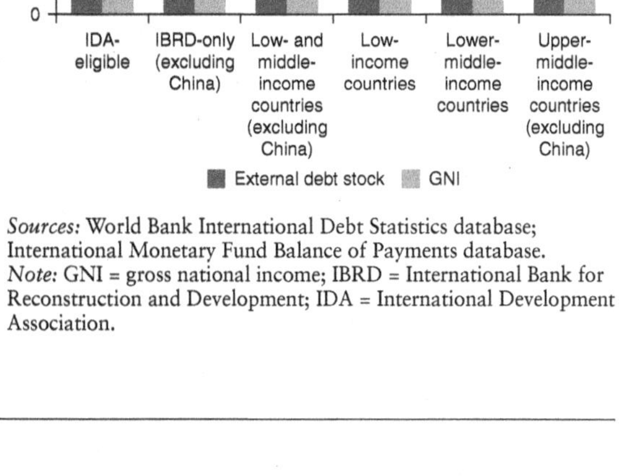

Sources: World Bank International Debt Statistics database; International Monetary Fund Balance of Payments database.
Note: GNI = gross national income; IBRD = International Bank for Reconstruction and Development; IDA = International Development Association.

outpaced debt accumulation, by 5 percentage points. Bosnia and Herzegovina, Grenada, and Serbia were able to decrease their debt-to-export ratios by more than 100 percentage points each during the past decade; at the other end of the spectrum, Colombia, Ecuador, and Suriname increased their ratios by more than 100 percentage points each.

Debt Servicing Costs, 2012–22

Excluding China, interest costs as a percentage of GNI have been growing over the past decade, and the increase was even more pronounced in IDA-eligible countries. Interest costs are expected to continue to grow because of rising global interest rates. Despite a slight decrease in the ratio of total debt service to exports among IDA-eligible countries, these countries remain vulnerable to a drop in export income or an increase in interest rates.

Despite the rapid accumulation of external debt by LMICs over the past decade, the low interest rate regime that prevailed until 2021 kept interest costs relatively low and stable in relation to GNI. For all LMICs combined, interest costs on total external debt stocks rose marginally, from 0.79 percent of GNI in 2012 to 0.83 percent in 2022. However, this stability is attributable in part to China's strong economic growth. Excluding China, interest costs for other LMICs rose from 0.94 percent of GNI in 2012 to peak at 1.33 percent in 2019 before falling back to 1.06 percent in 2022 following the post-COVID-19 rebound in growth. IDA-eligible countries registered the most significant rise in interest costs, from 0.35 percent of GNI in 2012 to 0.89 percent in 2019, reflecting not only the rapid accumulation of external debt but also the increased share owed to private creditors. The ratio of interest costs to GNI moderated to an average of 0.76 percent in 2020–21 because of payment deferrals accorded in the context of the Debt Service Suspension Initiative, but it rose again in 2022 to 0.85 percent as the initiative terminated and interest payments to bilateral creditors resumed.

In nominal terms interest payments on total external debt stock by IDA-eligible countries have quadrupled since 2012 to an all-time high of US$23.6 billion in 2022 (figure 1.9). Going forward, interest costs both in nominal terms and in relation to GNI are expected to increase given the aggressive rise in global interest rates to tame inflation and the fact that variable-rate loans account for 42 percent of the external debt stock of LMICs and 34 percent of that of IDA-eligible countries.

As a share, interest payments on external debt of IDA-eligible countries accounted for 27 percent of the total debt service payments due in 2022, a 3-percentage-point increase from 2021. This share is expected to increase in the future given the 2.7 percent increase in total external debt stock that countries in this group experienced in 2022 and the resumption of debt service payments from Debt Service Suspension Initiative agreements.

Closely related to the repayment capacity of countries is the total debt service-to-export ratio, which indicates how much of

Figure 1.9 **Total Debt Service and Interest Payments on External Debt for IDA-Eligible Countries, 2012–22**
US$ (billion)

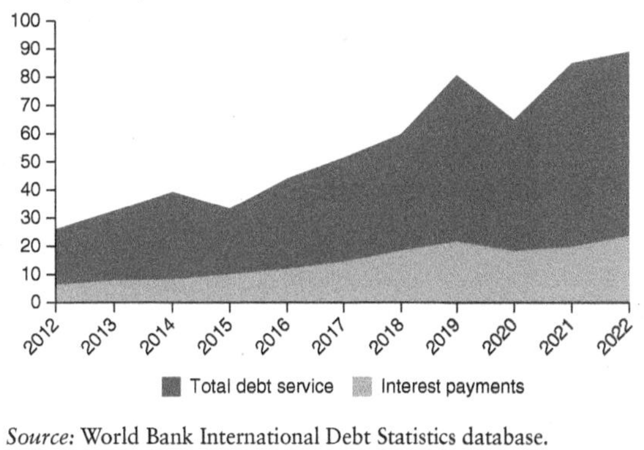

Source: World Bank International Debt Statistics database.
Note: IDA = International Development Association.

13

a country's export revenue will be used to service its debt. Total debt service of IDA-eligible countries increased 4.8 percent in 2022, to US$88.9 billion. However, because export earnings increased by 17 percent in 2022 for this group, to US$574.5 billion, the total debt service-to-export ratio *decreased* from 17.3 percent in 2021 to 15.5 percent in 2022. Despite the increase in export earnings, interest payments as a share of export earnings increased slightly to 4.1 percent in 2022, putting IDA-eligible countries under increased liquidity and solvency pressure. This rising pressure could trigger a crisis via a sharp drop in export earnings or an increase in foreign and/or domestic interest rates.

Trends in External Debt Flows, 2012–22

Total net debt flows (loan disbursements minus principal repayments) to LMICs turned negative in 2022 and became outflows, driven by a contraction in both short- and long-term debt flows, with the latter reaching record lows and turning negative for the first time since the beginning of the millennium. LMICs registered net debt outflows of US$185 billion in 2022, a sharp contrast to net inflows of US$556 billion recorded in 2021 (figure 1.10). These financial flows came under pressure in 2022 because of a combination of factors affecting the global economy.

This reversal was attributable to a contraction in both long-term and short-term debt flows: long-term debt flows swung from a net inflow of US$264.3 billion in 2021 to a US$94.5 billion net outflow in 2022. Short-term debt flows also contracted and turned negative, falling to an outflow of US$90.6 billion from an inflow of US$291.4 billion in 2021 (table 1.2).

The fall in net long-term debt inflows was due entirely to a drop in inflows from private creditors, reflecting a sharp retrenchment in bond issuance by sovereigns and other public and private sector borrowers, as well as in lending by commercial banks and other private entities. Inflows from bondholders turned negative in 2022, to an outflow of US$127.1 billion, as compared to a US$140.6 billion inflow in 2021. Inflows from banks and other private creditors also turned negative, from an inflow of US$61 billion in 2021 to an outflow of US$62.4 billion in 2022.

Central to this debt trajectory was China, which accounted for 73 percent of net debt flows to LMICs. China's external debt stock declined as of end-2022, driven by a decrease in net debt flows, which turned negative on obligations due to all creditor categories. Net debt flows contracted from a US$344.7 billion inflow in 2021 to an outflow of US$296.8 billion in 2022, led by a sharp decline in short-term debt flows which turned to a negative US$181 billion in 2022, and an outflow of US$114.2 billion in long-term private creditor flows. See box 1.5 for a more detailed discussion of China's borrowing.

In LMICs excluding China, net debt inflows fell 47 percent to US$111.8 billion in 2022. This decline was driven by an 84 percent drop in long-term debt inflows to

Figure 1.10 **Net Debt Inflows to Low- and Middle-Income Countries, by Maturity, 2012–22**
US$ (billion)

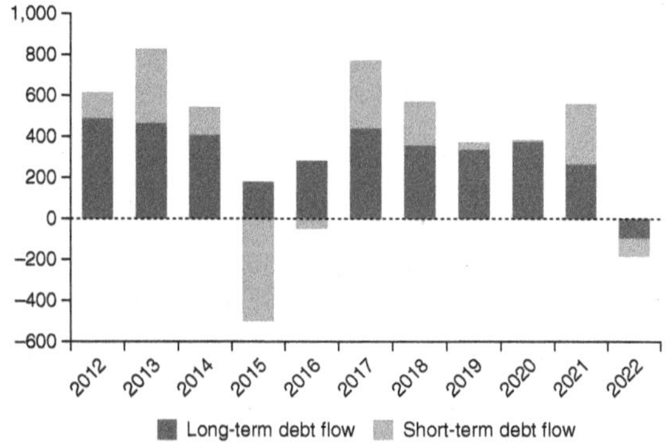

Source: World Bank International Debt Statistics database.

Table 1.2 Net Debt Inflows to Low- and Middle-Income Countries, 2012–22
US$ (billion)

	2012	2013	2014	2015	2016	2017	2018	2019	2020	2021	2022
Net debt inflows	612.5	825.9	541.8	–323.1	230.9	771.4	569.4	369.0	380.4	555.7	–185.0
Long-term	488.6	465.6	406.0	177.3	279.3	438.1	356.6	334.9	373.3	264.3	–94.5
Official creditors	35.6	33.0	51.9	55.9	58.4	59.2	83.7	64.7	123.7	62.7	95.0
Bilateral creditors	16.4	23.8	24.5	14.3	17.3	23.1	20.0	6.1	12.2	11.3	13.6
Multilateral creditors	19.2	9.2	27.4	41.6	41.2	36.1	63.7	58.6	111.5	51.4	81.4
World Bank (IBRD and IDA)	12.0	13.3	14.7	17.9	15.3	12.5	14.8	19.3	26.5	20.5	27.8
IMF (Use of credit and SDR allocations)	–6.4	–11.7	–2.1	7.2	6.4	4.4	30.7	20.9	44.8	1.1	14.0
Private creditors	453.0	432.6	354.0	121.5	220.9	378.9	272.9	270.2	249.6	201.6	–189.4
Bonds	220.4	166.3	165.8	73.2	121.1	291.2	199.1	235.5	229.1	140.6	–127.1
Banks and other private	232.6	266.2	188.3	48.3	99.8	87.7	73.8	34.7	20.6	61.0	–62.4
Short-term	123.9	360.3	135.9	–500.4	–48.4	333.4	212.8	34.1	7.1	291.4	–90.6
Memorandum item											
Long-term public and publicly guaranteed	219.5	211.3	201.5	116.6	139.8	279.7	246.3	213.9	257.0	179.5	50.6
Long-term private nonguaranteed	269.1	254.2	204.5	60.7	139.5	158.3	110.3	121.0	116.3	84.8	–145.1

Sources: World Bank International Debt Statistics database.
Note: IBRD = International Bank for Reconstruction and Development; IDA = International Development Association; IMF = International Monetary Fund; SDR = special drawing rights.

Box 1.5 China: The Largest Borrower among Low- and Middle-Income Countries

From 2012 to 2022, China received 40 percent of total net financial flows to low- and middle-income countries from external creditors. Net financial inflows to China in this period totaled US$4 trillion, of which 32 percent were debt-creating flows and 68 percent equity inflows comprising foreign direct investment and portfolio equity. Aggregate financial flows to China turned negative in 2022 for the first time since 2015, resulting in an outflow of US$103 billion, a marked contrast to the decade-high inflow of US$728 billion in 2021 (figure B1.5.1). Driving the downturn was a debt outflow of US$297 billion and a 49 percent fall in net equity inflows to US$194 billion.

The gross national income of China grew less than 1 percent in 2022, one of its worst performances in decades, the result of months of COVID-19 lockdowns, extreme weather conditions, and a historic downturn in the

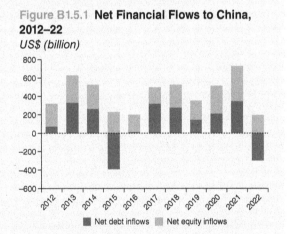

Figure B1.5.1 Net Financial Flows to China, 2012–22
US$ (billion)

■ Net debt inflows ■ Net equity inflows

Sources: World Bank International Debt Statistics database, International Monetary Fund, State Administration of Foreign Exchange of the People's Republic of China, and Bank for International Settlements.

property market. China's external debt accumulation slowed sharply in 2022. After rising on average 13.1 percent per annum in 2020–21, external debt stock, including domestic and foreign currency–denominated debt, fell 11.6 percent to US$2.4 trillion. Relative to gross national income, external debt stock remained moderate, at 13.0 percent, on par with its 2012 level. Short-term debt stock fell 13 percent but continued to account for the largest share of China's external debt stock, 53 percent at end-2022, largely unchanged from 2021. The 11 percent fall in long-term debt was driven by the sharp drop in net inflows from private creditors, particularly bondholders, which account for 91 percent of long-term debt external stock.

(Box continues on next page)

Box 1.5 **China: The Largest Borrower among Low- and Middle-Income Countries (*continued*)**

Nonresident participation in the China Interbank Bond Market (CIBM), the world's second-largest bond market after the United States, began in 2016 when the market was opened to foreign investors. Chinese authorities implemented various programs and measures to facilitate nonresident access to the CIBM, including automated links between the markets in Hong Kong SAR, China; London; and Shanghai. Inclusion of yuan bonds in the Bloomberg Barclays Global Aggregate Index and China-A shares in the FTSE Russell Emerging Market index also encourages foreign investors' appetite for Chinese bonds. Between 2019 and 2021, net inflows on bonds issued by Chinese entities, both public and private, accounted for, on average, 74 percent of annual long-term net debt inflows. By contrast, in 2022, 61 percent of the US$116 billion net debt outflow on long-term debt was accounted for by bondholders, reflecting global investors' withdrawal from the CIBM.

A major reason for the sharp sell-off of nonresident investors' holdings of Chinese yuan bonds in 2022 was the much smaller yield premium on Chinese bonds compared to those in Group of Seven bond markets. The Chinese economy did not rebound in 2022 and inflation remained low, unlike in Group of Seven economies that implemented aggressive policy tightening and raised interest rates to combat inflation. However, despite reduced nonresident participation, Chinese government bonds were resilient and outperformed most of their global peers, topping the list for positive returns in local currency terms in 2022. They also had the smallest losses in US dollar terms, aside from short-term US Treasury bonds.

US$21.3 billion, from US$129.6 billion in 2021, which was partially offset by higher short-term inflows, which rose 11 percent to US$90.5 billion. Long-term debt inflows were at their lowest level since 2002. Net long-term debt flows to nonguaranteed private sector borrowers, through both bond issuance and commercial bank lending, reflected a stark decline of 184 percent, turning to a negative US$33.5 billion in 2022. Net long-term debt flows to public sector borrowers fared better and fell less steeply; they dropped 39 percent to US$54.8 billion in 2022, reflecting a slowdown in bond issuance and commercial bank lending.

The reduction in the volume of flows and their composition varied significantly at the individual country level. Russia and Thailand combined accounted for US$59 billion in net long-term debt outflows from private nonguaranteed borrowers in 2022, whereas Brazil recorded inflows of US$27 billion. Regarding comparable net long-term debt flows to public sector borrowers, Russia recorded outflows of over US$40 billion whereas Mexico recorded a net inflow of US$11.2 billion. Most top-10 borrowers recorded an inflow of short-term debt in 2022, but the most significant were India (US$14.5 billion) and Türkiye (US$30 billion). Only Brazil and Russia recorded short-term debt outflows in 2022, of approximately US$11 billion each. Among other LMICs, Egypt recorded a US$17.4 billion short-term debt inflow, an increase of more than 19-fold from the 2021 volume.

The primary reason for the decline in long-term debt flows was bond issuance by public and private sector borrowers, which fell sharply in 2022 because of rising global interest rates, downgrades in selected borrower countries' credit ratings, and heightened overall perceived investor risks. When China is excluded, new bond issuance by public and private sector borrowers totaled US$101 billion in 2022, a 53 percent decline from the 2021 figure. New issuance by public sector borrowers was US$70 billion, 51.5 percent less than the comparable figure of 2021; new issuance by private sector borrowers faced an equally pronounced contraction of 56.8 percent from 2021, to US$32 billion (figure 1.11). In terms of net flows, the effect was even more pronounced because of changes in the share of maturing bonds. The combined effect of a decline in new issuances and a 4.2 percent increase in maturing bonds to US$52 billion reduced net flows to private nonguaranteed corporate borrowers to a negative

US$21 billion. Net flows to public sector borrowers turned to a negative US$35 billion in 2022, down from a net inflow of US$28 billion in the previous year due to a 9.1 percent decrease in maturing bonds, to US$105 billion in 2022, combined with a 51.5 percent decrease to US$69.7 billion in new bond issuances.

As global financial conditions have continued to tighten, and despite what happened to the bond market, LMICs have demonstrated a commitment to diversify their sources of financing and to tap innovative sources to finance investments that benefit the climate and increase the sustainable development impact. Some of the new and creative instruments developed to address these challenges include green, social, sustainability, and sustainability-linked bonds such as the World Bank Sustainable Development Bond, the African Development Bank's Green Bond, the Green Sukuk (Islamic Bond), Blue Bonds, and social bonds. New clauses have also been introduced in debt contracts, such as climate resilient debt clauses, which allow for automatic suspension of debt servicing payments in the event of natural disasters or health emergency crises, and majority voting provisions in syndicated loan contracts. Issuances of such sovereign thematic bonds positively affect a country's commitment to avoiding and adapting to climate change, and such sovereign issuances help diversify countries' portfolios and develop their markets by drawing participation from a different investor base.

In 2022, Egypt became the first country in the Middle East and North Africa region to issue a Samurai bond, a yen-denominated bond issued in Tokyo by non-Japanese companies and subject to Japanese regulations. Indonesia, a regular issuer of Samurai bonds, also used the instrument in 2022, in addition to a US$3.25 billion Shariah-compliant Sukuk format bond, which was its biggest Sukuk global sale in history. In 2022, the Bank of Industry of Nigeria, an official development bank, issued a US$700 million Eurobond with a sovereign guarantee, which marked the institution's first Eurobond issuance as well as the first provision of a Eurobond guarantee by the Federal Government of Nigeria. The Philippines issued a US$1 billion sustainability bond in March 2022 and a 70.1 billion Japanese yen sustainability bond in April 2022.

Despite these new forms of financing and the US$75.2 billion outflow recorded from private creditors, net flows to LMICs (excluding China) from official creditors, composed of bilateral and multilateral entities, were positive and rose 33.1 percent in 2022, to US$82.5 billion. Official creditors were the only group of creditors to mark an increase of financing in 2022 for LMICs, excluding China. Net debt inflows from multilateral creditors including the IMF in 2022 increased 61 percent, to US$81.8 billion, and accounted for an 85 percent share of official debt flows. For many countries, in particular the world's poorest, multilateral creditors were the primary source of external financing. Net debt inflows from bilateral creditors increased 19 percent to US$14.8 billion, but those creditors' share of official debt flows was modest at 15 percent. As financing from other creditor categories declined in 2022, borrowers increasingly turned to multilateral creditors, which serve as lenders of last resort.

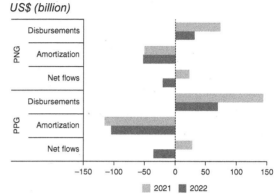

Figure 1.11 **Bond Flows to Low- and Middle-Income Countries (excluding China), by Borrower Type, 2021 vs. 2022**
US$ (billion)

Source: World Bank International Debt Statistics database.
Note: PNG = private nonguaranteed; PPG = public and publicly guaranteed.

The uncertain global economic outlook, limited fiscal space, and tightening financial conditions in international capital markets weighed heavily on LMICs in 2022, particularly those eligible for IDA financing. These countries depend significantly on official, concessional sources of financing, although over a third of them have gained market access during the last decade with bond issuances in international capital markets. Market access was severely curtailed for IDA-eligible countries in 2022, and net flows from other creditors declined, apart from multilateral creditors.

Net inflows from private creditors collapsed in 2022, falling 79 percent to US$6.1 billion. The downturn in net debt inflows from private creditors was intensified by a 43 percent fall in inflows from bilateral creditors to US$7.9 billion (from US$13.7 billion in 2021)—see figure 1.12. By contrast, net inflows from multilateral creditors rose 41 percent to US$30.4 billion (compared to a 48 percent decline in 2021), the only creditor category that experienced an upward net debt inflow trajectory in 2022.

Multilateral creditors' share of net long-term debt inflows rose to 68 percent from 33 percent in 2021. The World Bank accounted for 50 percent of multilateral debt flows during the year and reached an all-time high of US$15 billion. The Sub-Saharan Africa region received most of these debt flows, US$10.7 billion, which represents a 71 percent share of total flows received by IDA-eligible countries; the next biggest regional recipient was South Asia, with 16.9 percent (US$2.5 billion in 2022).

Looking beyond debt, net financial flows (debt and equity) dropped 77 percent in 2022, to US$291 billion (figure 1.13). After rebounding in 2021 from the pandemic, foreign direct investment (FDI) flows declined 28 percent in 2022, to US$479 billion, and portfolio equity flows dropped 81 percent to US$11 billion, as difficult global economic conditions and heightened geopolitical tensions affected investors' postcrisis risk perceptions. Despite experiencing a 47 percent decrease in FDI equity flows, China continued to be the largest recipient among LMICs, at US$159.7 billion. It accounted for 33 percent of total FDI flows, followed by Brazil (15 percent), India (10 percent), and Mexico (7 percent). Although on a downward trend, FDI equity flows as a volume remained positive and proved resilient, offsetting the fall and negative volumes in short- and long-term debt flows.

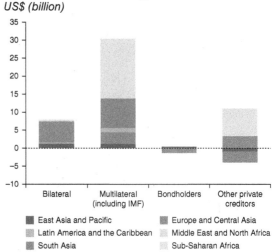

Figure 1.12 **Net Flows to IDA-Eligible Countries, by Region and Creditor Type, 2022**

US$ (billion)

Source: World Bank International Debt Statistics database.
Note: IDA = International Development Association; IMF = International Monetary Fund.

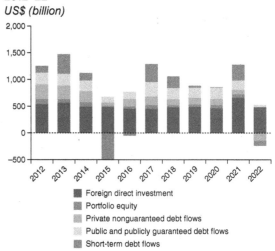

Figure 1.13 **Net Equity Inflows and External Debt Flows to Low- and Middle-Income Countries, 2012–22**

US$ (billion)

Sources: International Monetary Fund and United Nations Conference on Trade and Development.

New Debt Commitments, 2012–22

New commitments to LMICs plummeted in 2022, driven primarily by a steep decrease in private sector commitments; yet multilateral creditors stepped in to partly offset that drop with an increase in new commitments.

New commitments to public and publicly guaranteed (PPG) sector entities fell in 2022 for a second consecutive year, decreasing 23 percent to US$372 billion and reaching their lowest level since 2011. The main driver of the decrease was a 33 percent decline in new commitments from private creditors, which contracted to US$218 billion, also the lowest level since 2011. New PPG bonds issued in international markets by LMICs fell 51 percent in 2022 from the 2021 level, to US$114 billion. China, by far the largest bond issuer among LMICs, registered a sharp 74 percent decline in new bond issuance from PPG sector entities, to US$24 billion. Excluding China, new bond issuance by other LMICs decreased at a slower pace in 2022, falling 36 percent to US$89.7 billion.

IBRD-only countries are market-based borrowers that rely heavily on borrowing from private creditors, averaging 73 percent of new PPG commitments during the past decade. With the tightening of global financial conditions and increased risk aversion among private creditors, new borrowing from private creditors decreased 38 percent during the 2020–22 period, to US$208 billion in 2022, and this decrease was the primary reason for the drop in total new commitments to IBRD borrowers.

New PPG commitments from private creditors to IDA-eligible countries also decreased in 2022 by 72 percent, to US$9.7 billion, after experiencing a 56 percent increase in 2021. But these changes were much less significant for IDA-eligible countries, because these countries have far less exposure to private creditor borrowing, at just 14 percent of total new commitments (figure 1.14).

Commitments from Official Creditors

PPG commitments from official creditors—governments or other bilateral public entities and multilateral institutions such as the World Bank and regional development banks—decreased marginally in 2022, by 1.2 percent, to US$154 billion. But these overall figures for official creditors mask divergences between commitments originating from bilateral creditors and those from multilateral ones. New commitments from multilateral creditors, excluding the IMF, were three times larger than new bilateral commitments, and increased 1.5 percent to US$116 billion. Since the onset of the COVID-19 pandemic, multilateral creditors have provided an unprecedented level of support for countries to mitigate the economic and social impacts of the pandemic, which led to a surge in new commitments in 2020 and 2021. In 2022, multilateral creditors continued to step up and partly offset the decline in lending from private creditors. New commitments from the World Bank in 2022 increased by 1.3 percent, to US$53.5 billion, equivalent to 46 percent of

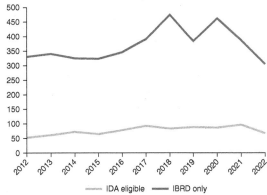

Figure 1.14 Loan Commitments to IDA-Eligible and IBRD-Only Countries, 2012–22

US$ (billion)

IDA eligible — IBRD only

Source: World Bank International Debt Statistics database.
Note: IBRD = International Bank for Reconstruction and Development; IDA = International Development Association.

new commitments by all multilateral institutions combined. New World Bank IDA commitments increased 11.3 percent to US$25.0 billion, while new IBRD commitments decreased by 6.4 percent to US$28.6 billion. In 2022, the World Bank also provided US$6.1 billion in grants to IDA-eligible countries. See box 1.6 for more on IDA grants.

Box 1.6 IDA Grants: Contributing to Reducing Debt Vulnerabilities

The International Development Association (IDA) provides sustained, highly concessional financing to its borrowers, and those at high risk of debt distress receive all or part of this financing in the form of grants. The terms of IDA financing to each IDA-eligible country vary based on an annual assessment of the country's gross national income per capita, its creditworthiness for borrowing from the International Bank for Reconstruction and Development, and its risk of debt distress and vulnerability. Outcomes of the Debt Sustainability Analysis, which assesses the risk of debt distress, translate to a "traffic light" system to determine the share of IDA grants and highly concessional IDA credits (loans) for each borrower. Before the 20th replenishment of IDA (IDA20), IDA-only countries with a per capita income below the IDA operational cutoff point (set at US$1,315 for fiscal year 2024) assessed at high risk of debt distress or in debt distress ("red light") received 100 percent grants; those at moderate risk ("yellow light") received 50 percent grants and 50 percent credits; and those at low risk ("green light") received only credits but with a grant element of at least 53 percent. Starting from IDA20, "red light" IDA-only countries with a gross national income per capita below the IDA cutoff point receive 100 percent grants, whereas "yellow light" countries, except those designated as small states, and "green light" countries receive 100 percent credits with a grant element of at least 36 percent and ranging up to 73 percent. IDA-only borrowers designated as small states are the only "yellow light" countries eligible for grant financing in IDA20: they receive 50 percent of IDA financing in grants. IDA20 retains the ceiling set under the 19th replenishment of IDA (IDA19) of US$1 billion grants per country allocation in any one fiscal year.

Of the current 75 IDA-eligible countries, 60 countries (including Sri Lanka, which reverse-graduated in December 2022) receive financing only from IDA and 15 countries are eligible for financing from both the International Bank for Reconstruction and Development and IDA (blend countries). A total of 28 countries are assessed at high risk of debt distress, and 11 are in distress. Twenty-seven countries are eligible for grants as part of their country allocation,[a] including two "yellow light" small states receiving 50 percent of their Performance Based Allocation as grants.

Throughout the past decade IDA has provided critical and increasing levels of support to its borrowers, particularly during times of crisis. Total net flows and net transfers[b] from IDA to IDA-eligible countries reporting to the Debtor Reporting System of loans and grants combined were US$19.7 billion and US$18.3 billion, respectively, in 2022. The comparable inflows at the start of the decade were US$7.8 billion and US$7.3 billion, respectively (figure B1.6.1).

a. IDA-only countries including those under the Small Island Economies Exception with a gross national income per capita below the IDA operational cutoff.

b. Net flows are gross disbursements minus principal payments on IDA credits. Net transfers are net flows minus interest and service fees on IDA credits.

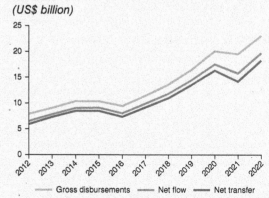

Figure B1.6.1 IDA Gross and Net Inflows of Credits and Grants to IDA-Eligible Countries, 2012–22

(US$ billion)

Gross disbursements — Net flow — Net transfer

Sources: World Bank International Debt Statistics database and International Development Association (IDA) accounts.

Other multilateral institutions also stepped up their financing during the pandemic. New commitments from the African Development Bank, Asian Development Bank, and Inter-American Development Bank combined reached a decade high of US$46.8 billion in 2020 (figure 1.15). In 2022, however, lending by these regional banks returned to prepandemic levels, with new commitments declining for the second consecutive year, by 7.7 percent, to US$26.9 billion. New commitments from other multilateral creditors increased by 9.8 percent to US$35.3 billion, and their share of new commitments from multilateral creditors rose from 25 percent in 2012 to 30 percent in 2022. In 2022, the largest amount of new commitments extended by these lenders was from the Asian Infrastructure Investment Bank, followed by the African Export-Import Bank and the European Investment Bank.

New commitments from bilateral creditors, of which Japan and China were the two largest, fell by 7.5 percent in 2022 to US$38.5 billion and accounted for only 25 percent of total commitments from official bilateral and multilateral creditors. New commitments from Japan increased 26.3 percent to US$11.1 billion in 2022, whereas those from China decreased 41.1 percent (to US$5.7 billion). New commitments from other non-Paris Club creditors rose 15.8 percent (to US$7.1 billion), while those from Paris Club creditors, excluding Japan, increased by a marginal 0.8 percent (to US$14.6 billion) (figure 1.16).

Commitments to IDA-Eligible Countries
Total new commitments (from all types of creditors, including official and private) to PPG sector entities in IDA-eligible coun-

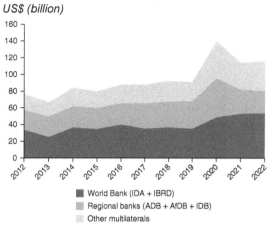

Figure 1.15 New Commitments from Multilateral Creditors to IDA-Eligible and IBRD-Only Countries, 2012–22
US$ (billion)

Legend:
- World Bank (IDA + IBRD)
- Regional banks (ADB + AfDB + IDB)
- Other multilaterals

Source: World Bank International Debt Statistics database.
Note: ADB = Asian Development Bank; AfDB = African Development Bank; IBRD = International Bank for Reconstruction and Development; IDA = International Development Association; IDB = Inter-American Development Bank.

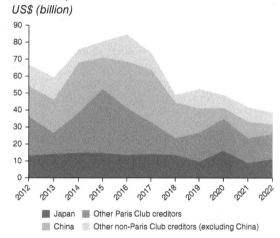

Figure 1.16 New Commitments from Bilateral Creditors to IDA-Eligible and IBRD-Only Countries, 2012–22
US$ (billion)

Legend:
- Japan
- China
- Other Paris Club creditors
- Other non-Paris Club creditors (excluding China)

Source: World Bank International Debt Statistics database.
Note: IBRD = International Bank for Reconstruction and Development; IDA = International Development Association.

tries totaled US$67 billion in 2022, a 30 percent decrease from the all-time high in 2021; this drop was primarily due to the decline in commitments from private sector creditors, which fell 72 percent to US$9.7 billion. New commitments to IDA-eligible countries from bilateral creditors also decreased by 30 percent to US$14.2 billion. By contrast, new commitments from multilateral creditors increased by 4 percent to US$43 billion. And new commitments by the World Bank (including IBRD and IDA lending) accounted for 58 percent of total multilateral creditor commitments, increasing by 8 percent in 2022 to an all-time high of US$25.2 billion. Nigeria and Tanzania were the top recipients of new financing from the World Bank in 2022, at US$2.9 billion and US$2.7 billion, respectively.

IDA-eligible countries continued to rely primarily on financing from official creditors, which accounted for 86 percent of new commitments to the PPG sector in 2022. The composition of creditors for the IDA-eligible group has shifted over the past decade, with new commitments from bilateral creditors decreasing from 43 to 21 percent, from multilateral creditors increasing from 41 to 64 percent, and from private creditors remaining unchanged at about 15 percent

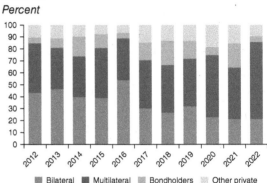

Figure 1.17 Percent Share of Loan Commitments to IDA-Eligible Countries, by Creditor Type, 2012–22
Percent

Source: World Bank International Debt Statistics database.
Note: IDA = International Development Association.

(figure 1.17). From the launch of the Belt and Road Initiative in 2013 until 2016, China averaged annual new commitments of US$16.3 billion and averaged 53 percent of total bilateral creditor commitments to IDA-eligible countries. The initiative aims to build an integrated international economic corridor encompassing more than 60 countries in various regions and provides financing for large-scale infrastructure projects to enable it. New commitments from Chinese bilateral creditors to IDA-eligible countries have been on a declining trend since 2016, however, reaching a decade low of US$3.6 billion in 2022, which represents 24 percent of total bilateral creditor commitments. New commitments from other bilateral creditors also decreased in 2022, by 14.7 percent to US$10.7 billion. See box 1.7 for more on China's lending.

Box 1.7 China: Low- and Middle-Income Countries' Largest Bilateral Creditor

Over the past two decades, China has been one of the world's fastest-growing economies, with annual gross national income growth averaging over 13 percent, a pace the World Bank described as "the fastest sustained expansion by a major economy in history."[a] This, combined with China's "Going Global Strategy," initiated in 1999 to foster Chinese investment abroad, propelled Chinese overseas investment and lending. In the process China became not only the largest borrower among low- and middle-income countries (LMICs) but also one of their largest creditors.

LMICs' combined public and publicly guaranteed external debt obligations to China totaled US$180 billion at end-2022 (figure B1.7.1).[b] To put this figure in context, LMICs' obligations to the International Bank

Figure B1.7.1 Low- and Middle-Income Countries' Debt to China, by Region, 2012–22
US$ (billion)

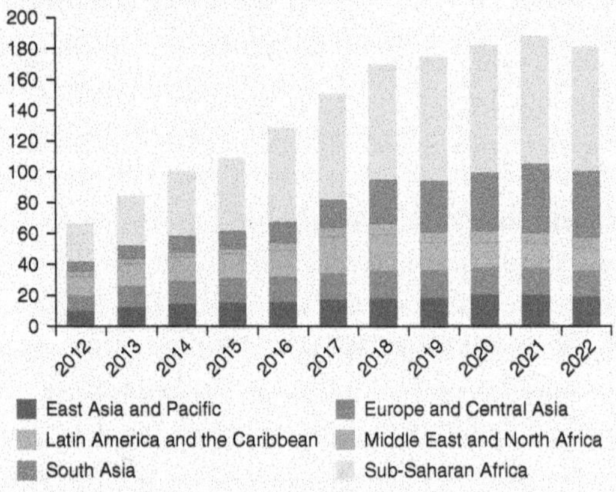

East Asia and Pacific · Europe and Central Asia · Latin America and the Caribbean · Middle East and North Africa · South Asia · Sub-Saharan Africa

Source: World Bank International Debt Statistics database.

(Box continues on next page)

Box 1.7 China as Low- and Middle-Income Countries' Largest Bilateral Creditor (*continued*)

for Reconstruction and Development and International Development Association, including US$16 billion owed by China, were US$223 billion and US$183 billion, respectively, at end-2022. Moreover, the figure for debt obligations to China does not include significant lending by China to private sector entities in LMICs without a sovereign guarantee.[c] Most of the public and publicly guaranteed external debt owed to China relates to large infrastructure projects and operations in the extractive industries. Countries in Sub-Saharan Africa (SSA), led by Angola, have seen some of the sharpest rises in Chinese lending since 2012, although the pace of accumulation has slowed since 2018. The SSA region accounted for 44 percent of LMICs' obligations to China at end-2022. In South Asia, external debt obligations to China rose nearly sevenfold over 11 years, from US$6.4 billion in 2012 to US$42.9 billion in 2022, of which two-thirds was accounted for by Pakistan.

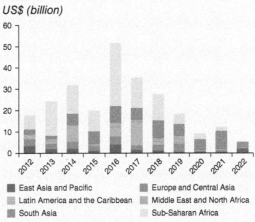

Figure B1.7.2 Commitments from China to Low- and Middle-Income Countries, by Region 2012–22

US$ (billion)

Legend:
- East Asia and Pacific
- Europe and Central Asia
- Latin America and the Caribbean
- Middle East and North Africa
- South Asia
- Sub-Saharan Africa

Source: World Bank International Debt Statistics database.

Commitments serve as a leading indicator of changes in financing patterns and how debt stocks are likely to evolve. From 2012 to 2022, commitments from China to public and publicly guaranteed borrowers in LMICs totaled US$254 billion. Lending was directed primarily to (a) oil-producing countries, (b) neighboring countries to China and those along the Belt and Road corridor, and (c) mineral-rich and other large countries in SSA. Annual commitments rose rapidly in the first half of the decade to peak at US$52 billion in 2016, of which 57 percent went to countries in SSA (figure B1.7.2). Since then, however, commitments have fallen sharply to an all-time low of US$5.4 billion in 2022, of which 80 percent went to China's neighboring countries and those in the South Asia region. New loan commitments to countries in SSA were a negligible US$145 million. Factors accounting for this downturn include changes in China's own economic environment and a steep contraction in its current account surplus, the failure of some overseas projects to come to fruition or realize anticipated financial dividends, and an increase in debt vulnerabilities in borrowing countries that has led some of them to default to China.

How China Lends

Chinese lending to public and private sector entities in LMICs falls into four main categories. First are concessional loans at very low interest rates or interest-free, funded from tax revenues, denominated in yuan, and managed by the China International Development Cooperation Agency. Second, the Export–Import Bank of China offers concessional loans managed by the Preferential Loans Department, including (a) concessional loans denominated in yuan funded by the Chinese government and (b) US dollar-denominated "preferential buyers" credits financed from the Export–Import Bank of China's own resources. Third, policy banks—including the Export–Import Bank of China, China Development Bank, and Agricultural Development Bank of China—extend nonconcessional dollar-denominated loans, which they fund through bond issuance in the domestic and international capital markets, and which are often insured by China's official export credit agency, SINOSURE. Fourth, Chinese commercial banks and suppliers extend short- and medium-term loans, usually insured by SINOSURE.

a. The World Bank, China Overview, https://www.worldbank.org/en/country/china/overview.

b. This figure does not include obligations of the Russian Federation, which may be substantial.

c. Lending to private sector entities not publicly guaranteed or through special purpose vehicles is captured in private nonguaranteed debt. These data are reported to the Debtor Reporting System in aggregate, and creditors cannot be separately identified.

Notes

1. The 10 countries are Argentina, Brazil, Colombia, India, Indonesia, Mexico, the Russian Federation, South Africa, Thailand, and Türkiye.
2. China participates formally in the creditor committee of the Common Framework but negotiates separately from other creditors with borrowers, including Zambia and, more recently, Sri Lanka.

References

IDA (International Development Association). 2023. "Sustainable Development Finance Policy of the International Development Association: Mid-Term Implementation Review (English)." World Bank, Washington, DC.

IMF (International Monetary Fund). 2009. *Balance of Payments and International Investment Position Manual, 6th edition*. Washington, DC: IMF.

IMF (International Monetary Fund). 2014. *Government Finance Statistics Manual 2014*. Washington, DC: IMF.

IMF (International Monetary Fund). 2021. "IMF Governors Approve a Historic US$650 Billion SDR Allocation of Special Drawing Rights." IMF Press Release No. 21/235, August 2, 2021. https://www.imf.org/en/News/Articles/2021/07/30/pr21235-imf-governors-approve-a-historic-us-650-billion-sdr-allocation-of-special-drawing-rights.

2. The Macroeconomic and Debt Outlook for 2023 and Beyond

Introduction

Global growth is expected to slow in 2023, and the outlook is weaker still for countries with elevated fiscal and financial vulnerabilities. This expected deceleration is due to short- and long-term factors that range from inflation and rising interest rates to global trade and investment fragmentation and adverse climate-related events. And it will occur amid significant debt accumulation in low- and middle-income countries (LMICs), with ratios of debt to gross national income (GNI) elevated by historical standards and similar to the debt wave of the 1980s. In addition, the composition of creditors has changed in recent years, with nontraditional official creditors and commercial lenders holding larger shares of LMICs' external debt, which makes debt resolutions and rollovers more challenging. Furthermore, a higher share of foreign currency–denominated debt results in greater exchange rate risks. Meanwhile, debt service burdens remain sizeable in these countries, which could crowd out spending on other priorities.

Global gross domestic product (GDP) growth is set to slow in 2023. According to the World Bank's latest projections, global growth in 2023 is expected to slow to 2.1 percent, a significant deceleration from 3.1 percent in 2022 (figure 2.1). GDP growth in LMICs is forecast to be 4.2 percent in 2023, but mainly because of China. Excluding China, LMICs' growth is projected to be 3.1 percent in 2023, down from 3.8 percent in 2022.

The outlook is particularly weak for countries with elevated fiscal and financial vulnerabilities. LMICs with weaker sovereign credit ratings have experienced slower growth and more adverse financial developments, including exchange rate depreciation and rising sovereign spreads. By the end of 2024, economic activity in LMICs is projected to be 5 percent below prepandemic projections. In about one-third of these countries, per capita income in 2024 will still fall below the 2019 level, and growth over the 2020–24 period is projected to be the weakest nonoverlapping five-year average since the mid-1990s.

Both short- and long-term factors have driven recent weakness in the global economy.

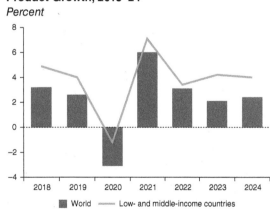

Figure 2.1 **Percent Change in Gross Domestic Product Growth, 2018–24**

Percent

Source: World Bank 2023.
Note: Aggregate GDP growth rates are calculated as weighted averages, based on real GDP in constant 2010–19 prices, expressed in US dollars, as weights. Data for 2023 are estimates and data for 2024 are forecasts.

Short-term factors include elevated inflation and the monetary policy tightening that resulted from it. In particular, the current hiking cycle in the United States has been the sharpest in nearly four decades. Although headline inflation has been easing globally, core inflation remains high, implying that policy interest rates are expected to be kept higher for longer. Monetary tightening in advanced economies has adverse effects in LMICs—for instance, through tighter financial conditions in general and by depressing external demand. In the long term, global potential output growth is expected to weaken further because of a broad-based decline in the fundamental drivers of growth (Kose and Ohnsorge 2023).

Risks to the outlook in LMICs are tilted to the downside. They include elevated geopolitical tensions, a heightened risk of financial stress, persistent inflation, and weaker external demand. These downside risks, if they materialize, could result in even more subdued economic activity.

- *An escalation of geopolitical tensions could adversely affect LMICs through disruptions in commodity markets and fragmentation of trade and financial links.* Elevated geopolitical tensions, especially in commodity-exporting countries or regions, could result in a surge in global commodity prices and policy uncertainty, reducing investment and economic activity in LMICs. An escalation of tensions and conflicts could also cause fragmentation of international trade and financial networks, as supply chains are damaged and cross-border capital flows are restricted, including the implementation of international sanctions.
- *Borrowing costs have been increasing in LMICs.* For about one-fourth of these countries, sovereign spreads exceed 10 percentage points, which indicates a loss of market access and a heightened risk of default. There have been 18 sovereign default occurences since 2020, above the 15 default events that occurred during the previous two decades.[1] Moreover, LMICs could experience even higher borrowing costs if high-income economies encounter financial stress. In countries with greater fiscal and financial vulnerabilities, negative financial spillovers could be amplified through undercapitalized banks, the sovereign-bank nexus,[2] or high debt levels.
- *Persistent inflation in both high-income economies and LMICs could lead to even tighter monetary policy and further depress economic activity.* Spillovers from monetary tightening in high-income economies could exacerbate vulnerabilities in LMICs by putting pressure on domestic financial systems via currency depreciation, which increases the likelihood of capital outflows as well as the potential for currency crises.
- *Long-term growth expectations have been weakening.* Fundamental growth drivers have been softening in many LMICs over the past few decades. Future growth could be further weakened by global trade and investment fragmentation and adverse climate-related events. However, if structural reforms are implemented to boost growth, strengthen confidence, and moderate the adverse impacts of climate change, the decline in potential growth might be mitigated. Successful implementation of reforms requires strong governance and institutional frameworks.

Amid slowing growth and heightened downside risks, several LMICs have accumulated significant external debt over the past decade. Excluding China, the external debt-to-GNI ratio among LMICs rose to 33.5 percent in 2022, 6 percentage points higher than the 2012 ratio. In low-income countries, where debt accumulated at an even more rapid pace, external debt rose to 45 percent of GNI in 2022, from 29 percent in 2012. This trajectory corresponds to the current global wave of debt growth that began in the wake of the 2009 global recession, when increasing debt levels were accompanied by slowing economic growth and the emergence of new lenders (Kose et al. 2021).

After the 2020 global recession, external debt stocks declined by 5 percentage points of GNI by 2022, but they are anticipated to remain elevated. External public and publicly guaranteed (PPG) debt also declined by 2 percentage points between 2020 and 2022 in LMICs. The reduction was larger in commodity exporting LMICs (by 5 percentage points) than in commodity importers, even when China was excluded from the group (by 2 percentage points), partly because exporting countries benefited from a rise in commodity prices, which allowed them to improve their external positions. In most LMICs, however, external debt remains elevated compared to prepandemic levels. Relative to the previous three waves of debt accumulation, the annual average change in external debt during the current wave has been almost as large as the change in the 1980s in low-income countries (figure 2.2). In the 1980s, these countries borrowed heavily from official creditors to finance domestic industry and some of them subsequently suffered debt crises amid rising global interest rates. Countries eligible for resources from the International Development Association (IDA-eligible countries) have also seen an increase in external debt during the current wave, following consecutive declines over the previous two waves.

The composition of external creditors has changed significantly over the past decade. In particular, the increasing shares of nontraditional official creditors (such as non-Paris Club countries[3]) and commercial lenders holding external debt stocks have raised concerns about debt resolution and rollover of debt in LMICs. Loan arrangements with non-Paris Club countries are often complex, and loan information is not always made public. This situation poses challenges to accurately pricing sovereign risks in such countries (Horn, Reinhart, and Trebesch 2021). Because loans from private sources are mostly made at market rates, borrowers are more exposed to refinancing risks, especially when a surge occurs in borrowing costs (Essl et al. 2019). In LMICs, bondholders and commercial banks accounted for more than half (53 percent) of external PPG debt stocks in 2022, an increase of 4 percentage points from 2012. By contrast, in IDA-eligible countries, the share of bondholders and commercial banks has been lower than in LMICs. However, the rate of increase has been higher because of a large shift to market borrowings, as the share of these private sources increased by 12 percentage points to 20 percent of external PPG debt stocks over 2012–22. In low-income countries that do not have the capacity to access international markets on a durable and substantial basis, the share of concessional term debt has been rising since the mid-2010s, though it was still about 50 percent of external PPG debt in 2022. For this group of countries, Paris Club countries accounted for about 27 percent of external bilateral PPG debt in 2022.

LMICs have become more vulnerable to currency risk as the share of external PPG debt in foreign currencies has increased. General government debt in foreign currencies in LMICs accounted for 25 percent in 2022, a significant increase from 17 percent a decade ago (Kose et al. 2022). This increase in government debt denominated in foreign currencies makes these countries more vulnerable to rising debt service costs through exchange rate movements. More than 80 percent of external PPG debt in LMICs was in US dollars in 2022, an increase from 76 percent a decade ago. In low-income countries, external PPG

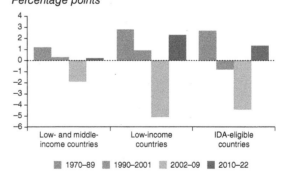

Figure 2.2 **Changes in External Debt-to-GNI Ratios, 1970–2022**
Percentage points

Source: World Bank International Debt Statistics database.
Note: The figure shows annual average changes in external debt, computed as changes in external debt-to-GNI ratios over the respective periods, divided by the number of years in each of them. For the period 1970–89, data for low-income countries start in 1981. GNI = gross national income; IDA = International Development Association.

debt in US dollars accounted for about 64 percent of external debt in 2022, up from 58 percent in 2012. Heavy reliance on debt denominated in a single currency could also increase vulnerability to sudden movements in exchange rates. With ongoing monetary policy tightening in the United States, LMICs may face continued depreciation pressures.

PPG debt service payments (including the International Monetary Fund) totaled US$443.5 billion in 2022, the highest level in history, and will remain sizable in LMICs. PPG external debt service due over 2023–24 is expected to be 10 percent higher than it was during the 2021–22 period. Excluding China, PPG debt service payments of LMICs are expected to rise by 12 percent.

The rise in debt service burdens is worse in low-income countries, and it could create significant challenges related to spending. The amount to service external PPG debt for the next two years will increase by 39 percent in low-income countries relative to the amount for the previous two years, assuming payment during the same period of current accumulated interest and principal arrears. This increase is attributable to a hike in principal repayments, as they are expected to rise by 56 percent over the same period. In contrast, the interest expense on external PPG debt over 2023–24 will remain stable, compared to the level seen in 2021–22. The debt service burden, on both domestic and external debt, has also been significant for government debt in low-income countries. Interest expense in these countries was 9 percent of government spending in 2020–21, up from 5 percent in the 2010s (figure 2.3). Amid high and rising global interest rates, the elevated level of debt service could have dire implications for overall government spending. In countries with large debt service burdens, the challenge is to redirect spending to areas in need and reallocate resources to promote potential growth and increase resilience. Improving government spending efficiency through strengthened institutions and domestic governance is another challenge in countries with limited spending capacity.

Domestic revenue mobilization efforts can help reduce vulnerabilities associated with elevated debt levels in LMICs. Amid persistently weak growth, revenue collection is a major challenge for many LMICs, reflecting less developed markets and limited institutional capacity, particularly in low-income countries. Countries can mobilize revenue and improve collection mechanisms by introducing measures to broaden the tax base and strengthen revenue administration.

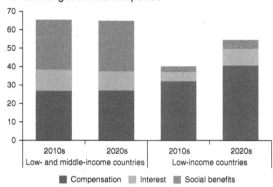

Figure 2.3 Composition of Government Expenditures in Low- and Middle-Income Countries, 2010s vs. 2020s
Percent of government expense

Sources: International Monetary Fund and World Bank.
Note: Compensation refers to employee compensation and includes wages, salaries, and social contributions. In some countries, data are for central governments. Data for 2020s cover 2020–21.

Notes

1. The information is based on long-term sovereign ratings by Fitch Ratings, as of end-October 2023. A default event is identified when a local-currency rating or a foreign-currency rating, or both, is changed to a default category. Therefore, a country can have multiple default events even within the same year. The 18 defaults since 2020 occurred in 10 middle-income countries: Argentina, Belarus, Ecuador, El Salvador, Ghana, Lebanon, Sri Lanka, Suriname, Ukraine, and Zambia.

2. The pandemic left many LMIC banks holding record levels of government debt, creating a new level of interdependence between banks and governments, with attendant risks. This is known as sovereign-bank nexus risk.

3. The Paris Club is a group of official creditors formed in 1956 to find coordinated solutions to payment difficulties experienced by debtor countries.

References

Essl, Sebastian, Sinem Kilic Celik, Patrick Kirby, and Andre Proite. 2019. "Debt in Low-Income Countries: Evolution, Implications, and Remedies." Policy Research Working Paper 8794, World Bank, Washington, DC.

Horn, Sebastian, Carmen M. Reinhart, and Christoph Trebesch. 2021. "China's Overseas Lending." *Journal of International Economics* 133: 103539. https://doi.org/10.1016/j.jinteco.2021.103539.

Kose, M. Ayhan, Sergei Kurlat, Franziska Ohnsorge, and Naotaka Sugawara. 2022. "A Cross-Country Database of Fiscal Space." *Journal of International Money and Finance* 128: 102682.

Kose, M. Ayhan, Peter Nagle, Franziska Ohnsorge, and Naotak Sugawara. 2021. *Global Waves of Debt: Causes and Consequences.* Washington, DC: World Bank.

Kose, M. Ayhan, and Franziska Ohnsorge, eds. 2023. *Falling Long-Term Growth Prospects: Trends, Expectations, and Policies.* Washington, DC: World Bank.

World Bank. 2023. *Global Economic Prospects.* June. Washington, DC: World Bank.

3. Charting Improvement in Public Debt Transparency and the Quality of Debt Reporting

Efforts to Improve Debt Transparency

Amid rising debt vulnerabilities in low- and middle-income countries and calls for greater debt transparency from the international community, the International Monetary Fund (IMF) and the World Bank began implementing a multipronged approach (MPA) to address debt vulnerabilities in 2018. Intensified debt risks owing to the COVID-19 pandemic heightened the urgency of implementing the MPA and highlighted the importance of debt sustainability and transparency for long-term financing for development. The MPA is designed to (a) strengthen debt transparency by helping borrowing countries, and by reaching out to creditors, to make better public sector debt data available; (b) support capacity development in public debt management to avert and mitigate debt vulnerabilities; (c) provide suitable tools to analyze debt developments and risks; and (d) adapt IMF and World Bank lending policies to better address debt risks and promote efficient resolution of debt crises.

The Sustainable Development Finance Policy (SDFP), launched by the International Development Association (IDA) on July 1, 2020, aims to incentivize IDA-eligible countries to move toward transparent and sustainable financing and to further enhance coordination between IDA and other creditors in support of reform efforts. The policy has two mutually reinforcing pillars: the Debt Sustainability Enhancement Program (DSEP) and the Program of Creditor Outreach (PCO). The DSEP pillar requires all IDA-eligible countries with elevated risk of debt distress to implement Performance and Policy Actions (PPAs) to address vulnerabilities in debt transparency, debt management, and fiscal sustainability systematically and proactively over a medium- to long-term time horizon. PPAs are designed and agreed upon through an intensive dialogue with country authorities, calibrated to countries' capacity constraints, and underpinned by core diagnostics. Support with implementation and institutionalization of reforms is provided through multiple channels, including development policy operations.

Under the PCO pillar, IDA promotes sustainable lending practices and provides a platform for information sharing. It also acts as a convener and works closely with the IMF and other multilateral development banks to promote stronger collective action, greater debt transparency, and closer coordination among borrowers and creditors to mitigate debt-related risks. PCO activities include regular global, regional, and in-country events that are designed to support IDA countries to improve debt sustainability and enhance debt transparency in the broader context of the World Bank's debt agenda. The PCO pillar aims to advance dialogue among a broader range of development partners to promote good practices of supporting information sharing, to facilitate coordination at the country-level among different creditors, and to scale up efforts on communication in the context of existing multilateral development bank consultation. Creditor outreach activities complement the DSEP pillar and other work by the World Bank to support countries' efforts to improve debt and fiscal sustainability, including through the joint IMF–World Bank MPA to address debt vulnerabilities and lending operations and technical assistance.

Since the inception of the SDFP in July 2020, 130 PPAs were approved in 55 countries in fiscal year 2021 (FY2021), 141 PPAs in 58 countries in FY2022, and 147 PPAs in 60 countries in FY2023. Implementation of these PPAs has required significant effort by IDA-eligible countries against a backdrop of overlapping crises and climate events that exacerbated existing challenges and diminished fiscal buffers. COVID-19 heightened public debt vulnerabilities, particularly in the world's poorest countries, as economic growth plummeted, expenditures rose, and revenues contracted.

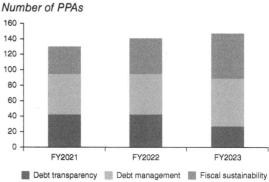

Figure 3.1 **Performance and Policy Actions, July 1, 2020, to June 30, 2023**
Number of PPAs

Debt transparency | Debt management | Fiscal sustainability

Source: IDA 2023.
Note: FY = fiscal year; PPAs = Performance and Policy Actions.

In FY2021, out of a total of 130 PPAs approved, 42 focused on debt transparency, 53 focused on debt management, and 35 focused on fiscal sustainability (figure 3.1). In FY2022, out of a total of 141 approved PPAs, 42 focused on debt transparency, 53 focused on debt management, and 46 focused on fiscal sustainability. In FY2023, out of a total of 147 PPAs, 27 focused on debt transparency, 62 focused on debt management, and 58 focused on fiscal sustainability. Debt transparency is intrinsically linked to debt management, so many of the actions that enable debt transparency, such as legislative and institutional reforms and strengthening debt monitoring and recording processes, are embedded in debt management PPAs.

In FY2021 and FY2022, more than 90 percent of countries satisfactorily implemented their PPAs. In FY2023, the share of countries that satisfactorily implemented their PPAs is about 80 percent. PPAs for the first two years of implementation focused primarily on debt transparency and debt management to reduce debt vulnerabilities, given the crisis context and the significant fiscal constraints faced by governments. In FY2023, as countries sought to unwind the supportive fiscal stance of previous years, PPAs had a greater focus on fiscal sustainability. In the context of the World Bank's Evolution Roadmap (World Bank 2023), the SDFP provides a platform to incentivize tax reforms given the increasing focus on domestic resource mobilization. Although the shift to more advanced, complex policy actions on fiscal sustainability is welcome, it has proved challenging. This highlights the importance of identifying the technical assistance requirements early in the process and building the necessary capacity in countries facing implementation challenges.

Direct and Indirect Disclosure of Public Debt Data

Public debt transparency requires the disclosure of comprehensive, accurate, detailed, and timely information on the volume and terms of public and publicly guaranteed (PPG) debt that is sufficiently detailed for scrutiny and accountability of government actions.

Debt transparency also equates with making this information available *directly* at the national level to legislatures, auditors, the media, and civil society, and *indirectly* to creditors, rating agencies, and the broader international community through reporting to international data collection systems. Timely and accurate loan-by-loan reporting to the World Bank Debtor Reporting System (DRS) on a quarterly and annual basis is a mandatory requirement for all countries borrowing from the International Bank for Reconstruction and Development or IDA. Data drawn from the DRS and disseminated by the World Bank in the International Debt Statistics database constitutes the only international, cross-country comparable data set of external debt of low- and middle-income countries.

The World Bank Debt Reporting Heat Map,[1] introduced in 2020 and updated annually, provides an assessment of direct reporting of the volume and composition of debt in official reports made publicly available by national authorities. It also charts the accountability of public borrowing through publication of medium-term debt strategies and annual borrowing plans and the extent to which data on guarantees, debt-related contingent liabilities, and loan collateral are made public. Implementation of PPAs to enhance debt transparency and strengthen debt management is reflected in improved outcomes.

The Heat Map shows that 43 percent of IDA-eligible countries recorded an improvement in direct reporting between 2020 and 2022. For example, greater debt transparency ranged from institutionalizing and publishing an annual debt report for the first time in countries such as Burundi and Tajikistan, to introducing more frequent quarterly reports and expanding the coverage of debt reports. Enhancements may be incremental and supported by successive PPAs. For example, Cabo Verde improved reporting of nonguaranteed debt of state-owned enterprises (SOEs) through publication of a quarterly SOE bulletin with fiscal risk assessment of the six largest SOEs (FY2022 PPA) and broadened the coverage of the quarterly public debt bulletin to include SOE debt and guaranteed debt from municipalities (FY2023 PPA). In Pakistan, the Debt Management Office published a semiannual debt bulletin for July–December 2021 with a creditor-wise breakdown of outstanding debt (FY2022 PPA); it also published an annual report on public debt that compares debt management strategy implementation with targets for end-FY2022, and provincial finance departments published semiannual debt bulletins for July–December 2022, following international reporting standards for Public Sector Debt Statistics (FY2023 PPA).

The improvements in debt transparency reflected in direct reporting of public debt at the national level, leveraged by PPAs and identified by the Heat Map, have led to concomitant improvements in the coverage, quality, and timeliness of reporting to the DRS. Publication of debt reports by national debt offices necessitates establishing and maintaining effective debt recording systems that continue to make incremental improvements in the overall coverage and accuracy of public debt data. The annual DRS status report assessed an improvement in the quality of reporting for the 2021 and 2022 submissions to the DRS for 13 IDA-eligible countries: Burkina Faso, Burundi, the Democratic Republic of Congo, The Gambia, the Lao People's Democratic Republic, Lesotho, Liberia, Mozambique, Myanmar, Senegal, Somalia, St. Lucia, and Tajikistan. Most of these countries[2] had at least one PPA focusing on debt transparency, and all satisfactorily implemented those PPAs. Similarly, PPAs focused on extending the legislative authority of national debt offices to capture comprehensive information on borrowing by SOEs and other contingent liabilities are laying the groundwork for data collection systems that will capture this information at the loan level and close gaps in reporting to the DRS. For example, to further enhance debt transparency and reporting and reduce debt and guarantees, the Sierra Leone Ministry of Finance will expand the coverage and publish an updated version of the "Report on the Outstanding Loans of Major State-Owned Enterprises" to include all guarantees and debt stock of all 17 registered SOEs as of end-December 2022 and disaggregate these by SOE (FY2023 PPA).

Harmonizing the formulation of PPAs with DRS reporting requirements also has a direct impact on the quality of the data disseminated annually in the International Debt Statistics database. In the case of Mozambique, these data were compromised by inconsistencies between historical stocks and flows data, unreported transactions, and the nonreporting of arrears, resulting in partial estimates at the aggregate level. To address these issues, the FY2023 PPA on debt transparency required the Mozambique government to prepare a comprehensive report using accurate external PPG and private nonguaranteed debt and addressing the severe inconsistencies between stocks and flows identified in the 2021 DRS report, and then publish an error-free debt report for 2022. As a result of satisfactory implementation of this PPA, the authorities prepared a comprehensive technical note that accompanied the annual 2022 DRS report and resolved all inconsistencies between stocks and flows identified in prior DRS reports. In addition, the authorities also produced and published a comprehensive debt report for 2022 that included error-free data on external PPG debt as well as information on borrowing by SOEs and for liquid natural gas projects, which have been important drivers of debt accumulation in recent years.

Enhancing debt transparency is critical to ensuring that debt-related vulnerabilities are known and contained, to enabling the creation of additional fiscal space, to raising external financing, and, when required, to supporting debt restructuring and debt relief. Policies like the SDFP, technical assistance, and lending operations are central to the goals of the 20th replenishment of IDA (or IDA20)—enhancing public debt transparency and the management of debt-related contingent liabilities. They also support IDA countries in publishing comprehensive PPG debt reports or fiscal risk statements. The World Bank is committed to the dissemination of comprehensive, timely, and transparent debt data, which are the foundation of sustainable borrowing and lending practices.

Notes

1. For more on the Debt Reporting Heat Map, see https://www.worldbank.org/en/topic/debt/brief/debt-transparency -report/2022.
2. Myanmar is not required to prepare PPAs because it is at low risk of debt distress (based on Low-Income Country Debt Sustainability Analysis).

Reference

World Bank. 2023. "World Bank Group Statement on Evolution Roadmap." News release, January 13, 2023. https://www .worldbank.org/en/news/statement/2023/01/13/world-bank-group-statement-on-evolution-roadmap.

4. The Debtor Reporting System and the Need for Innovative Approaches to Debt Management

Introduction

Not only is the World Bank Debtor Reporting System (DRS) an effective and transparent system for collecting, recording, and disseminating the external debt obligations of World Bank borrowers, but it can also help countries manage their debt.

The universe of debt instruments available to support the financing needs of low- and middle-income countries (LMICs) is vast. Debt managers therefore must consider numerous factors when constructing a debt portfolio appropriate to financing their countries' priorities. The most obvious of these factors is a debt instrument's interest rate, but other factors are also critical and include the currency mix, the share of fixed versus floating interest rates in the portfolio, the maturity profile, the choice of domestic versus external debt, and the share of nominal versus inflation-indexed instruments.

In the current environment of rising global interest rates, elevated interest payments, and shorter maturities offered on many loans, these choices are as challenging as ever. And elevated debt vulnerabilities and debt burdens in LMICs that have resulted from a decade-long mismatch between economic growth and debt accumulation only add to the difficulty of building and managing an appropriate and cost-efficient debt portfolio.

In this era of adverse financial market conditions and increasing debt vulnerabilities across LMICs, a close analysis of a country's debt portfolio—followed by portfolio optimization through active debt management—offers an avenue to easing debt service burdens.

Portfolio Analysis

That close analysis begins with a portfolio analysis, which can identify high-cost instruments and fees within a country's outstanding loans. In fact, such high costs and fees are all too common in the debt portfolios of LMICs. Drawing on the extensive and granular data in the DRS, it has been possible to highlight sharp variations in loan terms extended by official and private creditors in countries eligible only for concessional lending from the International Development Association (IDA), referred to as IDA-only countries (Mihalyi and Rivetti, forthcoming).

Research using DRS data examined over 10,000 loans to 53 such countries and focused on two features: loans with high interest rates and loans with high commitment fees.[1] It found that the average borrowing terms of debtor countries often mask large differences even within broad creditor groups, where a handful of loans may carry significantly worse terms. The research documented that, although most lending is done at low interest rates (below or near concessional thresholds), one-quarter of the lending is at rates higher than 5 percent. Such high-interest-rate loans are widespread across borrowers and are not limited to private sector creditors. In addition, many loans have additional fees attached. For example, 30 percent of low-income countries' outstanding debt has commitment fees of 0.25 percent or higher. Such fees can add up to substantial amounts when only a small fraction of the loan is drawn down.

Figure 4.1 shows the overall distribution of outstanding external public and publicly guaranteed debt in 2022 across the 53 IDA borrowing countries combined. The debt portfolio relies in large part on credit owed to multilateral creditors (especially IDA and regional multilaterals' concessional windows) with interest rates around 1 percent.[2] Many other official lenders offer concessional lending at rates below or around 2 percent, but

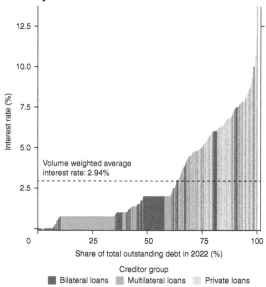

Figure 4.1 **Distribution of Interest Rates on Outstanding External Public Debt across IDA-Only Countries**

Source: World Bank Debtor Reporting System.
Note: Public and publicly guaranteed external debt across 53 IDA-only countries. IDA = International Development Association.

most countries will also incur some more expensive forms of borrowing from a mix of private and official borrowers. A quarter of the outstanding debt is at an interest rate above 5 percent. And the average borrowing rate (weighted by volume) is 2.94 percent.

Individual country portfolios show similar patterns. Interest rates cover a large range, and most countries have at least some loans that carry rates above 5 percent, including loans from multilateral, bilateral, and private lenders. Out of the 53 countries analyzed, 45 have at least one loan from an official sector creditor with an interest rate above 5 percent.

The cost of a loan is typically measured by the interest rate charged, but additional fees contribute to its all-in cost. One of the most important of these is the commitment fee, which the lender receives in exchange for keeping the option for the borrower to draw down the rest of the credit at the preagreed rate in the future. Although interest costs generally dwarf commitment fees in the case of commercial credit, these fees can often be a substantial cost factor for certain project loans that are drawn down more slowly.[3] This slower drawdown may be increasingly common as governments—because of debt sustainability concerns—consider suspending the disbursements on funds they have already secured for projects.

Figure 4.2 shows the distribution of commitment fees across the more than 10,000 official loans to IDA-only countries in the DRS. According to the World Bank analysis, over a third (37 percent) of these loans attract a (nonzero) commitment fee. The most typical fee is 0.5 percent of the undisbursed loan amount. Nonzero commitment fees exist across all creditor types.

Drawing down a loan in full can often take up to 10 years or longer (Mihalyi and Rivetti, forthcoming). In fact, whereas budget support loans typically have staggered disbursements that depend on the disbursement conditions being met, project loans are disbursed in line with project implementation progress. Borrowers experiencing macroeconomic difficulties or other forms of uncertainty (for example, political instability or climate shocks) may see further delays in project execution compared to normal timelines. As a result, commitment fees of 0.25 percent to 0.50 percent (and higher) add up to substantial additional costs over a 10-year period.

A key lesson from the analysis presented in the preceding paragraphs is that governments should closely scrutinize the terms of their debt instruments, because fees and high interest rates may be increasing their debt service burdens. For the same creditor categories (multilateral, bilateral, and commercial) providing credit to borrowers with similar income during the same period, there might be considerable differences in both interest rates and fees. Data from the DRS can be used as benchmarks against which the terms of new loans can be measured and compared.

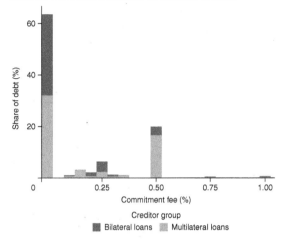

Figure 4.2 **Histogram of Commitment Fees across the Debt Portfolio of Official Loans**

Source: World Bank Debtor Reporting System.
Note: The distribution shown is volume weighted based on 2022 outstanding loan amounts. Loans with fees above 1 percent (outliers) are shown as 1.00.

To fully appreciate the cost of various debt instruments in a portfolio, as well as the overall cost of the portfolio, each borrowing country needs to conduct regular and detailed debt portfolio analyses. A granular country-level debt portfolio analysis may reveal loans that fall into the categories above, identify additional risky elements in the portfolio, and provide an estimate of the costs of loans in the portfolio. DRS data, compiled by country authorities and collected and curated by the World Bank, provide comprehensive information for such analysis.

Active Portfolio Management

Once a portfolio analysis is conducted, debt managers can employ an active debt management strategy—including repurchases, swaps, and cancellations. If done correctly, such a strategy can optimize the profile of their public debt and potentially achieve considerable financial gains. Such a strategy can be achieved primarily through loan renegotiations or, more often, through liability management operations, the most common of which are debt buybacks and debt exchanges, or switches (World Bank 2015).

Debt buybacks can be used not only as a risk management tool but also as an extraordinary operation aimed at reducing a country's stock of nominal debt if the debt is trading at a deep discount, as in the case of several emerging markets and LMICs, given the recent rise of international interest rates. Buybacks are most commonly used by sovereigns to mitigate refinancing risk by reducing the amount of short-term maturities. Many IDA-eligible countries that have issued bonds in international capital markets have bought back all or part of prior issues in order to lower interest rates and lengthen maturities. For example, Cameroon and Rwanda both recently repurchased Eurobonds nearing maturity using proceeds from new debt with longer maturities.

In external markets, buybacks are most commonly executed through primary market operations called tender offers, whereby the issuer announces its intention to buy back a certain bond.

The process is similar to the book-building process used to sell international bonds. As a primary market operation, tender offers carry some risk that the market can move against the issuer—that is, prices rise with the expectation that the issuer wants to buy it. The other risk involved in tender offers is a lack of interest from investors in selling the bond if it is considered a scarce asset. In these cases, a debt exchange, through which the investor can keep its credit exposure, might be more effective. Some countries execute external buybacks in a discrete way through the secondary markets. This option reduces the risk of the market moving against the issuer but requires the sovereign to have capacity to execute secondary market operations or hire a financial agent to do so.

Debt exchanges involve swapping outstanding debt for new debt. By doing so, these instruments allow governments to lengthen the average maturity of their debt portfolio and to reduce short-term maturities. Debt exchanges should be voluntary and carried out at market prices. In fact, any non-NPV-neutral[4] exchange would inevitably trigger a rating action or be rejected by creditors. Some countries have regular debt exchange auctions as part of their borrowing plan to reduce refinancing risk and debt service costs, modify the characteristics of the debt portfolio, provide liquidity to newly created benchmarks, and redeem off-the-run bonds.

International financial institutions and other official creditors can play an active role in facilitating these liability management operations. For instance, a multilateral or bilateral creditor may judge that paying down certain high-interest loans or bonds is a more efficient use of funds than providing new borrowing. This was the case in Benin in 2018 when the country conducted a debt reprofiling operation that was financed by an international financial institution with a partial guarantee provided by the World Bank. The guarantee amounted to €154.8 million for a commercial loan in the amount of €387 million. A portion of the funds was used to buy back debt owed to the West African Development Bank and repay domestic debt (World Bank 2022). This case also presents an example of the trade-offs of swapping one risk for another—in this case high-interest-rate domestic debt for a low-interest-rate external loan with a currency risk.

Debt-for-nature swaps are liability management operations instruments that have gained renewed attention in the context of growing environmental, social, and governance investments and increasing donor interest in green investments (Chamon et al. 2022). These swaps are intended to combine debt relief to participating sovereigns with partial earmarking of the freed-up resources for green projects. Recent debt-for-nature swaps involved several LMICs including Belize, Ecuador, and Gabon, and entailed buying back existing debt at a discount thanks to donor subsidies provided through cash or credit enhancements on new debt.

These options typically apply to marketable debt. For project loans, there are two other options to consider to effectively manage debt. First, the drawdown of certain loans may be prioritized to avoid additional commitment fees. Second, if a country finds itself in debt distress, some of its loans can be canceled if additional disbursement is not efficient from a cost/risk perspective. The decision should take into consideration the rate of the commitment fee, cancellation fees (if any), and the expected loan disbursement schedule. For example, after declaring default in 2021, Zambian authorities reviewed their entire project loan portfolio and canceled some loans, despite the initial disbursements.

LMICs are facing increasing difficulties in servicing their debts and need additional mechanisms to help address their debt vulnerabilities. Debt portfolio analysis and active debt management—both of which can use the DRS as an important resource—are a large part of the solution.

Notes

1. This analysis is centered on IDA-only borrowing countries, which are eligible solely for concessional financing (IDA) in fiscal year 2023 from the World Bank and which report to the World Bank's Debtor Reporting System (reporting is a requirement for accessing World Bank funds), except Sudan and Sri Lanka. The analysis excludes Sudan because the country has yet to reach the Heavily Indebted Poor Countries (HIPC) Initiative completion point and still has large pre-HIPC debts with especially high interest rates (15 percent and higher). Sri Lanka is excluded from the analysis because it reverse graduated in December 2022.
2. Variable interest rates are converted into fixed rates at the prevailing swap rate (September 2023) for the outstanding maturity of the loan plus spread. The swap rate reflects the cost of converting a variable rate loan into a fixed rate loan. Over 95 percent of the loans (in value) are in either special drawing rights or one of the currencies it is composed of (Chinese yuan, euro, Japanese yen, British pound, and US dollar).
3. Multilateral creditors may also waive the commitment fees for certain periods.
4. NPV neutrality implies that the net present value (or NPV) of the new debt is the same as that for the old debt.

References

Chamon, Marcos D., Erik Klok, Vimal V. Thakoor, and Jeromin Zettelmeyer. 2022. *Debt-for-Climate Swaps: Analysis, Design, and Implementation*. IMF Working Paper 2022/162. Washington, DC: International Monetary Fund.

Mihalyi, David, and Rivetti, Diego. Forthcoming. "Optimizing Debt Portfolio in Low-Income Countries." EMFMD note, World Bank, Washington, DC.

World Bank. 2015. "Bond Buybacks and Exchanges: Background Note." World Bank Group Government Bond Markets Advisory Services Program background notes series, World Bank, Washington, DC.

World Bank. 2022. *World Development Report 2022: Finance for an Equitable Recovery*. Washington, DC: World Bank.

5. The International Debt Statistics Database: A Gold Mine for Researchers

Introduction

Debt distress is all too common among low- and middle-income countries (LMICs) today. Much can be done in response to debt distress events, yet being able to identify and predict the likelihood of such events in advance would be of enormous help. Fortunately, International Debt Statistics (IDS)—the World Bank's comprehensive database of debt and debt-related data, and the only source of consistent, cross-country comparisons of those data—contains the information needed to predict distress events and allow policy makers to take proactive, rather than exclusively reactive, measures to avoid or mitigate those events and their dire consequences.

A Wealth of Data

The World Bank has been collecting external debt data from LMICs since the 1950s, each year adding additional detailed information on stocks and flows of external debt, including country-specific data and aggregated information on debt trends.

Today the World Bank collects data on 122 countries, including more than 45,000 active loans (with 2,500 to 3,000 new loans added annually), individual loan terms and conditions, annual stocks and flows for each loan, and historical series. It also has pipeline data for scheduled debt service payments on existing loans through 2030.

In collecting all that information, the World Bank has created a virtual gold mine for researchers and policy makers, who can tap the IDS database for information not available elsewhere. And today the data contained in the IDS are more critical than ever.

Over the past decade, debt distress risks have been rising in the developing world, particularly among the world's poorest countries. Nearly 60 percent of countries eligible for International Development Association (IDA) resources are currently in debt distress or at high risk of it, double the number from 10 years ago (figure 5.1). Over the same period, the share of IDA-eligible countries that face only low risk of debt distress has decreased by more than two-thirds.

There is much the global community can do in response. For example, it can increase financing for low-income countries to help them invest in critical sectors such as health, education, and infrastructure; accelerate debt restructuring to deliver the relief that was announced several years ago; and double down on the reform agenda by ensuring that global initiatives to bolster low-income countries are complemented by ambitious domestic measures. These efforts would go a long way toward mitigating the impact of rising debt burdens in LMICs (Gill and Kose 2023).

Improving the accuracy of debt distress predictions in LMICs would also be of enormous help, because countries can often take measures before a potential distress event to avoid or mitigate the event and its dire consequences. Recent research by a group of World Bank economists (Graf von Luckner et al., forthcoming) combines IDS debt with a volume of other macroeconomic data to create a model to predict external debt servicing difficulties ("sovereign debt distress") in low-income countries. At the heart of the research is an empirical model that links the risk of debt distress to indicators of the debt burden and debt carrying capacity. Data series in the IDS database play crucial roles on both sides of this model, in identifying debt distress events and in constructing suitable variables that can accurately predict them.

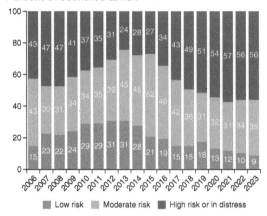

Figure 5.1 **Risk of External Debt Distress among IDA-Eligible Countries, 2006–23**
Percent of countries at risk

■ Low risk ■ Moderate risk ■ High risk or in distress

Source: Joint World Bank–International Monetary Fund Debt Sustainability Framework for Low-Income Countries (LIC DSF) database.
Note: The figure shows risk assessments for all IDA-eligible countries with an available LIC DSF risk rating as of August 2023. IDA = International Development Association.

Using IDS Arrears Data to Identify Debt Distress Events

To date, identifying debt distress events in LMICs has proved challenging because of a lack of systematic data on payment defaults for most creditor types. Generally, comprehensive data exist on the incidence of debt restructurings, but these events mark the resolution, rather than the onset, of a debt crisis and are therefore of secondary interest in debt prediction exercises (Das, Papaioannou, and Trebesch 2012). Detailed and systematic data on missed payments (defaults) are available for external bondholders, and those data are tracked meticulously by rating agencies, academic researchers, and the financial press (see for example Asonuma and Trebesch 2016). Yet no systematic data are available on the incidence and magnitude of payment defaults toward nonbond private and bilateral external creditors. Given that bondholders account for about 15 percent of external public and publicly guaranteed (PPG) debt in IDA-eligible countries, unobserved default events represent a major data gap for country surveillance and debt sustainability analysis (Horn, Reinhart, and Trebesch 2021).

In the absence of detailed default data, IDS data series on the accumulation of principal and interest arrears offer an indispensable proxy measure for the timing and magnitude of payment defaults. The empirical relationship between arrears and default events is not straightforward: positive arrears do not automatically imply the occurrence of a debt distress event (Farah-Yacoub, Graf von Luckner, and Reinhart 2022). Temporary or limited buildups of arrears might have benign reasons, such as low debt-management capacity, or they might be a cost-efficient way of obtaining short-term finance in underdeveloped capital markets. Sovereign debt contracts typically include grace periods for missed payments (Gelpern et al. 2021). For World Bank loans, for example, a default is declared when a payment is overdue for 180 days.

The academic literature has therefore defined arrears accumulation thresholds above which arrears are assumed to be systematically associated with sovereign debt distress (see for example Detragiache and Spilimbergo 2001; Kraay and Nehru 2006; Medas et al. 2018). The Graf von Luckner et al. (forthcoming) research follows the literature and treats country-year observations as distress episodes if a sovereign has outstanding interest or principal arrears that exceed 5 percent of its total external PPG debt stock for three consecutive years. This measure provides a highly useful indicator to track the incidence of debt distress over time, both in a broad cross-section of countries and when analyzing individual country histories.

According to this arrears-based default metric, more than a dozen IDA-eligible countries are currently in external sovereign debt distress and several have been so for decades.[1] This finding underscores the widespread debt service difficulties that the world's poorest countries face, even if only few of them are assessed to be in default by rating agencies.

Using IDS Data to Predict Debt Distress Events

Past debt distress episodes can be used to analyze the potential of different macroeconomic, financial, and political variables to serve as early warning indicators for crises. For this purpose, Graf von Luckner et al. (forthcoming) developed an algorithm to systematically evaluate the out-of-sample predictive performance of more than 600,000 linear debt distress prediction models. Their analysis compares the performance of different combinations of more than 20 predictor variables that have been commonly used in the academic literature, for example, a country's debt profile, as well as its fiscal, external, political, and institutional characteristics (see Badia et al. 2022 for a literature review). This set of variables includes a variety of measures that, for a broad cross-section of low-income countries, are available only through the IDS. These measures include the external PPG debt stock, the net present value of external debt, and different measures of a country's debt servicing costs.

Figure 5.2 Projected Debt Service Payments and External Default Episodes, Selected Countries, 1970–2021
Projected debt service as percent of exports

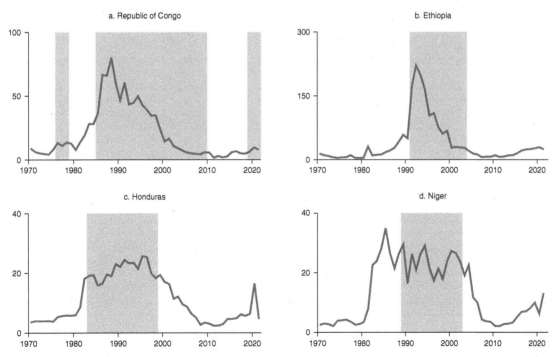

Sources: World Bank International Debt Statistics and World Development Indicators databases.
Note: This figure shows one-year-ahead projected debt service payments through principal and interest in percent of lagged exports (green lines) and external sovereign default episodes as measured by the arrears-based proxy (see text for definition).

The systematic analysis of the predictive performance of these variables shows that, besides measures of institutional strength, IDS-derived variables on debt servicing costs are most informative in predicting external debt distress episodes in low-income countries. More specifically, the granular data on individual loan terms that underlie the IDS data allow for the construction of one-year-ahead projections of a country's principal and interest payments due to external creditors.

The analysis shows that an increase in projected debt service payments is a robust and significant predictor of debt distress episodes. In fact, out of the 100 top performing models designed to predict debt distress episodes identified by Graf von Luckner et al. (forthcoming), all 100 include projected debt service payments as a predictor variable. Figure 5.2 illustrates this empirical link for selected country cases by plotting the debt service indicator (green line) as well as the arrears-based proxy of distress episodes (gray shaded areas).

These findings clearly illustrate the enormous value of the granular IDS debt data to inform and predict debt distress in LMICs. They are just one example of the potential usefulness of the 70 years of data that reside within International Debt Statistics database.

Note

1. These countries include Chad, the Democratic Republic of Congo, Djibouti, Eritrea, Grenada, Mozambique, Myanmar, Somalia, Sudan, Syrian Arab Republic, Tanzania, Yemen, Zambia, and Zimbabwe.

References

Asonuma, Tamon, and Christoph Trebesch. 2016. "Sovereign Debt Restructurings: Preemptive or Post-Default." *Journal of the European Economic Association* 14 (1): 175–214.

Badia, Marialuz Moreno, Paulo Medas, Pranav Gupta, and Yuan Xiang. 2022. "Debt Is Not Free." *Journal of International Money and Finance* 127 (October): 102654.

Das, Udaibir, Michael Papaioannou, and Christoph Trebesch. 2012. *Sovereign Debt Restructurings 1950–2010: Literature Survey, Data, and Stylized Facts.* IMF Working Paper 2012/203. Washington, DC: International Monetary Fund.

Detragiache, Enrica, and Antonio Spilimbergo. 2001. *Crises and Liquidity: Evidence and Interpretation.* IMF Working Paper No. 2001/02. Washington, DC: International Monetary Fund.

Farah-Yacoub, Juan, Clemens Graf von Luckner, and Carmen Reinhart. 2022. "Chasing the Storm: Debt Distress, Arrears, and Defaults." Presentation at the conference, "DebtCon 5," Florence, Italy, May 25–26. https://fbf.eui.eu/wp-content /uploads/2022/06/von-Luckne_presentation.pdf.

Gelpern, Anna, Sebastian Horn, Scott Morris, Bradley Parks, and Christoph Trebesch. 2021. "How China Lends: A Rare Look into 100 Debt Contracts with Foreign Governments." *Economic Policy*, eiac054. https://doi.org/10.1093/epolic /eiac054.

Gill, Indermit, and Ayhan Kose. 2023. "A Tragedy Is Unfolding in the Poorest Countries." Project Syndicate, September 18, 2023. https://www.project-syndicate.org/commentary/low-income-countries-debt-distress-instability-declining -prospects-by-indermit-gill-and-m-ayhan-kose-2023-09.

Graf von Luckner, Clemens, Sebastian Horn, Aart Kraay, and Rita Ramalho. Forthcoming. "An Empirical Model for Debt Distress in Low-Income Countries." Policy Research Working Paper, World Bank, Washington, DC.

Horn, Sebastian, Carmen M. Reinhart, and Christoph Trebesch. 2021. "China's Overseas Lending." *Journal of International Economics* 133: 103539. https://doi.org/10.1016/j.jinteco.2021.103539.

Kraay, Aart, and Vikram Nehru. 2006. "When Is External Debt Sustainable?" *World Bank Economic Review* 20 (3): 341–65.

Medas, Paulo, Tigran Poghosyan, Yizhi Xu, Juan Farah-Yacoub, and Kerstin Gerling. 2018. "Fiscal Crises." *Journal of International Money and Finance* 88: 191–207.

PART 2

Aggregate and Country Tables

(US$ billion, unless otherwise indicated)

Snapshot	2022
Total external debt stocks	**8,966**
External debt stocks as % of	
Exports	89
GNI	24
Debt service as % of	
Exports	13
GNI	4
Net financial flows, debt and equity	**305**
Net debt inflows	-185
Net equity inflows	490
GNI	**37,404**
Population (million)	**6,579**

Figure 1 Public and publicly guaranteed debt, by creditor and creditor type in 2022, including IMF credit

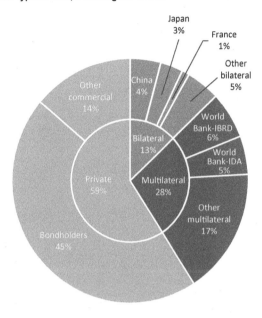

Figure 2 Average terms on new debt commitments from official and private creditors

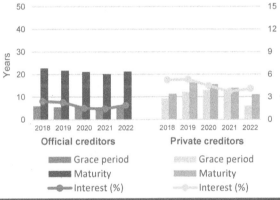

Summary External Debt Data	2010	2018	2019	2020	2021	2022
Total external debt stocks	**4,326**	**7,879**	**8,250**	**8,644**	**9,277**	**8,966**
Long-term external debt stocks	**3,022**	**5,631**	**5,947**	**6,278**	**6,427**	**6,207**
Public and publicly guaranteed debt from:	1,565	2,945	3,139	3,371	3,489	3,448
Official creditors	822	1,101	1,142	1,257	1,285	1,324
Multilateral	467	659	694	779	811	860
of which: World Bank	239	323	341	377	390	407
Bilateral	355	442	448	478	473	464
Private creditors	743	1,844	1,996	2,115	2,205	2,123
Bondholders	462	1,360	1,513	1,632	1,706	1,626
Commercial banks and others	281	483	483	482	498	498
Private nonguaranteed debt from:	1,457	2,686	2,809	2,906	2,937	2,760
Bondholders	210	488	573	676	694	618
Commercial banks and others	1,248	2,198	2,236	2,230	2,243	2,142
Use of IMF credit and SDR allocations	**134**	**151**	**171**	**224**	**415**	**408**
IMF credit	49	74	94	145	142	149
SDR allocations	85	77	77	80	273	260
Short-term external debt stocks	**1,169**	**2,097**	**2,132**	**2,142**	**2,435**	**2,350**
Disbursements, long-term	**647**	**1,115**	**1,209**	**1,217**	**1,195**	**908**
Public and publicly guaranteed sector	285	476	454	504	472	338
Private sector not guaranteed	362	639	755	713	723	571
Principal repayments, long-term	**362**	**790**	**895**	**888**	**932**	**1,017**
Public and publicly guaranteed sector	135	261	261	292	294	301
Private sector not guaranteed	227	529	634	596	638	716
Interest payments, long-term	**99**	**211**	**230**	**203**	**221**	**210**
Public and publicly guaranteed sector	47	108	123	107	114	113
Private sector not guaranteed	52	103	108	95	108	98

(US$ billion, unless otherwise indicated)

Snapshot	2022
Total external debt stocks	**3,345**
External debt stocks as % of	
Exports	65
GNI	16
Debt service as % of	
Exports	11
GNI	3
Net financial flows, debt and equity	**-31**
Net debt inflows	-289
Net equity inflows	258
GNI	**20,509**
Population (million)	**2,069**

Figure 1 Public and publicly guaranteed debt, by creditor and creditor type in 2022, including IMF credit

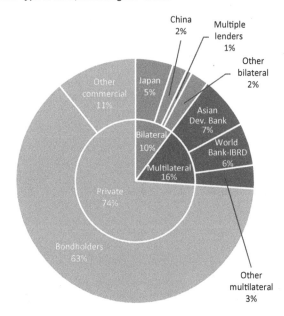

Figure 2 Average terms on new debt commitments from official and private creditors

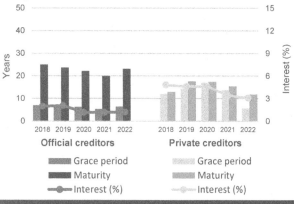

Summary External Debt Data	2010	2018	2019	2020	2021	2022
Total external debt stocks	**1,193**	**2,805**	**2,999**	**3,274**	**3,676**	**3,345**
Long-term external debt stocks	**559**	**1,416**	**1,623**	**1,852**	**1,974**	**1,814**
Public and publicly guaranteed debt from:	319	647	733	838	911	884
Official creditors	217	211	214	235	234	229
Multilateral	87	111	116	130	135	138
of which: World Bank	47	60	62	66	68	69
Bilateral	130	100	98	105	99	91
Private creditors	102	436	520	603	676	655
Bondholders	73	372	451	535	591	559
Commercial banks and others	29	64	69	68	86	96
Private nonguaranteed debt from:	240	768	890	1,014	1,064	930
Bondholders	20	216	276	371	393	337
Commercial banks and others	220	553	614	643	671	593
Use of IMF credit and SDR allocations	**18**	**17**	**17**	**18**	**75**	**72**
IMF credit	0	0	0	1	1	1
SDR allocations	18	16	16	17	74	70
Short-term external debt stocks	**616**	**1,373**	**1,359**	**1,403**	**1,626**	**1,460**
Disbursements, long-term	**117**	**408**	**513**	**501**	**487**	**339**
Public and publicly guaranteed sector	48	132	130	150	166	83
Private sector not guaranteed	69	276	383	350	321	256
Principal repayments, long-term	**65**	**253**	**314**	**281**	**343**	**461**
Public and publicly guaranteed sector	29	34	44	60	77	91
Private sector not guaranteed	36	219	270	221	266	371
Interest payments, long-term	**16**	**47**	**58**	**53**	**64**	**66**
Public and publicly guaranteed sector	9	18	23	23	29	33
Private sector not guaranteed	7	29	35	30	35	32

(US$ billion, unless otherwise indicated)

Snapshot	2022
Total external debt stocks	1,448
External debt stocks as % of	
Exports	95
GNI	36
Debt service as % of	
Exports	18
GNI	7
Net financial flows, debt and equity	-42
Net debt inflows	-38
Net equity inflows	-3
GNI	4,042
Population (million)	397

Figure 1 Public and publicly guaranteed debt, by creditor and creditor type in 2022, including IMF credit

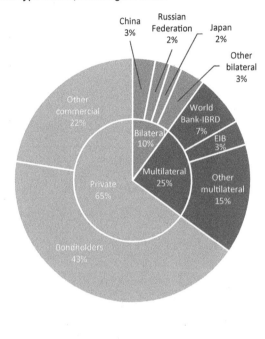

Figure 2 Average terms on new debt commitments from official and private creditors

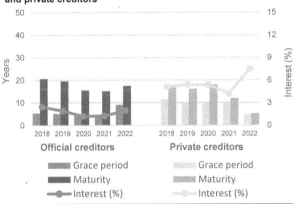

Summary External Debt Data	2010	2018	2019	2020	2021	2022
Total external debt stocks	1,166	1,425	1,438	1,470	1,504	1,448
Long-term external debt stocks	891	1,185	1,179	1,192	1,171	1,092
Public and publicly guaranteed debt from:	341	495	513	535	529	507
Official creditors	96	140	141	150	150	168
Multilateral	62	90	89	98	99	114
of which: World Bank	33	40	40	42	42	44
Bilateral	34	50	52	52	51	54
Private creditors	245	355	372	385	379	339
Bondholders	85	206	234	248	252	223
Commercial banks and others	160	149	137	137	127	117
Private nonguaranteed debt from:	551	690	666	656	642	585
Bondholders	34	75	81	83	78	68
Commercial banks and others	517	615	585	574	564	517
Use of IMF credit and SDR allocations	46	29	27	31	64	63
IMF credit	28	13	11	15	14	15
SDR allocations	17	16	15	16	50	48
Short-term external debt stocks	228	212	232	247	269	294
Disbursements, long-term	219	199	213	227	194	152
Public and publicly guaranteed sector	84	74	81	95	62	56
Private sector not guaranteed	135	126	132	133	133	96
Principal repayments, long-term	159	224	212	226	201	217
Public and publicly guaranteed sector	40	81	62	83	57	69
Private sector not guaranteed	119	144	150	143	143	148
Interest payments, long-term	32	44	43	43	42	37
Public and publicly guaranteed sector	8	20	20	20	20	17
Private sector not guaranteed	24	24	24	23	22	20

(US$ billion, unless otherwise indicated)

Snapshot	2022
Total external debt stocks	**1,989**
External debt stocks as % of	
Exports	132
GNI	40
Debt service as % of	
Exports	18
GNI	5
Net financial flows, debt and equity	**224**
Net debt inflows	71
Net equity inflows	153
GNI	**5,005**
Population (million)	**585**

Figure 2 Average terms on new debt commitments from official and private creditors

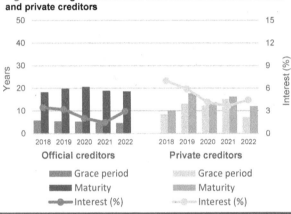

Figure 1 Public and publicly guaranteed debt, by creditor and creditor type in 2022, including IMF credit

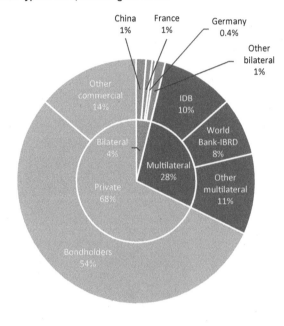

Summary External Debt Data	2010	2018	2019	2020	2021	2022
Total external debt stocks	**1,007**	**1,866**	**1,902**	**1,895**	**1,948**	**1,989**
Long-term external debt stocks	**836**	**1,587**	**1,596**	**1,618**	**1,619**	**1,649**
Public and publicly guaranteed debt from:	426	849	857	890	896	902
Official creditors	158	209	209	225	235	246
Multilateral	121	162	168	184	195	208
of which: World Bank	48	58	60	67	71	77
Bilateral	36	47	41	41	40	38
Private creditors	268	640	648	665	661	655
Bondholders	227	500	506	531	528	522
Commercial banks and others	41	140	142	134	134	133
Private nonguaranteed debt from:	411	738	739	728	723	747
Bondholders	133	171	184	185	179	168
Commercial banks and others	278	567	555	543	543	580
Use of IMF credit and SDR allocations	**19**	**45**	**62**	**78**	**113**	**116**
IMF credit	2	29	47	62	57	63
SDR allocations	17	15	15	16	56	54
Short-term external debt stocks	**151**	**234**	**243**	**199**	**216**	**224**
Disbursements, long-term	**190**	**280**	**250**	**283**	**294**	**241**
Public and publicly guaranteed sector	83	128	100	132	95	83
Private sector not guaranteed	108	153	150	151	198	158
Principal repayments, long-term	**83**	**177**	**235**	**225**	**243**	**187**
Public and publicly guaranteed sector	39	75	91	72	78	57
Private sector not guaranteed	44	102	144	153	166	130
Interest payments, long-term	**35**	**73**	**79**	**63**	**71**	**58**
Public and publicly guaranteed sector	19	44	50	37	37	34
Private sector not guaranteed	15	29	29	26	34	25

MIDDLE EAST AND NORTH AFRICA

(US$ billion, unless otherwise indicated)

Snapshot	2022
Total external debt stocks	**431**
External debt stocks as % of	
Exports	..
GNI	27
Debt service as % of	
Exports	..
GNI	3
Net financial flows, debt and equity	**31**
Net debt inflows	17
Net equity inflows	13
GNI	**1,595**
Population (million)	**412**

Figure 2 **Average terms on new debt commitments from official and private creditors**

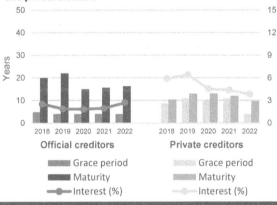

Figure 1 **Public and publicly guaranteed debt, by creditor and creditor type in 2022, including IMF credit**

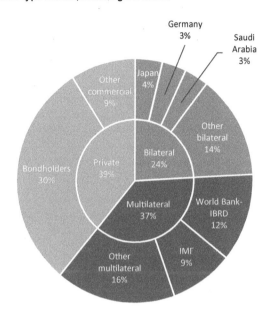

Summary External Debt Data	2010	2018	2019	2020	2021	2022
Total external debt stocks	**210**	**350**	**369**	**398**	**421**	**431**
Long-term external debt stocks	**161**	**278**	**289**	**301**	**299**	**290**
Public and publicly guaranteed debt from:	130	221	237	258	261	256
Official creditors	91	134	138	151	147	147
Multilateral	37	62	66	76	77	79
of which: World Bank	13	27	30	33	34	35
Bilateral	54	72	73	75	70	68
Private creditors	39	87	99	108	114	109
Bondholders	27	71	79	86	91	84
Commercial banks and others	12	17	20	22	23	25
Private nonguaranteed debt from:	31	56	52	43	37	34
Bondholders	1	1	1	1	1	1
Commercial banks and others	30	56	51	42	36	33
Use of IMF credit and SDR allocations	**11**	**23**	**26**	**36**	**52**	**49**
IMF credit	1	14	17	27	26	24
SDR allocations	10	9	9	9	26	24
Short-term external debt stocks	**38**	**49**	**55**	**61**	**70**	**92**
Disbursements, long-term	**23**	**52**	**39**	**36**	**38**	**26**
Public and publicly guaranteed sector	14	34	31	34	35	25
Private sector not guaranteed	9	18	8	2	2	1
Principal repayments, long-term	**18**	**24**	**27**	**29**	**32**	**28**
Public and publicly guaranteed sector	11	14	15	17	25	24
Private sector not guaranteed	8	11	12	12	7	4
Interest payments, long-term	**6**	**10**	**11**	**9**	**8**	**9**
Public and publicly guaranteed sector	5	7	9	6	7	7
Private sector not guaranteed	2	2	3	2	2	2

SOUTH ASIA

(US$ billion, unless otherwise indicated)

Snapshot	2022
Total external debt stocks	**919**
External debt stocks as % of	
Exports	100
GNI	21
Debt service as % of	
Exports	10
GNI	2
Net financial flows, debt and equity	**58**
Net debt inflows	23
Net equity inflows	34
GNI	**4,304**
Population (million)	**1,919**

Figure 2 **Average terms on new debt commitments from official and private creditors**

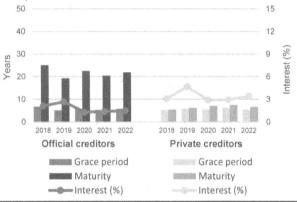

Figure 1 **Public and publicly guaranteed debt, by creditor and creditor type in 2022, including IMF credit**

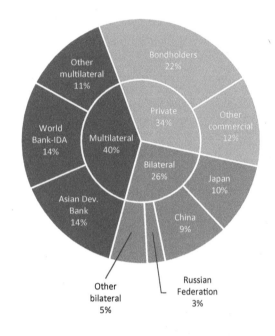

Summary External Debt Data	2010	2018	2019	2020	2021	2022
Total external debt stocks	**410**	**744**	**804**	**831**	**913**	**919**
Long-term external debt stocks	**323**	**598**	**652**	**680**	**719**	**712**
Public and publicly guaranteed debt from:	189	341	366	387	417	419
Official creditors	156	204	220	249	264	273
Multilateral	101	122	130	146	154	161
of which: World Bank	64	72	75	82	84	83
Bilateral	56	82	90	103	110	112
Private creditors	33	137	147	138	153	146
Bondholders	18	95	104	93	99	95
Commercial banks and others	15	41	43	45	54	51
Private nonguaranteed debt from:	134	257	285	293	302	293
Bondholders	13	14	19	27	33	34
Commercial banks and others	120	243	266	266	269	260
Use of IMF credit and SDR allocations	**20**	**16**	**17**	**20**	**42**	**41**
IMF credit	11	8	9	11	10	10
SDR allocations	9	8	8	9	32	30
Short-term external debt stocks	**67**	**130**	**135**	**131**	**152**	**166**
Disbursements, long-term	**52**	**84**	**104**	**98**	**101**	**73**
Public and publicly guaranteed sector	31	43	50	49	64	44
Private sector not guaranteed	22	40	54	50	38	29
Principal repayments, long-term	**24**	**58**	**52**	**77**	**53**	**65**
Public and publicly guaranteed sector	9	29	26	35	27	30
Private sector not guaranteed	15	29	26	42	26	34
Interest payments, long-term	**6**	**19**	**18**	**16**	**17**	**20**
Public and publicly guaranteed sector	3	6	8	6	7	8
Private sector not guaranteed	4	12	10	10	10	13

SUB-SAHARAN AFRICA

(US$ billion, unless otherwise indicated)

Snapshot	2022
Total external debt stocks	**833**
External debt stocks as % of	
Exports	157
GNI	43
Debt service as % of	
Exports	16
GNI	4
Net financial flows, debt and equity	**65**
Net debt inflows	31
Net equity inflows	35
GNI	**1,957**
Population (million)	**1,196**

Figure 2 Average terms on new debt commitments from official and private creditors

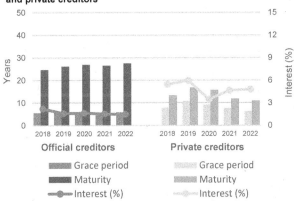

Figure 1 Public and publicly guaranteed debt, by creditor and creditor type in 2022, including IMF credit

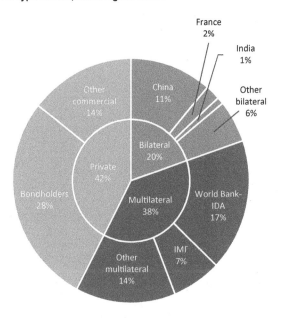

Summary External Debt Data	2010	2018	2019	2020	2021	2022
Total external debt stocks	**340**	**689**	**738**	**776**	**816**	**833**
Long-term external debt stocks	**252**	**568**	**608**	**634**	**645**	**650**
Public and publicly guaranteed debt from:	160	392	431	462	475	480
Official creditors	104	202	220	247	255	262
Multilateral	59	111	125	145	151	161
of which: World Bank	34	65	74	86	91	99
Bilateral	45	91	95	102	104	101
Private creditors	57	190	211	216	220	218
Bondholders	32	117	139	139	146	143
Commercial banks and others	24	73	72	77	74	75
Private nonguaranteed debt from:	91	176	177	172	169	171
Bondholders	9	12	12	10	11	10
Commercial banks and others	83	164	164	162	159	160
Use of IMF credit and SDR allocations	**19**	**22**	**23**	**41**	**69**	**68**
IMF credit	6	9	11	29	33	34
SDR allocations	14	12	12	13	35	34
Short-term external debt stocks	**68**	**100**	**107**	**101**	**103**	**114**
Disbursements, long-term	**45**	**92**	**90**	**71**	**81**	**77**
Public and publicly guaranteed sector	26	65	62	44	51	46
Private sector not guaranteed	18	27	28	27	31	31
Principal repayments, long-term	**13**	**54**	**55**	**49**	**60**	**58**
Public and publicly guaranteed sector	7	29	25	24	30	31
Private sector not guaranteed	6	24	30	25	30	28
Interest payments, long-term	**4**	**18**	**21**	**19**	**18**	**20**
Public and publicly guaranteed sector	3	12	15	15	14	14
Private sector not guaranteed	1	6	7	4	4	6

AFGHANISTAN

(US$ million, unless otherwise indicated)

Snapshot	2022
Total external debt stocks	**3,393**
External debt stocks as % of	
Exports	..
GNI	..
Debt service as % of	
Exports	..
GNI	..
Net financial flows, debt and equity	**-91**
Net debt inflows	-91
Net equity inflows	..
GNI	..
Population (million)	**41**

Figure 1 **Public and publicly guaranteed debt, by creditor and creditor type in 2022, including IMF credit**

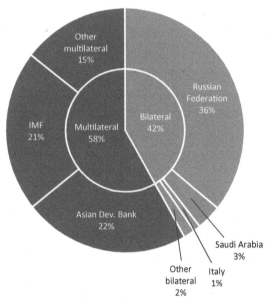

Figure 2 **Average terms on new debt commitments from official and private creditors**

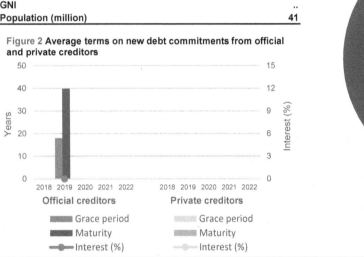

Summary External Debt Data	2010	2018	2019	2020	2021	2022
Total external debt stocks	**2,436**	**2,679**	**2,662**	**3,040**	**3,556**	**3,393**
Long-term external debt stocks	**1,976**	**1,970**	**1,965**	**1,976**	**1,926**	**1,877**
Public and publicly guaranteed debt from:	1,976	1,949	1,944	1,958	1,908	1,859
Official creditors	1,976	1,949	1,944	1,958	1,908	1,859
Multilateral	1,016	983	955	968	919	872
of which: World Bank	406	348	338	344	329	303
Bilateral	959	965	989	991	989	987
Private creditors	0	..	..	..	..	..
Bondholders	..	..	..	..	..	..
Commercial banks and others	0	..	..	..	..	..
Private nonguaranteed debt from:	..	22	21	18	18	18
Bondholders	..	..	..	..	..	..
Commercial banks and others	..	22	21	18	18	18
Use of IMF credit and SDR allocations	**355**	**275**	**277**	**629**	**1,185**	**1,122**
IMF credit	116	59	62	405	534	502
SDR allocations	239	216	215	224	652	620
Short-term external debt stocks	**105**	**434**	**420**	**435**	**445**	**394**
Disbursements, long-term	**76**	**16**	**29**	**0**	**..**	**..**
Public and publicly guaranteed sector	76	16	29	0	..	..
Private sector not guaranteed	..	..	..	..	..	..
Principal repayments, long-term	**1**	**31**	**31**	**26**	**14**	**9**
Public and publicly guaranteed sector	1	25	25	22	14	9
Private sector not guaranteed	..	6	6	5	..	..
Interest payments, long-term	**8**	**9**	**9**	**8**	**5**	**3**
Public and publicly guaranteed sector	8	8	7	7	5	3
Private sector not guaranteed	..	1	1	1	..	..

ALBANIA

(US$ million, unless otherwise indicated)

Snapshot	2022
Total external debt stocks	**10,455**
External debt stocks as % of	
Exports	136
GNI	56
Debt service as % of	
Exports	10
GNI	4
Net financial flows, debt and equity	**1,511**
Net debt inflows	100
Net equity inflows	1,410
GNI	**18,535**
Population (million)	**3**

Figure 2 Average terms on new debt commitments from official and private creditors

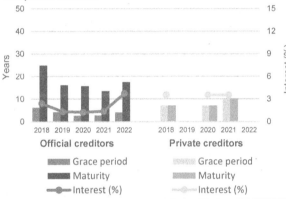

Figure 1 Public and publicly guaranteed debt, by creditor and creditor type in 2022, including IMF credit

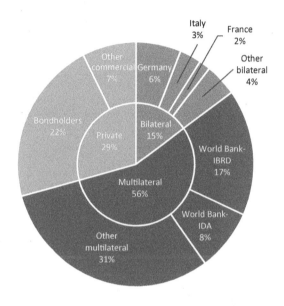

Summary External Debt Data	2010	2018	2019	2020	2021	2022
Total external debt stocks	**5,437**	**9,651**	**9,275**	**10,477**	**11,055**	**10,455**
Long-term external debt stocks	**4,564**	**7,277**	**8,220**	**9,180**	**9,364**	**8,805**
Public and publicly guaranteed debt from:	3,210	4,334	4,160	4,896	5,303	4,860
Official creditors	2,175	3,037	3,004	3,254	3,411	3,327
Multilateral	1,521	2,362	2,338	2,547	2,639	2,537
of which: World Bank	875	1,301	1,330	1,418	1,409	1,310
Bilateral	654	675	666	708	773	790
Private creditors	1,035	1,298	1,156	1,642	1,892	1,533
Bondholders	477	718	642	1,116	1,441	1,142
Commercial banks and others	558	580	514	526	451	391
Private nonguaranteed debt from:	1,354	2,942	4,060	4,284	4,061	3,945
Bondholders	69	329	306	284	267	248
Commercial banks and others	1,285	2,614	3,754	4,000	3,794	3,697
Use of IMF credit and SDR allocations	**129**	**470**	**448**	**627**	**734**	**632**
IMF credit	58	406	383	560	482	393
SDR allocations	72	65	64	67	252	240
Short-term external debt stocks	**743**	**1,904**	**607**	**670**	**957**	**1,018**
Disbursements, long-term	**866**	**1,037**	**457**	**1,162**	**1,532**	**604**
Public and publicly guaranteed sector	631	699	207	880	1,234	318
Private sector not guaranteed	235	338	250	283	298	286
Principal repayments, long-term	**250**	**922**	**498**	**948**	**693**	**499**
Public and publicly guaranteed sector	174	554	263	537	369	283
Private sector not guaranteed	76	368	234	410	323	216
Interest payments, long-term	**110**	**147**	**112**	**146**	**115**	**151**
Public and publicly guaranteed sector	66	119	95	96	102	128
Private sector not guaranteed	44	28	17	50	13	23

ALGERIA

(US$ million, unless otherwise indicated)

Snapshot	2022
Total external debt stocks	**7,129**
External debt stocks as % of	
Exports	10
GNI	4
Debt service as % of	
Exports	0
GNI	0
Net financial flows, debt and equity	**107**
Net debt inflows	39
Net equity inflows	68
GNI	**187,922**
Population (million)	**45**

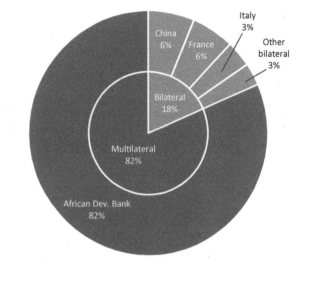

Figure 1 **Public and publicly guaranteed debt, by creditor and creditor type in 2022, including IMF credit**

Figure 2 **Average terms on new debt commitments from official and private creditors**

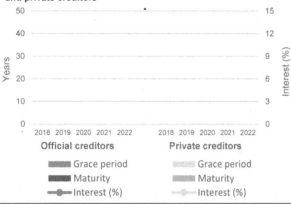

Official creditors   Private creditors

- Grace period   Grace period
- Maturity   Maturity
- Interest (%)   Interest (%)

Summary External Debt Data	2010	2018	2019	2020	2021	2022
Total external debt stocks	**7,253**	**5,710**	**5,492**	**5,178**	**7,379**	**7,129**
Long-term external debt stocks	**3,630**	**1,725**	**1,571**	**1,669**	**1,476**	**1,291**
Public and publicly guaranteed debt from:	2,662	1,523	1,398	1,436	1,240	1,056
Official creditors	1,986	1,512	1,393	1,433	1,239	1,056
Multilateral	10	1,031	1,007	1,095	984	860
of which: World Bank	9	..	..	..	..	..
Bilateral	1,976	481	386	338	256	195
Private creditors	676	11	6	3	1	0
Bondholders	..	..	..	..	..	..
Commercial banks and others	676	11	6	3	1	0
Private nonguaranteed debt from:	968	202	173	232	236	235
Bondholders	..	..	..	..	..	..
Commercial banks and others	968	202	173	232	236	235
Use of IMF credit and SDR allocations	**1,845**	**1,666**	**1,657**	**1,726**	**4,306**	**4,095**
IMF credit	0	0	0	0	0	0
SDR allocations	1,845	1,666	1,657	1,726	4,306	4,095
Short-term external debt stocks	**1,778**	**2,319**	**2,264**	**1,784**	**1,597**	**1,744**
Disbursements, long-term	**42**	**44**	**33**	**98**	**70**	**53**
Public and publicly guaranteed sector	40	0	0	0	0	0
Private sector not guaranteed	2	44	33	98	70	53
Principal repayments, long-term	**557**	**151**	**118**	**119**	**147**	**161**
Public and publicly guaranteed sector	324	122	93	77	101	107
Private sector not guaranteed	234	29	25	41	46	54
Interest payments, long-term	**95**	**29**	**25**	**23**	**22**	**18**
Public and publicly guaranteed sector	64	26	23	22	22	18
Private sector not guaranteed	31	3	2	1	1	..

Note: Figure 2 shows no data values because the country did not have new commitments from 2018 to 2022.

ANGOLA

(US$ million, unless otherwise indicated)

Snapshot	2022
Total external debt stocks	60,107
External debt stocks as % of	
Exports	120
GNI	61
Debt service as % of	
Exports	30
GNI	16
Net financial flows, debt and equity	-5,406
Net debt inflows	-5,406
Net equity inflows	..
GNI	98,720
Population (million)	36

Figure 1 **Public and publicly guaranteed debt, by creditor and creditor type in 2022, including IMF credit**

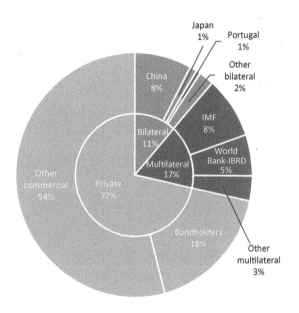

Figure 2 **Average terms on new debt commitments from official and private creditors**

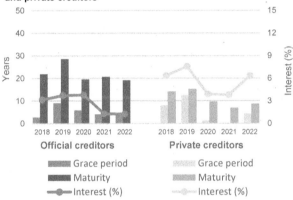

Summary External Debt Data	2010	2018	2019	2020	2021	2022
Total external debt stocks	**26,796**	**61,791**	**62,292**	**65,387**	**66,087**	**60,107**
Long-term external debt stocks	20,926	57,586	57,848	57,044	55,575	50,330
Public and publicly guaranteed debt from:	15,662	47,078	47,597	47,366	46,712	47,817
Official creditors	4,746	10,461	9,643	9,926	10,635	10,528
Multilateral	445	2,268	2,847	3,069	3,857	4,559
of which: World Bank	378	1,042	1,636	1,746	2,481	3,235
Bilateral	4,301	8,193	6,796	6,857	6,777	5,969
Private creditors	10,916	36,618	37,954	37,440	36,078	37,289
Bondholders	..	5,000	8,000	8,000	8,000	9,114
Commercial banks and others	10,916	31,618	29,954	29,440	28,078	28,175
Private nonguaranteed debt from:	5,264	10,507	10,251	9,679	8,862	2,513
Bondholders	..	..	..	..	..	..
Commercial banks and others	5,264	10,507	10,251	9,679	8,862	2,513
Use of IMF credit and SDR allocations	1,302	1,374	1,861	2,992	5,872	5,584
IMF credit	882	994	1,484	2,599	4,497	4,277
SDR allocations	420	380	378	393	1,375	1,307
Short-term external debt stocks	4,568	2,832	2,583	5,351	4,639	4,193
Disbursements, long-term	**6,714**	**12,182**	**8,105**	**3,950**	**6,194**	**7,604**
Public and publicly guaranteed sector	4,082	12,182	8,105	3,950	6,194	7,604
Private sector not guaranteed	2,632	..	..	..	..	..
Principal repayments, long-term	**2,639**	**9,141**	**7,803**	**5,129**	**7,574**	**12,564**
Public and publicly guaranteed sector	2,113	6,907	7,546	4,557	6,758	6,214
Private sector not guaranteed	526	2,234	257	572	816	6,350
Interest payments, long-term	**257**	**2,704**	**2,820**	**2,571**	**2,236**	**2,525**
Public and publicly guaranteed sector	177	2,338	2,480	2,408	2,129	2,477
Private sector not guaranteed	80	367	340	163	106	48

ARGENTINA

(US$ million, unless otherwise indicated)

Snapshot	2022
Total external debt stocks	**247,681**
External debt stocks as % of	
Exports	232
GNI	40
Debt service as % of	
Exports	32
GNI	5
Net financial flows, debt and equity	**16,627**
Net debt inflows	10,305
Net equity inflows	6,322
GNI	**621,442**
Population (million)	**46**

Figure 1 **Public and publicly guaranteed debt, by creditor and creditor type in 2022, including IMF credit**

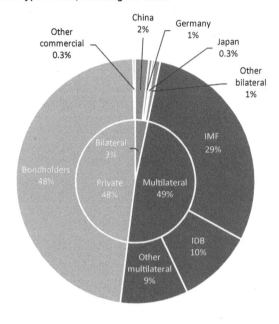

Figure 2 **Average terms on new debt commitments from official and private creditors**

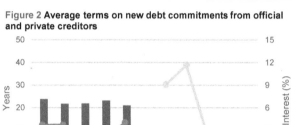

Summary External Debt Data	2010	2018	2019	2020	2021	2022
Total external debt stocks	**126,642**	**277,827**	**280,685**	**255,558**	**246,307**	**247,681**
Long-term external debt stocks	**107,119**	**179,134**	**166,744**	**164,078**	**154,278**	**146,301**
Public and publicly guaranteed debt from:	69,184	135,603	121,319	118,035	114,750	109,252
Official creditors	22,874	29,058	29,113	30,260	31,412	35,022
Multilateral	17,016	23,005	23,879	25,301	27,107	29,787
of which: World Bank	5,349	6,879	7,128	7,721	8,517	9,205
Bilateral	5,859	6,053	5,235	4,959	4,305	5,234
Private creditors	46,310	106,545	92,206	87,775	83,339	74,230
Bondholders	44,344	105,287	91,240	86,537	82,219	73,775
Commercial banks and others	1,966	1,258	966	1,238	1,119	455
Private nonguaranteed debt from:	37,934	43,531	45,425	46,042	39,527	37,049
Bondholders	7,855	15,933	15,378	15,742	15,354	13,617
Commercial banks and others	30,080	27,598	30,047	30,300	24,173	23,433
Use of IMF credit and SDR allocations	**3,111**	**30,923**	**46,924**	**48,874**	**48,055**	**52,290**
IMF credit	0	28,113	44,131	45,964	40,953	45,536
SDR allocations	3,111	2,809	2,793	2,909	7,103	6,754
Short-term external debt stocks	**16,413**	**67,770**	**67,016**	**42,607**	**43,974**	**49,090**
Disbursements, long-term	**6,923**	**66,555**	**25,171**	**23,155**	**14,562**	**8,562**
Public and publicly guaranteed sector	2,623	48,369	11,559	12,326	4,906	7,069
Private sector not guaranteed	4,300	18,186	13,612	10,830	9,656	1,493
Principal repayments, long-term	**11,690**	**28,202**	**29,842**	**21,686**	**16,661**	**10,045**
Public and publicly guaranteed sector	6,035	15,787	19,296	8,200	4,473	6,069
Private sector not guaranteed	5,655	12,415	10,546	13,485	12,189	3,977
Interest payments, long-term	**3,789**	**13,385**	**11,498**	**5,608**	**3,308**	**3,067**
Public and publicly guaranteed sector	2,700	10,996	8,883	2,484	1,290	1,929
Private sector not guaranteed	1,089	2,389	2,615	3,124	2,019	1,137

ARMENIA

(US$ million, unless otherwise indicated)

Snapshot	2022
Total external debt stocks	**14,715**
External debt stocks as % of	
Exports	138
GNI	79
Debt service as % of	
Exports	15
GNI	9
Net financial flows, debt and equity	**2,548**
Net debt inflows	1,632
Net equity inflows	915
GNI	**18,654**
Population (million)	**3**

Figure 1 **Public and publicly guaranteed debt, by creditor and creditor type in 2022, including IMF credit**

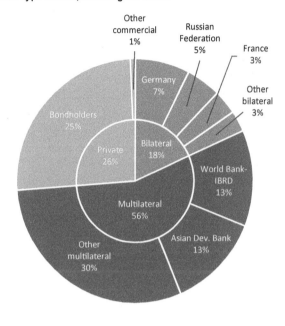

Figure 2 **Average terms on new debt commitments from official and private creditors**

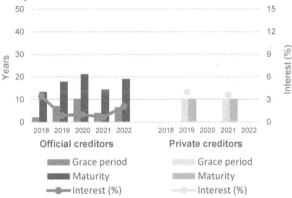

Summary External Debt Data	2010	2018	2019	2020	2021	2022
Total external debt stocks	**6,307**	**10,726**	**11,884**	**12,600**	**13,802**	**14,715**
Long-term external debt stocks	**4,775**	**9,141**	**9,915**	**10,352**	**11,543**	**10,715**
Public and publicly guaranteed debt from:	2,560	5,371	5,652	5,616	6,246	6,320
Official creditors	2,556	4,310	4,496	4,555	4,460	4,539
Multilateral	1,513	3,278	3,352	3,401	3,334	3,298
of which: World Bank	1,267	1,798	1,824	1,830	1,763	1,659
Bilateral	1,042	1,032	1,144	1,154	1,125	1,242
Private creditors	4	1,061	1,156	1,061	1,786	1,780
Bondholders	..	1,000	1,098	1,000	1,733	1,733
Commercial banks and others	4	61	59	61	53	47
Private nonguaranteed debt from:	2,216	3,770	4,262	4,735	5,296	4,396
Bondholders	..	..	..	300	300	300
Commercial banks and others	2,216	3,770	4,262	4,435	4,996	4,096
Use of IMF credit and SDR allocations	**876**	**451**	**375**	**646**	**735**	**758**
IMF credit	741	328	253	519	439	476
SDR allocations	136	122	122	127	296	281
Short-term external debt stocks	**656**	**1,134**	**1,595**	**1,603**	**1,524**	**3,242**
Disbursements, long-term	**1,734**	**1,678**	**2,377**	**1,827**	**3,033**	**950**
Public and publicly guaranteed sector	198	347	867	129	1,092	471
Private sector not guaranteed	1,536	1,331	1,510	1,698	1,941	479
Principal repayments, long-term	**857**	**1,282**	**1,586**	**1,538**	**1,626**	**1,095**
Public and publicly guaranteed sector	24	138	568	313	246	256
Private sector not guaranteed	833	1,144	1,018	1,225	1,380	839
Interest payments, long-term	**60**	**269**	**362**	**320**	**333**	**356**
Public and publicly guaranteed sector	35	162	189	167	145	162
Private sector not guaranteed	25	107	174	152	188	194

AZERBAIJAN

(US$ million, unless otherwise indicated)

Snapshot	2022
Total external debt stocks	**15,277**
External debt stocks as % of	
Exports	31
GNI	21
Debt service as % of	
Exports	3
GNI	2
Net financial flows, debt and equity	**-4,554**
Net debt inflows	-84
Net equity inflows	-4,470
GNI	**73,234**
Population (million)	**10**

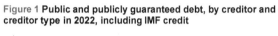

Figure 1 **Public and publicly guaranteed debt, by creditor and creditor type in 2022, including IMF credit**

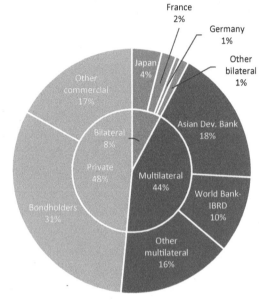

Figure 2 **Average terms on new debt commitments from official and private creditors**

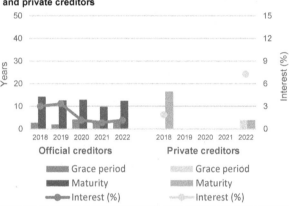

Summary External Debt Data	2010	2018	2019	2020	2021	2022
Total external debt stocks	**7,286**	**16,583**	**16,539**	**16,478**	**15,648**	**15,277**
Long-term external debt stocks	**6,004**	**15,800**	**15,710**	**15,805**	**14,908**	**14,067**
Public and publicly guaranteed debt from:	3,846	14,328	14,675	14,667	13,623	12,911
Official creditors	2,661	7,243	7,822	7,838	7,266	6,657
Multilateral	1,738	6,129	6,566	6,484	6,084	5,641
of which: World Bank	1,063	2,538	2,395	2,098	1,681	1,487
Bilateral	922	1,114	1,256	1,354	1,182	1,016
Private creditors	1,186	7,086	6,853	6,829	6,358	6,254
Bondholders	..	3,750	3,750	3,750	3,750	4,050
Commercial banks and others	1,186	3,336	3,103	3,079	2,608	2,204
Private nonguaranteed debt from:	2,158	1,471	1,035	1,138	1,284	1,156
Bondholders	..	..	..	500	500	500
Commercial banks and others	2,158	1,471	1,035	638	784	656
Use of IMF credit and SDR allocations	**282**	**214**	**212**	**221**	**740**	**704**
IMF credit	46	0	0	0	0	0
SDR allocations	237	214	212	221	740	704
Short-term external debt stocks	**999**	**570**	**617**	**452**	**0**	**506**
Disbursements, long-term	**2,643**	**3,503**	**1,412**	**1,080**	**1,094**	**513**
Public and publicly guaranteed sector	729	3,484	1,408	553	653	503
Private sector not guaranteed	1,914	19	4	527	442	11
Principal repayments, long-term	**306**	**2,123**	**1,463**	**1,298**	**1,703**	**1,104**
Public and publicly guaranteed sector	234	1,640	1,016	866	1,408	969
Private sector not guaranteed	72	483	447	432	296	135
Interest payments, long-term	**78**	**552**	**585**	**554**	**443**	**497**
Public and publicly guaranteed sector	65	461	519	496	403	448
Private sector not guaranteed	13	91	66	58	41	49

BANGLADESH

(US$ million, unless otherwise indicated)

Snapshot	2022
Total external debt stocks	97,012
External debt stocks as % of	
Exports	160
GNI	20
Debt service as % of	
Exports	11
GNI	1
Net financial flows, debt and equity	9,865
Net debt inflows	8,518
Net equity inflows	1,347
GNI	478,433
Population (million)	171

Figure 1 Public and publicly guaranteed debt, by creditor and creditor type in 2022, including IMF credit

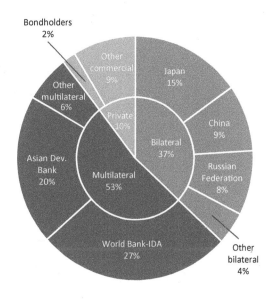

Figure 2 Average terms on new debt commitments from official and private creditors

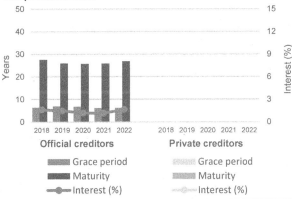

Summary External Debt Data	2010	2018	2019	2020	2021	2022
Total external debt stocks	26,572	57,125	62,468	73,551	91,478	97,012
Long-term external debt stocks	22,222	46,560	51,317	60,455	70,088	75,501
Public and publicly guaranteed debt from:	21,146	41,322	46,417	54,830	62,473	67,608
Official creditors	21,129	36,797	41,599	49,518	54,880	60,402
Multilateral	18,463	25,429	27,732	31,181	33,382	35,101
of which: World Bank	10,653	14,501	15,788	17,572	17,832	18,226
Bilateral	2,666	11,368	13,866	18,337	21,498	25,301
Private creditors	16	4,525	4,818	5,313	7,594	7,207
Bondholders	..	1,433	1,569	1,736	1,675	1,266
Commercial banks and others	16	3,092	3,249	3,577	5,919	5,941
Private nonguaranteed debt from:	1,076	5,238	4,901	5,625	7,615	7,892
Bondholders	..	..	..	..	..	..
Commercial banks and others	1,076	5,238	4,901	5,625	7,615	7,892
Use of IMF credit and SDR allocations	1,403	1,536	1,414	2,109	3,301	2,981
IMF credit	617	826	708	1,374	1,156	941
SDR allocations	786	710	706	735	2,145	2,040
Short-term external debt stocks	2,947	9,029	9,737	10,986	18,088	18,530
Disbursements, long-term	1,355	9,861	9,321	10,220	13,975	13,376
Public and publicly guaranteed sector	968	7,165	6,208	7,931	9,564	10,540
Private sector not guaranteed	388	2,696	3,113	2,289	4,410	2,835
Principal repayments, long-term	821	2,033	4,681	2,871	4,401	5,141
Public and publicly guaranteed sector	724	1,180	1,250	1,307	1,981	2,583
Private sector not guaranteed	97	853	3,431	1,565	2,420	2,558
Interest payments, long-term	203	641	809	863	900	1,037
Public and publicly guaranteed sector	195	528	657	707	798	819
Private sector not guaranteed	8	113	152	155	102	218

BELARUS

(US$ million, unless otherwise indicated)

Snapshot	2022
Total external debt stocks	**39,915**
External debt stocks as % of	
Exports	83
GNI	57
Debt service as % of	
Exports	14
GNI	9
Net financial flows, debt and equity	**-62**
Net debt inflows	-1,635
Net equity inflows	1,573
GNI	**70,254**
Population (million)	**9**

Figure 2 **Average terms on new debt commitments from official and private creditors**

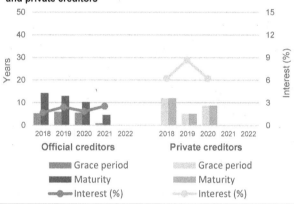

Figure 1 **Public and publicly guaranteed debt, by creditor and creditor type in 2022, including IMF credit**

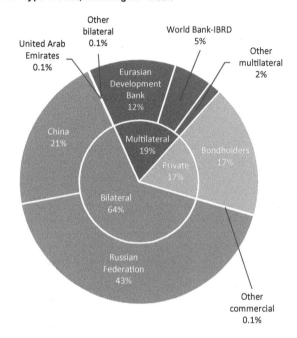

Summary External Debt Data	2010	2018	2019	2020	2021	2022
Total external debt stocks	**28,412**	**38,768**	**40,734**	**41,792**	**41,654**	**39,915**
Long-term external debt stocks	**12,486**	**28,729**	**30,026**	**31,180**	**29,859**	**28,476**
Public and publicly guaranteed debt from:	8,014	19,988	19,511	20,270	19,979	19,329
Official creditors	5,729	16,495	16,595	16,710	16,437	15,924
Multilateral	295	3,810	3,480	3,595	3,678	3,620
of which: World Bank	291	905	948	955	1,002	993
Bilateral	5,434	12,685	13,115	13,115	12,759	12,304
Private creditors	2,286	3,493	2,916	3,560	3,543	3,405
Bondholders	1,019	2,000	2,162	3,521	3,519	3,392
Commercial banks and others	1,266	1,493	755	39	23	13
Private nonguaranteed debt from:	4,471	8,741	10,514	10,910	9,880	9,147
Bondholders	..	..	..	368	367	371
Commercial banks and others	4,471	8,741	10,514	10,542	9,512	8,776
Use of IMF credit and SDR allocations	**4,063**	**513**	**510**	**531**	**1,430**	**1,360**
IMF credit	3,495	0	0	0	0	0
SDR allocations	568	513	510	531	1,430	1,360
Short-term external debt stocks	**11,864**	**9,526**	**10,199**	**10,082**	**10,365**	**10,079**
Disbursements, long-term	**3,810**	**3,743**	**4,106**	**4,099**	**1,691**	**3,767**
Public and publicly guaranteed sector	2,679	2,673	1,996	3,533	1,691	1,935
Private sector not guaranteed	1,132	1,070	2,111	566	..	1,832
Principal repayments, long-term	**1,265**	**4,130**	**2,900**	**2,881**	**2,968**	**5,105**
Public and publicly guaranteed sector	463	3,455	2,563	2,712	1,938	2,537
Private sector not guaranteed	802	675	338	169	1,030	2,568
Interest payments, long-term	**208**	**1,288**	**1,307**	**1,282**	**1,240**	**1,313**
Public and publicly guaranteed sector	128	1,022	1,015	892	853	862
Private sector not guaranteed	80	265	292	391	387	451

BELIZE

(US$ million, unless otherwise indicated)

Snapshot	2022
Total external debt stocks	1,465
External debt stocks as % of	
Exports	108
GNI	54
Debt service as % of	
Exports	6
GNI	3
Net financial flows, debt and equity	155
Net debt inflows	21
Net equity inflows	134
GNI	2,689
Population (thousand)	405

Figure 2 Average terms on new debt commitments from official and private creditors

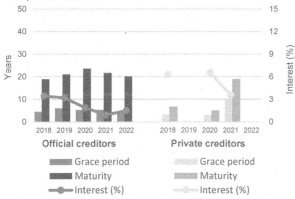

Figure 1 Public and publicly guaranteed debt, by creditor and creditor type in 2022, including IMF credit

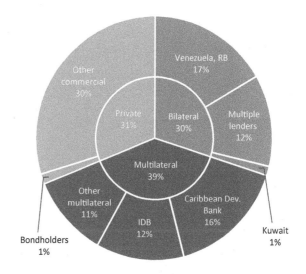

Summary External Debt Data	2010	2018	2019	2020	2021	2022
Total external debt stocks	**1,304**	**1,349**	**1,378**	**1,526**	**1,450**	**1,465**
Long-term external debt stocks	**1,262**	**1,320**	**1,349**	**1,492**	**1,380**	**1,398**
Public and publicly guaranteed debt from:	1,019	1,260	1,286	1,408	1,276	1,299
Official creditors	425	706	734	821	872	895
Multilateral	254	348	368	429	485	507
of which: World Bank	13	19	19	28	38	36
Bilateral	171	358	366	392	387	389
Private creditors	594	554	552	587	404	404
Bondholders	21	527	527	563	17	17
Commercial banks and others	573	27	25	24	387	387
Private nonguaranteed debt from:	243	61	63	84	103	98
Bondholders	..	..	..	..	..	..
Commercial banks and others	243	61	63	84	103	98
Use of IMF credit and SDR allocations	**35**	**25**	**25**	**26**	**61**	**58**
IMF credit	7	0	0	0	0	0
SDR allocations	28	25	25	26	61	58
Short-term external debt stocks	**7**	**4**	**4**	**8**	**10**	**10**
Disbursements, long-term	**39**	**77**	**79**	**153**	**482**	**65**
Public and publicly guaranteed sector	32	71	70	146	458	65
Private sector not guaranteed	7	6	9	7	24	..
Principal repayments, long-term	**69**	**65**	**50**	**45**	**599**	**43**
Public and publicly guaranteed sector	49	42	44	43	597	41
Private sector not guaranteed	20	22	6	2	2	2
Interest payments, long-term	**58**	**49**	**54**	**34**	**19**	**33**
Public and publicly guaranteed sector	47	43	50	32	17	31
Private sector not guaranteed	11	6	4	2	3	2

BENIN

(US$ million, unless otherwise indicated)

Snapshot	2022
Total external debt stocks	**7,307**
External debt stocks as % of	
Exports	177
GNI	42
Debt service as % of	
Exports	12
GNI	3
Net financial flows, debt and equity	**1,088**
Net debt inflows	821
Net equity inflows	267
GNI	**17,254**
Population (million)	**13**

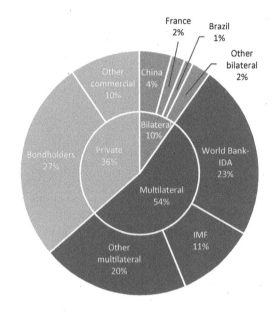

Figure 1 **Public and publicly guaranteed debt, by creditor and creditor type in 2022, including IMF credit**

Figure 2 **Average terms on new debt commitments from official and private creditors**

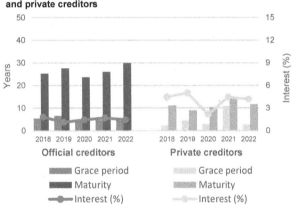

Summary External Debt Data	2010	2018	2019	2020	2021	2022
Total external debt stocks	**1,596**	**3,590**	**3,920**	**5,259**	**6,821**	**7,307**
Long-term external debt stocks	1,112	3,299	3,603	4,414	5,786	5,990
Public and publicly guaranteed debt from:	1,112	3,299	3,603	4,414	5,786	5,990
Official creditors	1,112	2,484	2,539	3,155	3,284	3,563
Multilateral	937	2,032	2,100	2,627	2,675	2,895
of which: World Bank	383	984	1,082	1,309	1,369	1,555
Bilateral	175	452	439	528	609	668
Private creditors	..	815	1,064	1,259	2,501	2,427
Bondholders	..	..	557	614	1,898	1,788
Commercial banks and others	..	815	508	646	603	639
Private nonguaranteed debt from:	..	..	..	..	..	..
Bondholders	..	..	..	..	..	..
Commercial banks and others	..	..	..	..	..	..
Use of IMF credit and SDR allocations	**146**	**245**	**267**	**563**	**699**	**944**
IMF credit	55	162	185	477	450	707
SDR allocations	91	82	82	85	249	237
Short-term external debt stocks	**339**	**46**	**50**	**283**	**336**	**373**
Disbursements, long-term	**175**	**1,061**	**761**	**631**	**2,290**	**796**
Public and publicly guaranteed sector	175	1,061	761	631	2,290	796
Private sector not guaranteed	..	..	..	..	..	..
Principal repayments, long-term	**26**	**170**	**416**	**99**	**623**	**292**
Public and publicly guaranteed sector	26	170	416	99	623	292
Private sector not guaranteed	..	..	..	..	..	..
Interest payments, long-term	**13**	**40**	**77**	**111**	**105**	**163**
Public and publicly guaranteed sector	13	40	77	111	105	163
Private sector not guaranteed	..	..	..	..	..	..

BHUTAN

(US$ million, unless otherwise indicated)

Snapshot	2022
Total external debt stocks	**2,960**
External debt stocks as % of	
Exports	363
GNI	..
Debt service as % of	
Exports	15
GNI	..
Net financial flows, debt and equity	**149**
Net debt inflows	146
Net equity inflows	3
GNI	**..**
Population (million)	**1**

Figure 2 **Average terms on new debt commitments from official and private creditors**

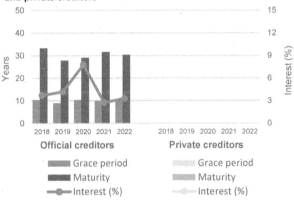

Official creditors — Grace period, Maturity, Interest (%)
Private creditors — Grace period, Maturity, Interest (%)

Figure 1 **Public and publicly guaranteed debt, by creditor and creditor type in 2022, including IMF credit**

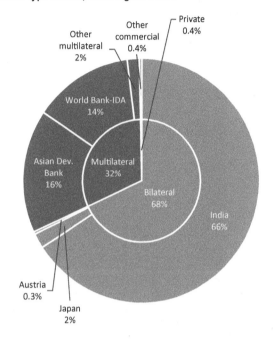

Summary External Debt Data	2010	2018	2019	2020	2021	2022
Total external debt stocks	**935**	**2,552**	**2,704**	**3,037**	**3,069**	**2,960**
Long-term external debt stocks	**919**	**2,539**	**2,668**	**3,027**	**3,030**	**2,921**
Public and publicly guaranteed debt from:	919	2,484	2,616	2,985	2,986	2,877
Official creditors	899	2,455	2,592	2,964	2,971	2,866
Multilateral	330	563	646	789	829	905
of which: World Bank	112	244	271	337	353	390
Bilateral	568	1,892	1,946	2,174	2,141	1,961
Private creditors	21	29	24	22	16	10
Bondholders	..	..	..	..	..	..
Commercial banks and others	21	29	24	22	16	10
Private nonguaranteed debt from:	..	55	51	41	44	44
Bondholders	..	..	..	..	..	..
Commercial banks and others	..	55	51	41	44	44
Use of IMF credit and SDR allocations	**9**	**8**	**8**	**9**	**36**	**34**
IMF credit	0	0	0	0	0	0
SDR allocations	9	8	8	9	36	34
Short-term external debt stocks	**6**	**4**	**28**	**1**	**3**	**6**
Disbursements, long-term	**178**	**168**	**198**	**408**	**138**	**215**
Public and publicly guaranteed sector	178	168	198	408	135	215
Private sector not guaranteed	..	..	1	..	3	..
Principal repayments, long-term	**47**	**51**	**28**	**37**	**73**	**71**
Public and publicly guaranteed sector	47	51	24	27	73	71
Private sector not guaranteed	..	1	5	10	..	..
Interest payments, long-term	**41**	**36**	**32**	**21**	**45**	**47**
Public and publicly guaranteed sector	41	34	31	20	43	44
Private sector not guaranteed	..	2	1	1	2	2

BOLIVIA

(US$ million, unless otherwise indicated)

Snapshot	2022
Total external debt stocks	**15,930**
External debt stocks as % of	
Exports	109
GNI	38
Debt service as % of	
Exports	16
GNI	6
Net financial flows, debt and equity	**393**
Net debt inflows	36
Net equity inflows	357
GNI	**41,822**
Population (million)	**12**

Figure 2 Average terms on new debt commitments from official and private creditors

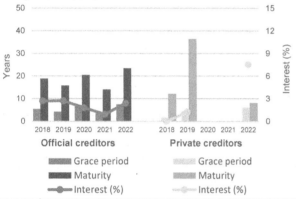

Official creditors · Private creditors

- Grace period · Grace period
- Maturity · Maturity
- Interest (%) · Interest (%)

Figure 1 Public and publicly guaranteed debt, by creditor and creditor type in 2022, including IMF credit

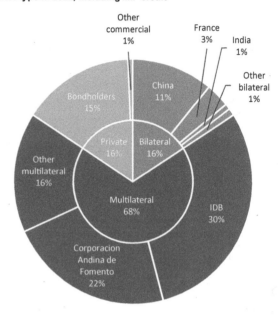

Summary External Debt Data	2010	2018	2019	2020	2021	2022
Total external debt stocks	**5,777**	**13,248**	**14,301**	**15,420**	**16,026**	**15,930**
Long-term external debt stocks	**5,187**	**12,317**	**13,437**	**14,260**	**14,714**	**14,775**
Public and publicly guaranteed debt from:	2,830	9,905	11,000	11,877	12,773	13,372
Official creditors	2,806	7,897	8,959	9,818	10,673	11,253
Multilateral	2,285	6,710	7,467	8,248	8,669	9,136
of which: World Bank	355	847	927	1,300	1,416	1,445
Bilateral	521	1,187	1,492	1,569	2,003	2,118
Private creditors	24	2,008	2,041	2,060	2,100	2,118
Bondholders	..	2,000	2,000	2,000	2,000	2,033
Commercial banks and others	24	8	41	60	100	85
Private nonguaranteed debt from:	2,358	2,412	2,437	2,383	1,942	1,403
Bondholders	..	..	..	..	..	..
Commercial banks and others	2,358	2,412	2,437	2,383	1,942	1,403
Use of IMF credit and SDR allocations	**253**	**228**	**227**	**582**	**552**	**525**
IMF credit	0	0	0	346	0	0
SDR allocations	253	228	227	236	552	525
Short-term external debt stocks	**336**	**703**	**637**	**577**	**759**	**631**
Disbursements, long-term	**548**	**1,373**	**1,741**	**1,445**	**1,456**	**2,123**
Public and publicly guaranteed sector	518	1,198	1,514	1,244	1,456	2,123
Private sector not guaranteed	30	176	227	201	..	..
Principal repayments, long-term	**569**	**640**	**658**	**764**	**936**	**1,959**
Public and publicly guaranteed sector	247	360	412	458	495	1,420
Private sector not guaranteed	322	280	246	306	441	539
Interest payments, long-term	**76**	**346**	**400**	**391**	**332**	**410**
Public and publicly guaranteed sector	54	316	371	363	307	389
Private sector not guaranteed	22	30	28	29	26	21

BOSNIA AND HERZEGOVINA

(US$ million, unless otherwise indicated)

Snapshot	2022
Total external debt stocks	**12,885**
External debt stocks as % of	
Exports	103
GNI	53
Debt service as % of	
Exports	11
GNI	6
Net financial flows, debt and equity	**797**
Net debt inflows	189
Net equity inflows	609
GNI	**24,343**
Population (million)	**3**

Figure 1 **Public and publicly guaranteed debt, by creditor and creditor type in 2022, including IMF credit**

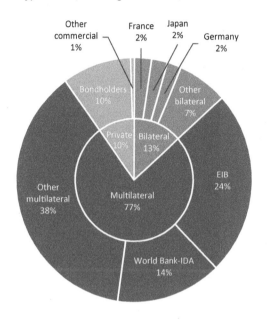

Figure 2 **Average terms on new debt commitments from official and private creditors**

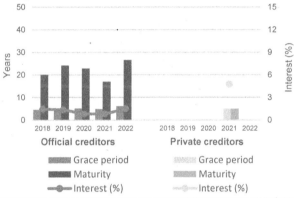

Summary External Debt Data	2010	2018	2019	2020	2021	2022
Total external debt stocks	**14,289**	**12,936**	**12,703**	**13,866**	**13,026**	**12,885**
Long-term external debt stocks	**12,372**	**9,502**	**9,500**	**10,081**	**9,205**	**8,978**
Public and publicly guaranteed debt from:	3,733	4,919	4,876	5,207	5,098	4,742
Official creditors	3,255	4,596	4,590	4,928	4,534	4,219
Multilateral	2,416	3,724	3,737	4,024	3,737	3,523
of which: World Bank	1,626	1,610	1,584	1,670	1,586	1,423
Bilateral	840	872	853	904	797	696
Private creditors	478	322	286	278	564	523
Bondholders	273	256	231	229	526	496
Commercial banks and others	204	66	55	50	37	28
Private nonguaranteed debt from:	8,638	4,584	4,624	4,875	4,106	4,235
Bondholders	..	..	..	..	..	..
Commercial banks and others	8,638	4,584	4,624	4,875	4,106	4,235
Use of IMF credit and SDR allocations	**769**	**466**	**398**	**796**	**1,115**	**1,039**
IMF credit	521	243	175	565	534	487
SDR allocations	248	224	222	232	581	552
Short-term external debt stocks	**1,149**	**2,967**	**2,805**	**2,988**	**2,707**	**2,868**
Disbursements, long-term	**566**	**4,065**	**942**	**1,126**	**1,142**	**986**
Public and publicly guaranteed sector	441	600	409	403	862	277
Private sector not guaranteed	125	3,465	533	723	280	710
Principal repayments, long-term	**373**	**1,034**	**895**	**707**	**1,337**	**938**
Public and publicly guaranteed sector	145	340	384	381	410	357
Private sector not guaranteed	227	694	512	327	926	581
Interest payments, long-term	**177**	**122**	**117**	**106**	**120**	**295**
Public and publicly guaranteed sector	55	77	80	82	68	77
Private sector not guaranteed	121	46	38	25	52	219

BOTSWANA

(US$ million, unless otherwise indicated)

Snapshot	2022
Total external debt stocks	**1,968**
External debt stocks as % of	
Exports	22
GNI	10
Debt service as % of	
Exports	2
GNI	1
Net financial flows, debt and equity	**59**
Net debt inflows	9
Net equity inflows	50
GNI	**19,538**
Population (million)	**3**

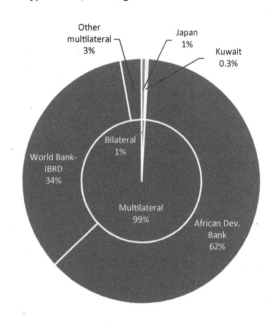

Figure 1 **Public and publicly guaranteed debt, by creditor and creditor type in 2022, including IMF credit**

Figure 2 **Average terms on new debt commitments from official and private creditors**

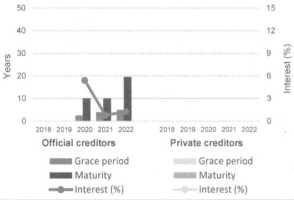

Official creditors — Private creditors

- Grace period — Grace period
- Maturity — Maturity
- Interest (%) — Interest (%)

Summary External Debt Data	2010	2018	2019	2020	2021	2022
Total external debt stocks	**1,807**	**1,782**	**1,565**	**1,597**	**1,982**	**1,968**
Long-term external debt stocks	**1,358**	**1,451**	**1,346**	**1,297**	**1,481**	**1,529**
Public and publicly guaranteed debt from:	1,358	1,451	1,334	1,278	1,466	1,524
Official creditors	1,357	1,447	1,334	1,278	1,466	1,524
Multilateral	1,219	1,389	1,287	1,242	1,443	1,511
of which: World Bank	11	174	172	194	470	521
Bilateral	138	58	47	37	24	14
Private creditors	1	4	0	..	..	..
Bondholders	..	..	..	..	..	..
Commercial banks and others	1	4	0	..	..	..
Private nonguaranteed debt from:	..	0	12	19	14	4
Bondholders	..	..	..	..	..	..
Commercial banks and others	..	0	12	19	14	4
Use of IMF credit and SDR allocations	**88**	**80**	**79**	**83**	**345**	**328**
IMF credit	0	0	0	0	0	0
SDR allocations	88	80	79	83	345	328
Short-term external debt stocks	**360**	**251**	**139**	**218**	**156**	**112**
Disbursements, long-term	**17**	**47**	**48**	**90**	**336**	**201**
Public and publicly guaranteed sector	17	47	26	74	329	201
Private sector not guaranteed	..	..	22	16	7	..
Principal repayments, long-term	**58**	**144**	**152**	**147**	**145**	**149**
Public and publicly guaranteed sector	58	144	141	138	135	140
Private sector not guaranteed	..	..	10	10	10	9
Interest payments, long-term	**18**	**31**	**40**	**32**	**14**	**20**
Public and publicly guaranteed sector	18	31	40	31	14	20
Private sector not guaranteed	..	..	1	1	0	0

BRALIZ

(US$ million, unless otherwise indicated)

Snapshot	2022
Total external debt stocks	**578,599**
External debt stocks as % of	
Exports	138
GNI	31
Debt service as % of	
Exports	30
GNI	7
Net financial flows, debt and equity	**96,364**
Net debt inflows	15,650
Net equity inflows	80,713
GNI	**1,859,747**
Population (million)	**215**

Figure 1 Public and publicly guaranteed debt, by creditor and creditor type in 2022, including IMF credit

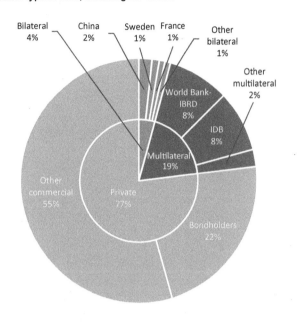

Figure 2 Average terms on new debt commitments from official and private creditors

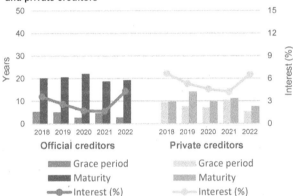

Summary External Debt Data	2010	2018	2019	2020	2021	2022
Total external debt stocks	**352,364**	**557,765**	**568,709**	**549,300**	**571,507**	**578,599**
Long-term external debt stocks	**282,426**	**486,906**	**485,537**	**476,159**	**473,901**	**492,901**
Public and publicly guaranteed debt from:	97,486	190,216	193,800	194,303	194,162	189,689
Official creditors	41,553	47,860	43,216	44,000	44,841	43,926
Multilateral	29,980	33,386	33,266	33,715	35,497	35,820
of which: World Bank	13,523	16,213	16,253	15,682	15,419	16,061
Bilateral	11,573	14,474	9,950	10,285	9,344	8,106
Private creditors	55,933	142,356	150,584	150,303	149,320	145,763
Bondholders	46,806	43,479	45,004	49,385	46,520	42,361
Commercial banks and others	9,127	98,878	105,580	100,918	102,801	103,401
Private nonguaranteed debt from:	184,940	296,690	291,737	281,856	279,739	303,212
Bondholders	83,032	32,686	37,553	35,903	31,375	27,194
Commercial banks and others	101,908	264,004	254,184	245,953	248,364	276,018
Use of IMF credit and SDR allocations	**4,446**	**4,015**	**3,992**	**4,158**	**18,853**	**17,927**
IMF credit	0	0	0	0	0	0
SDR allocations	4,446	4,015	3,992	4,158	18,853	17,927
Short-term external debt stocks	**65,492**	**66,844**	**79,179**	**68,983**	**78,753**	**67,772**
Disbursements, long-term	**85,379**	**105,082**	**114,564**	**126,754**	**156,033**	**132,921**
Public and publicly guaranteed sector	19,957	28,834	23,884	39,484	16,625	22,611
Private sector not guaranteed	65,422	76,249	90,680	87,270	139,408	110,310
Principal repayments, long-term	**32,026**	**74,509**	**123,463**	**109,833**	**132,311**	**106,289**
Public and publicly guaranteed sector	9,628	28,433	30,505	23,170	20,387	22,986
Private sector not guaranteed	22,398	46,077	92,958	86,663	111,924	83,303
Interest payments, long-term	**13,157**	**18,681**	**25,702**	**19,055**	**28,690**	**17,783**
Public and publicly guaranteed sector	5,172	5,679	11,385	7,764	8,520	7,980
Private sector not guaranteed	7,985	13,002	14,317	11,292	20,169	9,803

BULGARIA

(US$ million, unless otherwise indicated)

Snapshot	2022
Total external debt stocks	**47,206**
External debt stocks as % of	
Exports	75
GNI	55
Debt service as % of	
Exports	15
GNI	11
Net financial flows, debt and equity	**4,943**
Net debt inflows	2,870
Net equity inflows	2,074
GNI	**86,212**
Population (million)	**6**

Figure 2 **Average terms on new debt commitments from official and private creditors**

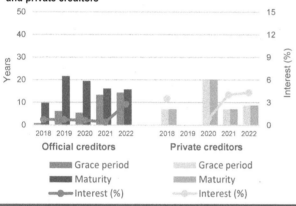

Figure 1 **Public and publicly guaranteed debt, by creditor and creditor type in 2022, including IMF credit**

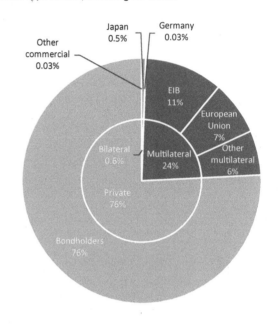

Summary External Debt Data	2010	2018	2019	2020	2021	2022
Total external debt stocks	**50,697**	**40,103**	**40,501**	**46,867**	**44,947**	**47,206**
Long-term external debt stocks	**34,613**	**29,708**	**29,762**	**34,112**	**34,421**	**35,260**
Public and publicly guaranteed debt from:	4,845	11,506	11,186	15,447	15,533	15,871
Official creditors	3,210	3,214	3,050	3,532	3,857	3,844
Multilateral	2,388	2,966	2,839	3,345	3,721	3,756
of which: World Bank	1,338	831	727	701	575	471
Bilateral	822	247	211	187	136	87
Private creditors	1,635	8,292	8,136	11,915	11,676	12,027
Bondholders	1,618	8,286	8,130	11,909	11,671	12,023
Commercial banks and others	17	6	6	6	5	4
Private nonguaranteed debt from:	29,768	18,202	18,576	18,665	18,888	19,389
Bondholders	134	1,405	1,489	1,465	1,537	1,412
Commercial banks and others	29,635	16,797	17,086	17,200	17,351	17,977
Use of IMF credit and SDR allocations	**941**	**850**	**845**	**880**	**2,057**	**1,956**
IMF credit	0	0	0	0	0	0
SDR allocations	941	850	845	880	2,057	1,956
Short-term external debt stocks	**15,143**	**9,546**	**9,895**	**11,876**	**8,468**	**9,991**
Disbursements, long-term	**1,620**	**5,052**	**4,554**	**7,908**	**6,269**	**8,986**
Public and publicly guaranteed sector	250	917	150	3,275	1,597	2,870
Private sector not guaranteed	1,370	4,135	4,405	4,633	4,672	6,115
Principal repayments, long-term	**3,550**	**5,055**	**4,286**	**3,919**	**4,680**	**7,643**
Public and publicly guaranteed sector	268	300	256	266	261	1,634
Private sector not guaranteed	3,282	4,754	4,029	3,653	4,418	6,009
Interest payments, long-term	**609**	**1,388**	**1,180**	**1,021**	**1,164**	**1,099**
Public and publicly guaranteed sector	180	269	276	280	313	303
Private sector not guaranteed	430	1,118	904	741	851	797

BURKINA FASO

(US$ million, unless otherwise indicated)

Snapshot	2022
Total external debt stocks	**10,381**
External debt stocks as % of	
Exports	184
GNI	58
Debt service as % of	
Exports	10
GNI	3
Net financial flows, debt and equity	**463**
Net debt inflows	342
Net equity inflows	121
GNI	**17,783**
Population (million)	**23**

Figure 1 Public and publicly guaranteed debt, by creditor and creditor type in 2022, including IMF credit

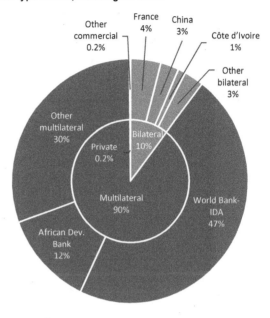

Figure 2 Average terms on new debt commitments from official and private creditors

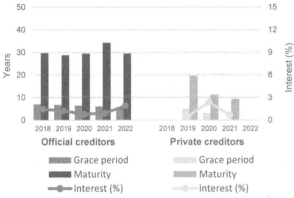

Summary External Debt Data	2010	2018	2019	2020	2021	2022
Total external debt stocks	**4,800**	**10,621**	**9,157**	**9,756**	**10,296**	**10,381**
Long-term external debt stocks	**4,582**	**10,352**	**8,847**	**9,290**	**9,710**	**9,847**
Public and publicly guaranteed debt from:	1,960	3,041	3,372	4,019	4,328	4,385
Official creditors	1,919	3,028	3,360	4,008	4,317	4,376
Multilateral	1,611	2,670	3,008	3,548	3,834	3,890
of which: World Bank	776	1,458	1,673	2,014	2,146	2,187
Bilateral	308	358	351	460	482	486
Private creditors	41	14	12	10	11	9
Bondholders	..	..	..	..	..	..
Commercial banks and others	41	14	12	10	11	9
Private nonguaranteed debt from:	2,622	7,311	5,475	5,271	5,382	5,461
Bondholders	..	..	..	..	..	..
Commercial banks and others	2,622	7,311	5,475	5,271	5,382	5,461
Use of IMF credit and SDR allocations	**217**	**269**	**310**	**466**	**586**	**534**
IMF credit	129	189	230	383	344	304
SDR allocations	89	80	80	83	242	230
Short-term external debt stocks	**0**	**0**	**0**	**0**	**0**	**0**
Disbursements, long-term	**1,392**	**344**	**463**	**2,084**	**1,046**	**819**
Public and publicly guaranteed sector	286	344	463	523	625	423
Private sector not guaranteed	1,106	..	..	1,560	421	396
Principal repayments, long-term	**293**	**2,384**	**1,933**	**1,864**	**412**	**454**
Public and publicly guaranteed sector	31	84	98	100	102	137
Private sector not guaranteed	262	2,300	1,836	1,764	310	317
Interest payments, long-term	**149**	**582**	**348**	**274**	**55**	**64**
Public and publicly guaranteed sector	18	32	32	36	41	46
Private sector not guaranteed	131	550	316	238	14	18

(US$ million, unless otherwise indicated)

Snapshot	2022
Total external debt stocks	**954.3**
External debt stocks as % of	
Exports	309.8
GNI	30.9
Debt service as % of	
Exports	10.7
GNI	1.1
Net financial flows, debt and equity	**28.2**
Net debt inflows	15.3
Net equity inflows	12.9
GNI	**3,087.4**
Population (million)	**12.9**

Figure 1 Public and publicly guaranteed debt, by creditor and creditor type in 2022, including IMF credit

Figure 2 Average terms on new debt commitments from official and private creditors

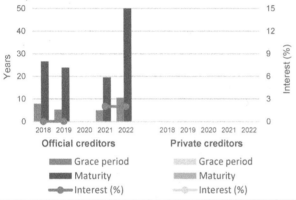

Summary External Debt Data	2010	2018	2019	2020	2021	2022
Total external debt stocks	**620.9**	**585.7**	**625.4**	**662.5**	**975.8**	**954.3**
Long-term external debt stocks	**381.8**	**419.0**	**476.0**	**529.8**	**575.6**	**577.6**
Public and publicly guaranteed debt from:	381.8	419.0	476.0	529.8	575.6	577.6
Official creditors	381.8	419.0	476.0	529.8	575.6	577.6
Multilateral	325.1	314.4	343.4	358.6	389.5	387.1
of which: World Bank	162.7	141.5	137.5	139.9	132.1	121.6
Bilateral	56.7	104.6	132.5	171.3	186.2	190.5
Private creditors	..	..	..	..	..	..
Bondholders	..	..	..	..	..	..
Commercial banks and others	..	..	..	..	..	..
Private nonguaranteed debt from:	..	..	..	..	..	..
Bondholders	..	..	..	..	..	..
Commercial banks and others	..	..	..	..	..	..
Use of IMF credit and SDR allocations	**223.4**	**166.4**	**149.1**	**132.4**	**399.9**	**376.4**
IMF credit	109.6	63.6	47.0	26.0	90.0	81.7
SDR allocations	113.7	102.7	102.1	106.4	309.9	294.7
Short-term external debt stocks	**15.7**	**0.3**	**0.3**	**0.3**	**0.3**	**0.3**
Disbursements, long-term	**31.6**	**14.2**	**74.0**	**50.8**	**64.5**	**39.4**
Public and publicly guaranteed sector	31.6	14.2	74.0	50.8	64.5	39.4
Private sector not guaranteed	..	..	..	..	..	..
Principal repayments, long-term	**2.4**	**9.1**	**16.0**	**10.3**	**13.0**	**20.3**
Public and publicly guaranteed sector	2.4	9.1	16.0	10.3	13.0	20.3
Private sector not guaranteed	..	..	..	..	..	..
Interest payments, long-term	**1.4**	**3.1**	**4.4**	**3.9**	**5.7**	**5.3**
Public and publicly guaranteed sector	1.4	3.1	4.4	3.9	5.7	5.3
Private sector not guaranteed	..	..	..	..	..	..

CABO VERDE

(US$ million, unless otherwise indicated)

Snapshot	2022
Total external debt stocks	**2,011**
External debt stocks as % of	
Exports	228
GNI	88
Debt service as % of	
Exports	11
GNI	4
Net financial flows, debt and equity	**191**
Net debt inflows	69
Net equity inflows	122
GNI	**2,286**
Population (million)	**1**

Figure 2 Average terms on new debt commitments from official and private creditors

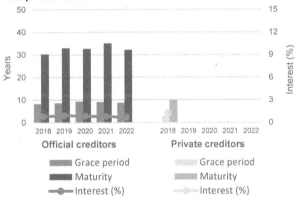

Figure 1 Public and publicly guaranteed debt, by creditor and creditor type in 2022, including IMF credit

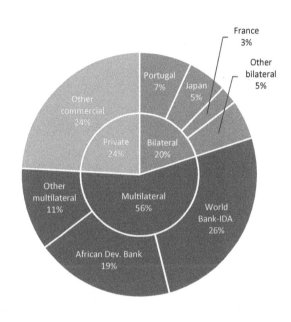

Summary External Debt Data	2010	2018	2019	2020	2021	2022
Total external debt stocks	**885**	**1,768**	**1,822**	**2,073**	**2,060**	**2,011**
Long-term external debt stocks	**862**	**1,755**	**1,810**	**2,025**	**1,983**	**1,922**
Public and publicly guaranteed debt from:	862	1,755	1,810	2,025	1,983	1,922
Official creditors	778	1,241	1,303	1,467	1,467	1,447
Multilateral	598	817	882	1,014	1,042	1,050
of which: World Bank	303	351	406	482	523	547
Bilateral	181	424	420	453	426	397
Private creditors	84	514	507	558	515	475
Bondholders	..	..	..	..	..	..
Commercial banks and others	84	514	507	558	515	475
Private nonguaranteed debt from:	..	..	..	..	..	..
Bondholders	..	..	..	..	..	..
Commercial banks and others	..	..	..	..	..	..
Use of IMF credit and SDR allocations	**23**	**13**	**13**	**47**	**78**	**89**
IMF credit	9	0	0	34	33	47
SDR allocations	14	13	13	13	45	42
Short-term external debt stocks	**0**	**0**	**0**	**0**	**0**	**0**
Disbursements, long-term	**203**	**75**	**118**	**124**	**115**	**131**
Public and publicly guaranteed sector	203	75	118	124	115	131
Private sector not guaranteed	..	..	..	..	..	..
Principal repayments, long-term	**25**	**37**	**41**	**43**	**44**	**77**
Public and publicly guaranteed sector	25	37	41	43	44	77
Private sector not guaranteed	..	..	..	..	..	..
Interest payments, long-term	**8**	**19**	**19**	**17**	**11**	**20**
Public and publicly guaranteed sector	8	19	19	17	11	20
Private sector not guaranteed	..	..	..	..	..	..

CAMBODIA

(US$ million, unless otherwise indicated)

Snapshot	2022
Total external debt stocks	**22,471**
External debt stocks as % of	
Exports	87
GNI	79
Debt service as % of	
Exports	10
GNI	9
Net financial flows, debt and equity	**6,431**
Net debt inflows	2,852
Net equity inflows	3,579
GNI	**28,457**
Population (million)	**17**

Figure 1 **Public and publicly guaranteed debt, by creditor and creditor type in 2022, including IMF credit**

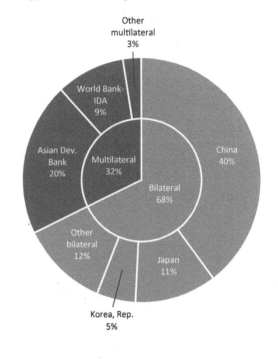

Figure 2 **Average terms on new debt commitments from official and private creditors**

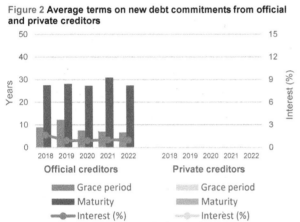

Summary External Debt Data	2010	2018	2019	2020	2021	2022
Total external debt stocks	**4,010**	**13,549**	**15,363**	**17,594**	**20,050**	**22,471**
Long-term external debt stocks	**3,502**	**11,066**	**11,834**	**13,691**	**15,261**	**17,526**
Public and publicly guaranteed debt from:	3,060	7,010	7,582	8,789	9,481	10,064
Official creditors	3,060	7,010	7,582	8,789	9,481	10,064
Multilateral	1,529	1,973	2,123	2,717	2,874	3,229
of which: World Bank	565	544	585	685	727	936
Bilateral	1,531	5,037	5,459	6,073	6,608	6,835
Private creditors	..	..	..	..	..	..
Bondholders	..	..	..	..	..	..
Commercial banks and others	..	..	..	..	..	..
Private nonguaranteed debt from:	442	4,056	4,252	4,902	5,779	7,462
Bondholders	..	300	300	650	550	550
Commercial banks and others	442	3,756	3,952	4,252	5,229	6,912
Use of IMF credit and SDR allocations	**129**	**117**	**116**	**121**	**352**	**335**
IMF credit	0	0	0	0	0	0
SDR allocations	129	117	116	121	352	335
Short-term external debt stocks	**379**	**2,366**	**3,413**	**3,782**	**4,437**	**4,610**
Disbursements, long-term	**596**	**2,757**	**2,070**	**2,945**	**3,687**	**4,778**
Public and publicly guaranteed sector	348	723	828	1,215	1,155	1,352
Private sector not guaranteed	248	2,033	1,242	1,729	2,532	3,426
Principal repayments, long-term	**33**	**1,109**	**1,263**	**1,344**	**1,946**	**2,097**
Public and publicly guaranteed sector	33	180	218	264	291	355
Private sector not guaranteed	..	928	1,045	1,079	1,654	1,743
Interest payments, long-term	**27**	**103**	**139**	**150**	**171**	**186**
Public and publicly guaranteed sector	26	85	93	95	103	113
Private sector not guaranteed	1	17	47	55	67	74

CAMEROON

(US$ million, unless otherwise indicated)

Snapshot	2022
Total external debt stocks	**15,096**
External debt stocks as % of	
Exports	170
GNI	35
Debt service as % of	
Exports	20
GNI	4
Net financial flows, debt and equity	**1,189**
Net debt inflows	301
Net equity inflows	889
GNI	**43,742**
Population (million)	**28**

Figure 1 Public and publicly guaranteed debt, by creditor and creditor type in 2022, including IMF credit

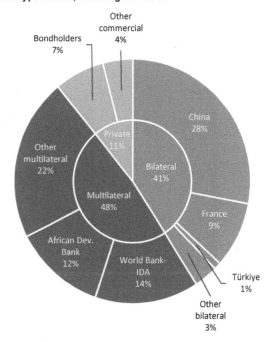

Figure 2 Average terms on new debt commitments from official and private creditors

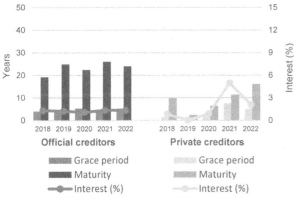

Summary External Debt Data	2010	2018	2019	2020	2021	2022
Total external debt stocks	**3,190**	**11,004**	**12,924**	**14,720**	**15,374**	**15,096**
Long-term external debt stocks	**2,737**	**9,856**	**11,787**	**13,083**	**12,944**	**12,343**
Public and publicly guaranteed debt from:	2,160	9,154	10,384	11,388	12,373	11,839
Official creditors	2,143	7,797	8,929	9,949	10,287	10,408
Multilateral	787	3,208	3,746	4,318	4,718	5,040
of which: World Bank	374	1,432	1,733	1,915	2,068	2,234
Bilateral	1,356	4,589	5,184	5,631	5,569	5,368
Private creditors	17	1,356	1,454	1,439	2,086	1,431
Bondholders	..	750	750	750	1,526	891
Commercial banks and others	17	606	704	689	560	540
Private nonguaranteed debt from:	577	703	1,403	1,695	571	504
Bondholders	..	..	..	..	..	..
Commercial banks and others	577	703	1,403	1,695	571	504
Use of IMF credit and SDR allocations	**445**	**714**	**760**	**1,269**	**1,777**	**1,874**
IMF credit	172	468	515	1,014	1,159	1,286
SDR allocations	273	247	245	255	618	588
Short-term external debt stocks	**9**	**433**	**377**	**368**	**652**	**879**
Disbursements, long-term	**278**	**1,796**	**2,588**	**1,723**	**1,851**	**1,346**
Public and publicly guaranteed sector	278	1,743	1,752	1,090	1,851	1,304
Private sector not guaranteed	..	53	837	633	0	42
Principal repayments, long-term	**160**	**623**	**762**	**962**	**1,648**	**1,489**
Public and publicly guaranteed sector	122	372	436	622	523	1,380
Private sector not guaranteed	38	250	325	341	1,125	109
Interest payments, long-term	**42**	**400**	**342**	**343**	**283**	**280**
Public and publicly guaranteed sector	27	232	230	330	276	275
Private sector not guaranteed	15	168	112	13	8	4

CENTRAL AFRICAN REPUBLIC

(US$ million, unless otherwise indicated)

Snapshot	2022
Total external debt stocks	**1,018**
External debt stocks as % of	
Exports	288
GNI	41
Debt service as % of	
Exports	6
GNI	1
Net financial flows, debt and equity	**-33**
Net debt inflows	-57
Net equity inflows	24
GNI	**2,509**
Population (million)	**6**

Figure 1 **Public and publicly guaranteed debt, by creditor and creditor type in 2022, including IMF credit**

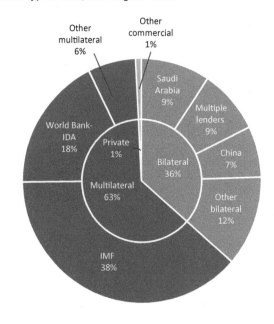

Figure 2 **Average terms on new debt commitments from official and private creditors**

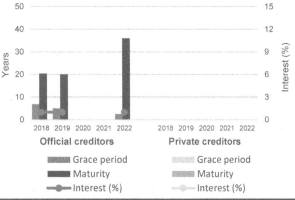

Summary External Debt Data	2010	2018	2019	2020	2021	2022
Total external debt stocks	**634**	**784**	**848**	**899**	**1,118**	**1,018**
Long-term external debt stocks	**376**	**417**	**420**	**411**	**437**	**434**
Public and publicly guaranteed debt from:	376	417	420	411	437	434
Official creditors	337	391	394	406	431	428
Multilateral	43	150	153	177	176	172
of which: World Bank	14	99	107	130	133	126
Bilateral	294	241	241	230	254	257
Private creditors	39	26	26	5	7	5
Bondholders	..	..	..	..	..	..
Commercial banks and others	39	26	26	5	7	5
Private nonguaranteed debt from:	..	..	..	..	..	..
Bondholders	..	..	..	..	..	..
Commercial banks and others	..	..	..	..	..	..
Use of IMF credit and SDR allocations	**173**	**279**	**296**	**355**	**518**	**483**
IMF credit	90	205	223	279	294	270
SDR allocations	82	74	74	77	224	213
Short-term external debt stocks	**86**	**88**	**132**	**133**	**162**	**102**
Disbursements, long-term	**35**	**67**	**22**	**26**	**33**	**13**
Public and publicly guaranteed sector	35	67	22	26	33	13
Private sector not guaranteed	..	..	..	..	..	..
Principal repayments, long-term	**2**	**10**	**15**	**3**	**6**	**5**
Public and publicly guaranteed sector	2	10	15	3	6	5
Private sector not guaranteed	..	..	..	..	..	..
Interest payments, long-term	**1**	**2**	**2**	**1**	**1**	**2**
Public and publicly guaranteed sector	1	2	2	1	1	2
Private sector not guaranteed	..	..	..	..	..	..

CHAD

(US$ million, unless otherwise indicated)

Snapshot	2022
Total external debt stocks	**3,471**
External debt stocks as % of	
Exports	61
GNI	28
Debt service as % of	
Exports	4
GNI	2
Net financial flows, debt and equity	**610**
Net debt inflows	-4
Net equity inflows	614
GNI	**12,516**
Population (million)	**18**

Figure 1 **Public and publicly guaranteed debt, by creditor and creditor type in 2022, including IMF credit**

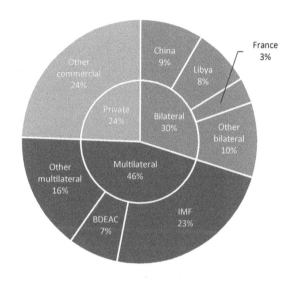

Figure 2 **Average terms on new debt commitments from official and private creditors**

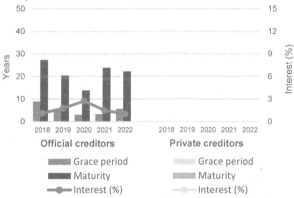

Summary External Debt Data	2010	2018	2019	2020	2021	2022
Total external debt stocks	**2,158**	**3,181**	**3,216**	**3,487**	**3,586**	**3,471**
Long-term external debt stocks	**2,049**	**2,755**	**2,720**	**2,778**	**2,639**	**2,441**
Public and publicly guaranteed debt from:	2,049	2,755	2,720	2,778	2,639	2,441
Official creditors	2,032	1,553	1,562	1,702	1,711	1,662
Multilateral	1,529	666	660	712	757	715
of which: World Bank	865	181	176	180	169	155
Bilateral	504	887	902	990	954	947
Private creditors	17	1,202	1,158	1,076	929	779
Bondholders	..	..	..	..	..	..
Commercial banks and others	17	1,202	1,158	1,076	929	779
Private nonguaranteed debt from:	..	..	..	..	..	..
Bondholders	..	..	..	..	..	..
Commercial banks and others	..	..	..	..	..	..
Use of IMF credit and SDR allocations	**99**	**395**	**470**	**678**	**914**	**996**
IMF credit	17	320	396	601	651	746
SDR allocations	83	75	74	77	263	250
Short-term external debt stocks	**9**	**31**	**27**	**31**	**32**	**34**
Disbursements, long-term	**366**	**52**	**49**	**123**	**174**	**62**
Public and publicly guaranteed sector	366	52	49	123	174	62
Private sector not guaranteed	..	..	..	..	..	..
Principal repayments, long-term	**45**	**116**	**74**	**135**	**270**	**194**
Public and publicly guaranteed sector	45	116	74	135	270	194
Private sector not guaranteed	..	..	..	..	..	..
Interest payments, long-term	**17**	**61**	**59**	**50**	**49**	**26**
Public and publicly guaranteed sector	17	61	59	50	49	26
Private sector not guaranteed	..	..	..	..	..	..

CHINA

(US$ million, unless otherwise indicated)

Snapshot	2022
Total external debt stocks	**2,388,742**
External debt stocks as % of	
Exports	61
GNI	13
Debt service as % of	
Exports	11
GNI	2
Net financial flows, debt and equity	**-102,732**
Net debt inflows	-296,816
Net equity inflows	194,084
GNI	**17,770,327**
Population (million)	**1,412**

Figure 2 **Average terms on new debt commitments from official and private creditors**

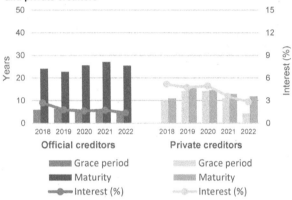

Figure 1 **Public and publicly guaranteed debt, by creditor and creditor type in 2022, including IMF credit**

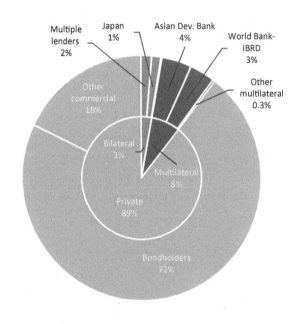

Summary External Debt Data	2010	2018	2019	2020	2021	2022
Total external debt stocks	**742,737**	**1,961,562**	**2,114,162**	**2,326,233**	**2,702,248**	**2,388,742**
Long-term external debt stocks	**219,650**	**732,940**	**899,184**	**1,079,933**	**1,205,349**	**1,075,368**
Public and publicly guaranteed debt from:	102,275	259,687	318,064	391,682	475,167	464,366
Official creditors	75,476	54,499	53,840	52,994	51,622	48,897
Multilateral	35,527	34,439	35,427	36,007	36,424	35,840
of which: World Bank	22,135	16,095	16,271	16,236	16,585	16,067
Bilateral	39,949	20,060	18,412	16,987	15,198	13,057
Private creditors	26,799	205,188	264,225	338,688	423,545	415,469
Bondholders	12,398	163,960	214,523	288,234	352,395	332,378
Commercial banks and others	14,401	41,228	49,701	50,454	71,150	83,091
Private nonguaranteed debt from:	117,375	473,254	581,120	688,252	730,182	611,001
Bondholders	5,561	179,902	234,623	323,512	340,414	285,907
Commercial banks and others	111,814	293,351	346,497	364,739	389,768	325,094
Use of IMF credit and SDR allocations	**10,764**	**9,721**	**9,665**	**10,067**	**50,674**	**48,185**
IMF credit	0	0	0	0	0	0
SDR allocations	10,764	9,721	9,665	10,067	50,674	48,185
Short-term external debt stocks	**512,323**	**1,218,901**	**1,205,312**	**1,236,232**	**1,446,225**	**1,265,190**
Disbursements, long-term	**39,167**	**247,559**	**338,220**	**361,370**	**361,062**	**209,424**
Public and publicly guaranteed sector	12,421	79,731	79,493	95,258	123,006	48,183
Private sector not guaranteed	26,746	167,828	258,727	266,112	238,056	161,241
Principal repayments, long-term	**18,782**	**160,494**	**180,617**	**181,917**	**226,388**	**325,205**
Public and publicly guaranteed sector	11,978	15,291	20,632	25,312	33,310	52,419
Private sector not guaranteed	6,803	145,203	159,985	156,605	193,078	272,786
Interest payments, long-term	**5,484**	**27,184**	**35,730**	**31,593**	**46,498**	**45,939**
Public and publicly guaranteed sector	1,819	6,135	8,670	8,506	17,050	20,444
Private sector not guaranteed	3,665	21,049	27,059	23,087	29,448	25,494

COLOMBIA

(US$ million, unless otherwise indicated)

Snapshot	2022
Total external debt stocks	**184,118**
External debt stocks as % of	
Exports	230
GNI	56
Debt service as % of	
Exports	34
GNI	8
Net financial flows, debt and equity	**27,441**
Net debt inflows	13,554
Net equity inflows	13,887
GNI	**330,444**
Population (million)	**52**

Figure 1 Public and publicly guaranteed debt, by creditor and creditor type in 2022, including IMF credit

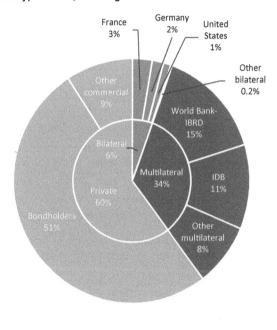

Figure 2 Average terms on new debt commitments from official and private creditors

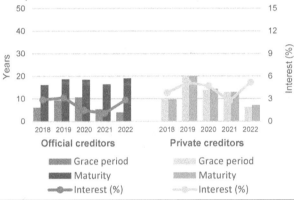

Summary External Debt Data	2010	2018	2019	2020	2021	2022
Total external debt stocks	**64,432**	**133,285**	**138,942**	**155,728**	**172,107**	**184,118**
Long-term external debt stocks	**55,383**	**117,341**	**122,285**	**135,364**	**147,224**	**156,418**
Public and publicly guaranteed debt from:	37,058	74,927	75,126	85,554	93,930	97,610
Official creditors	16,483	27,779	27,809	31,180	33,618	35,764
Multilateral	15,898	22,016	22,690	25,539	28,047	30,164
of which: World Bank	7,504	10,233	10,582	11,989	13,515	15,122
Bilateral	585	5,763	5,119	5,640	5,571	5,600
Private creditors	20,574	47,149	47,317	54,374	60,313	61,846
Bondholders	17,965	41,138	41,868	48,536	52,916	52,448
Commercial banks and others	2,609	6,011	5,450	5,838	7,397	9,398
Private nonguaranteed debt from:	18,325	42,414	47,159	49,810	53,294	58,808
Bondholders	3,329	9,521	10,481	8,954	9,604	8,249
Commercial banks and others	14,996	32,892	36,677	40,856	43,689	50,558
Use of IMF credit and SDR allocations	**1,137**	**1,027**	**1,021**	**6,464**	**9,024**	**8,581**
IMF credit	0	0	0	5,401	5,248	4,991
SDR allocations	1,137	1,027	1,021	1,063	3,776	3,590
Short-term external debt stocks	**7,912**	**14,918**	**15,635**	**13,900**	**15,858**	**19,119**
Disbursements, long-term	**12,970**	**22,912**	**17,189**	**27,645**	**31,053**	**30,004**
Public and publicly guaranteed sector	3,629	6,887	5,036	13,525	18,768	9,698
Private sector not guaranteed	9,340	16,025	12,153	14,120	12,286	20,306
Principal repayments, long-term	**6,566**	**17,863**	**12,081**	**15,066**	**18,344**	**19,710**
Public and publicly guaranteed sector	2,318	6,754	4,674	3,597	9,542	4,918
Private sector not guaranteed	4,248	11,109	7,408	11,469	8,802	14,792
Interest payments, long-term	**2,839**	**5,875**	**6,401**	**5,991**	**6,226**	**6,441**
Public and publicly guaranteed sector	2,121	3,581	3,802	3,478	3,808	3,880
Private sector not guaranteed	717	2,293	2,600	2,513	2,418	2,561

COMOROS

(US$ million, unless otherwise indicated)

Snapshot	2022
Total external debt stocks	**368.7**
External debt stocks as % of	
Exports	209.8
GNI	29.5
Debt service as % of	
Exports	2.7
GNI	0.4
Net financial flows, debt and equity	**39.1**
Net debt inflows	35.2
Net equity inflows	3.8
GNI	**1,248.7**
Population (million)	**0.8**

Figure 1 **Public and publicly guaranteed debt, by creditor and creditor type in 2022, including IMF credit**

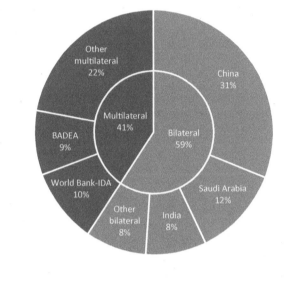

Figure 2 **Average terms on new debt commitments from official and private creditors**

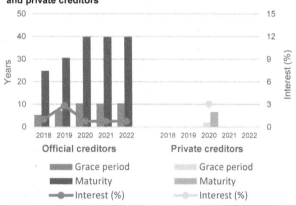

Summary External Debt Data	2010	2018	2019	2020	2021	2022
Total external debt stocks	**278.4**	**240.0**	**259.3**	**296.6**	**350.3**	**368.7**
Long-term external debt stocks	**248.5**	**216.5**	**226.6**	**252.9**	**285.7**	**309.8**
Public and publicly guaranteed debt from:	248.5	216.5	226.6	252.9	285.7	309.8
Official creditors	248.5	216.5	226.6	252.9	285.7	309.8
Multilateral	201.6	54.0	68.0	76.7	92.0	111.9
of which: World Bank	115.5	12.7	12.3	16.7	21.8	33.1
Bilateral	46.9	162.5	158.6	176.2	193.6	197.9
Private creditors	0.0	0.0	0.0	0.0	0.0	0.0
Bondholders	0.0	0.0	0.0	0.0	0.0	0.0
Commercial banks and others	0.0	0.0	0.0	0.0	0.0	0.0
Private nonguaranteed debt from:	0.0	0.0	0.0	0.0	0.0	0.0
Bondholders	0.0	0.0	0.0	0.0	0.0	0.0
Commercial banks and others	0.0	0.0	0.0	0.0	0.0	0.0
Use of IMF credit and SDR allocations	**25.4**	**22.3**	**30.7**	**41.9**	**62.9**	**57.3**
IMF credit	12.3	10.5	19.0	29.7	27.1	23.3
SDR allocations	13.1	11.8	11.8	12.2	35.8	34.0
Short-term external debt stocks	**4.4**	**1.2**	**1.9**	**1.8**	**1.8**	**1.6**
Disbursements, long-term	**0.0**	**68.2**	**14.5**	**18.7**	**33.8**	**38.9**
Public and publicly guaranteed sector	0.0	68.2	14.5	18.7	33.8	38.9
Private sector not guaranteed	0.0	0.0	0.0	0.0	0.0	0.0
Principal repayments, long-term	**3.1**	**2.0**	**1.8**	**1.8**	**1.1**	**1.2**
Public and publicly guaranteed sector	3.1	2.0	1.8	1.8	1.1	1.2
Private sector not guaranteed	0.0	0.0	0.0	0.0	0.0	0.0
Interest payments, long-term	**1.1**	**0.9**	**0.4**	**1.5**	**0.5**	**0.5**
Public and publicly guaranteed sector	1.1	0.9	0.4	1.5	0.5	0.5
Private sector not guaranteed	0.0	0.0	0.0	0.0	0.0	0.0

CONGO, DEMOCRATIC REPUBLIC OF

(US$ million, unless otherwise indicated)

Snapshot	2022
Total external debt stocks	**9,432**
External debt stocks as % of	
Exports	34
GNI	17
Debt service as % of	
Exports	2
GNI	1
Net financial flows, debt and equity	**2,375**
Net debt inflows	529
Net equity inflows	1,846
GNI	**55,545**
Population (million)	**99**

Figure 1 **Public and publicly guaranteed debt, by creditor and creditor type in 2022, including IMF credit**

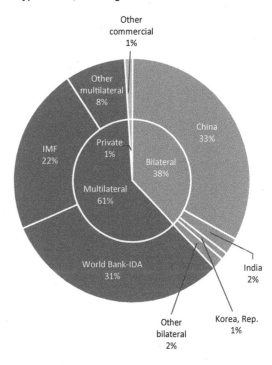

Figure 2 **Average terms on new debt commitments from official and private creditors**

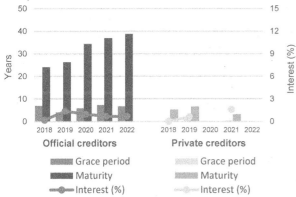

Summary External Debt Data	2010	2018	2019	2020	2021	2022
Total external debt stocks	**6,127**	**5,826**	**6,487**	**7,084**	**9,186**	**9,432**
Long-term external debt stocks	**4,583**	**4,778**	**4,976**	**5,212**	**5,414**	**5,351**
Public and publicly guaranteed debt from:	4,583	4,778	4,976	5,212	5,414	5,351
Official creditors	4,505	4,748	4,873	5,115	5,314	5,278
Multilateral	2,585	2,043	2,128	2,290	2,448	2,689
of which: World Bank	849	1,098	1,288	1,521	1,772	2,125
Bilateral	1,920	2,705	2,745	2,825	2,866	2,589
Private creditors	77	30	102	97	99	74
Bondholders	..	..	..	..	..	..
Commercial banks and others	77	30	102	97	99	74
Private nonguaranteed debt from:	..	..	..	..	..	..
Bondholders	..	..	..	..	..	..
Commercial banks and others	..	..	..	..	..	..
Use of IMF credit and SDR allocations	**1,110**	**839**	**1,130**	**1,511**	**3,317**	**3,560**
IMF credit	323	129	423	775	1,172	1,520
SDR allocations	787	710	706	736	2,145	2,040
Short-term external debt stocks	**435**	**209**	**382**	**362**	**455**	**521**
Disbursements, long-term	**178**	**311**	**433**	**301**	**484**	**584**
Public and publicly guaranteed sector	178	311	433	301	484	584
Private sector not guaranteed	..	..	..	..	..	..
Principal repayments, long-term	**89**	**181**	**196**	**161**	**257**	**528**
Public and publicly guaranteed sector	89	181	196	161	257	528
Private sector not guaranteed	..	..	..	..	..	..
Interest payments, long-term	**124**	**46**	**773**	**59**	**54**	**116**
Public and publicly guaranteed sector	124	46	773	59	54	116
Private sector not guaranteed	..	..	..	..	..	..

CONGO, REPUBLIC OF

(US$ million, unless otherwise indicated)

Snapshot	2022
Total external debt stocks	7,895
External debt stocks as % of	
Exports	67
GNI	58
Debt service as % of	
Exports	7
GNI	6
Net financial flows, debt and equity	292
Net debt inflows	-241
Net equity inflows	532
GNI	13,582
Population (million)	6

Figure 2 Average terms on new debt commitments from official and private creditors

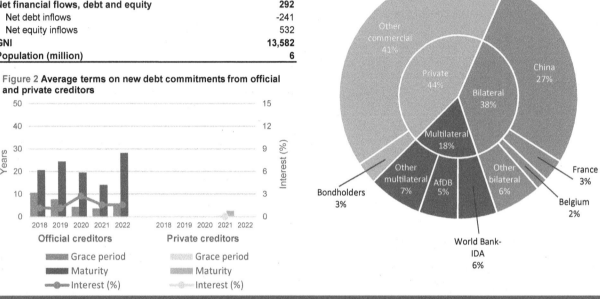

Figure 1 Public and publicly guaranteed debt, by creditor and creditor type in 2022, including IMF credit

Summary External Debt Data	2010	2018	2019	2020	2021	2022
Total external debt stocks	2,796	7,044	8,397	8,224	8,254	7,895
Long-term external debt stocks	2,450	6,653	8,006	7,778	7,590	7,174
Public and publicly guaranteed debt from:	2,450	6,653	8,006	7,772	7,581	7,164
Official creditors	1,023	3,795	4,101	4,081	4,061	3,924
Multilateral	182	640	869	985	1,021	1,108
of which: World Bank	84	192	243	342	413	543
Bilateral	842	3,155	3,232	3,096	3,039	2,816
Private creditors	1,426	2,858	3,905	3,691	3,521	3,241
Bondholders	454	322	295	268	241	213
Commercial banks and others	973	2,536	3,610	3,423	3,280	3,027
Private nonguaranteed debt from:	..	..	..	6	9	10
Bondholders	..	..	..	..	..	..
Commercial banks and others	..	..	..	6	9	10
Use of IMF credit and SDR allocations	150	115	157	162	374	528
IMF credit	27	4	47	48	45	216
SDR allocations	123	111	110	115	329	313
Short-term external debt stocks	197	276	234	284	290	193
Disbursements, long-term	882	269	639	189	201	330
Public and publicly guaranteed sector	882	269	639	183	195	327
Private sector not guaranteed	..	..	..	6	5	3
Principal repayments, long-term	95	390	418	543	320	658
Public and publicly guaranteed sector	95	390	418	543	318	656
Private sector not guaranteed	..	..	..	..	2	2
Interest payments, long-term	24	77	80	94	69	171
Public and publicly guaranteed sector	24	77	80	93	68	170
Private sector not guaranteed	..	..	..	0	1	1

COSTA RICA

(US$ million, unless otherwise indicated)

Snapshot	2022
Total external debt stocks	**38,946**
External debt stocks as % of	
Exports	137
GNI	62
Debt service as % of	
Exports	6
GNI	3
Net financial flows, debt and equity	**8,216**
Net debt inflows	4,928
Net equity inflows	3,288
GNI	**62,618**
Population (million)	**5**

Figure 2 **Average terms on new debt commitments from official and private creditors**

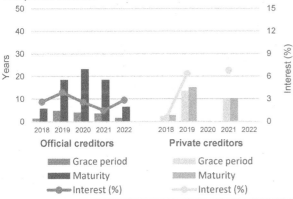

Figure 1 **Public and publicly guaranteed debt, by creditor and creditor type in 2022, including IMF credit**

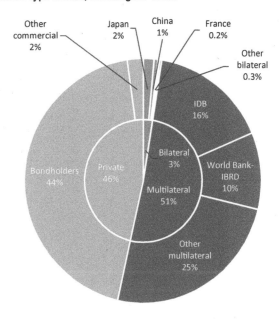

Summary External Debt Data	2010	2018	2019	2020	2021	2022
Total external debt stocks	**8,154**	**28,369**	**29,801**	**31,269**	**34,108**	**38,946**
Long-term external debt stocks	**5,482**	**24,782**	**26,829**	**26,570**	**27,904**	**30,128**
Public and publicly guaranteed debt from:	3,822	11,941	13,392	12,577	12,706	14,061
Official creditors	2,196	4,662	4,910	4,924	5,383	6,921
Multilateral	1,767	4,199	4,443	4,448	4,916	6,539
of which: World Bank	570	903	955	1,021	1,292	1,562
Bilateral	430	464	466	476	467	382
Private creditors	1,626	7,278	8,482	7,652	7,323	7,140
Bondholders	1,310	6,250	7,600	6,983	6,800	6,800
Commercial banks and others	316	1,028	882	669	523	340
Private nonguaranteed debt from:	1,660	12,841	13,437	13,994	15,198	16,067
Bondholders	0	2,100	2,100	2,100	1,250	1,250
Commercial banks and others	1,660	10,741	11,337	11,894	13,948	14,817
Use of IMF credit and SDR allocations	**241**	**218**	**216**	**757**	**1,520**	**1,995**
IMF credit	0	0	0	532	806	1,315
SDR allocations	241	218	216	225	715	680
Short-term external debt stocks	**2,431**	**3,370**	**2,755**	**3,942**	**4,683**	**6,824**
Disbursements, long-term	**1,455**	**4,418**	**3,569**	**1,873**	**3,210**	**2,783**
Public and publicly guaranteed sector	928	1,701	2,486	497	1,066	1,914
Private sector not guaranteed	528	2,716	1,083	1,375	2,144	869
Principal repayments, long-term	**617**	**2,024**	**1,959**	**2,150**	**1,852**	**548**
Public and publicly guaranteed sector	342	897	1,073	1,311	913	548
Private sector not guaranteed	275	1,127	886	839	939	0
Interest payments, long-term	**313**	**1,261**	**1,123**	**769**	**1,144**	**1,135**
Public and publicly guaranteed sector	213	687	674	311	578	610
Private sector not guaranteed	100	574	448	458	566	525

CÔTE D'IVOIRE

(US$ million, unless otherwise indicated)

Snapshot	2022
Total external debt stocks	**31,960**
External debt stocks as % of	
Exports	185
GNI	47
Debt service as % of	
Exports	12
GNI	3
Net financial flows, debt and equity	**4,889**
Net debt inflows	3,305
Net equity inflows	1,584
GNI	**67,835**
Population (million)	**28**

Figure 2 Average terms on new debt commitments from official and private creditors

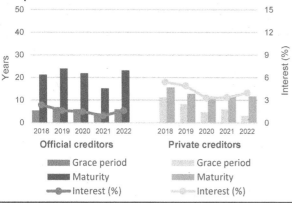

Figure 1 Public and publicly guaranteed debt, by creditor and creditor type in 2022, including IMF credit

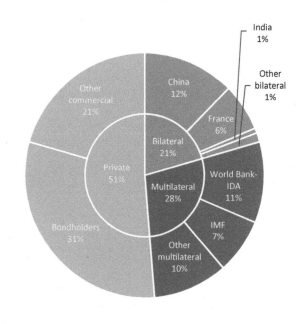

Summary External Debt Data	2010	2018	2019	2020	2021	2022
Total external debt stocks	**11,703**	**16,198**	**19,831**	**25,246**	**29,895**	**31,960**
Long-term external debt stocks	**10,431**	**14,246**	**17,027**	**21,142**	**24,060**	**26,971**
Public and publicly guaranteed debt from:	9,413	13,234	15,748	20,152	23,311	26,447
Official creditors	9,301	5,200	5,972	8,101	10,205	11,605
Multilateral	2,373	2,024	2,609	4,010	4,755	5,844
of which: World Bank	1,763	883	1,204	1,882	2,488	3,117
Bilateral	6,928	3,176	3,363	4,090	5,450	5,761
Private creditors	112	8,034	9,776	12,051	13,106	14,842
Bondholders	0	7,230	7,589	8,532	9,010	8,592
Commercial banks and others	112	804	2,187	3,519	4,097	6,251
Private nonguaranteed debt from:	1,018	1,011	1,279	991	749	524
Bondholders	..	..	..	..	..	..
Commercial banks and others	1,018	1,011	1,279	991	749	524
Use of IMF credit and SDR allocations	**861**	**1,814**	**1,915**	**3,047**	**3,647**	**3,303**
IMF credit	383	1,382	1,485	2,600	2,339	2,060
SDR allocations	479	432	430	448	1,308	1,243
Short-term external debt stocks	**411**	**138**	**890**	**1,056**	**2,188**	**1,686**
Disbursements, long-term	**599**	**3,867**	**5,083**	**4,308**	**4,989**	**5,212**
Public and publicly guaranteed sector	244	3,747	4,511	4,308	4,989	5,212
Private sector not guaranteed	355	120	572	..	..	..
Principal repayments, long-term	**623**	**1,036**	**2,247**	**1,565**	**803**	**1,240**
Public and publicly guaranteed sector	438	702	1,946	1,226	603	1,043
Private sector not guaranteed	185	334	302	340	200	197
Interest payments, long-term	**114**	**453**	**556**	**701**	**701**	**614**
Public and publicly guaranteed sector	58	407	518	671	685	602
Private sector not guaranteed	56	47	38	29	17	12

DJIBOUTI

(US$ million, unless otherwise indicated)

Snapshot	2022
Total external debt stocks	3,170
External debt stocks as % of	
Exports	65
GNI	92
Debt service as % of	
Exports	2
GNI	2
Net financial flows, debt and equity	164
Net debt inflows	-26
Net equity inflows	191
GNI	3,448
Population (million)	1

Figure 1 **Public and publicly guaranteed debt, by creditor and creditor type in 2022, including IMF credit**

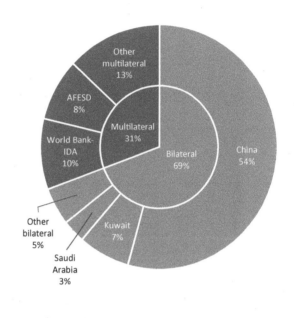

Figure 2 **Average terms on new debt commitments from official and private creditors**

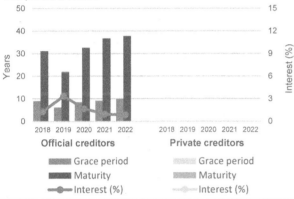

Summary External Debt Data	2010	2018	2019	2020	2021	2022
Total external debt stocks	**769**	**2,321**	**2,553**	**2,900**	**3,207**	**3,170**
Long-term external debt stocks	**612**	**2,045**	**2,146**	**2,575**	**2,427**	**2,439**
Public and publicly guaranteed debt from:	612	2,045	2,146	2,354	2,407	2,409
Official creditors	595	2,045	2,146	2,354	2,407	2,409
Multilateral	406	551	611	660	692	708
of which: World Bank	155	152	161	191	215	230
Bilateral	189	1,494	1,534	1,694	1,715	1,701
Private creditors	16	..	..	..	..	..
Bondholders	..	..	..	..	..	..
Commercial banks and others	16	..	..	..	..	..
Private nonguaranteed debt from:	..	..	..	221	21	30
Bondholders	..	..	..	219	20	20
Commercial banks and others	..	..	..	2	1	10
Use of IMF credit and SDR allocations	**35**	**37**	**32**	**72**	**109**	**103**
IMF credit	12	16	11	51	45	42
SDR allocations	23	21	21	22	64	61
Short-term external debt stocks	**122**	**240**	**375**	**253**	**670**	**628**
Disbursements, long-term	**35**	**141**	**136**	**435**	**86**	**75**
Public and publicly guaranteed sector	35	141	136	214	86	66
Private sector not guaranteed	..	..	..	221	..	9
Principal repayments, long-term	**22**	**27**	**35**	**28**	**30**	**33**
Public and publicly guaranteed sector	22	27	35	28	28	33
Private sector not guaranteed	..	..	..	..	1	..
Interest payments, long-term	**8**	**32**	**29**	**33**	**21**	**20**
Public and publicly guaranteed sector	8	32	29	25	20	19
Private sector not guaranteed	..	..	..	8	1	1

(US$ million, unless otherwise indicated)

Snapshot	2022
Total external debt stocks	**400.7**
External debt stocks as % of	
Exports	200.0
GNI	65.6
Debt service as % of	
Exports	15.0
GNI	4.9
Net financial flows, debt and equity	**60.0**
Net debt inflows	30.6
Net equity inflows	29.3
GNI	**610.4**
Population (thousand)	**72.7**

Figure 1 Public and publicly guaranteed debt, by creditor and creditor type in 2022, including IMF credit

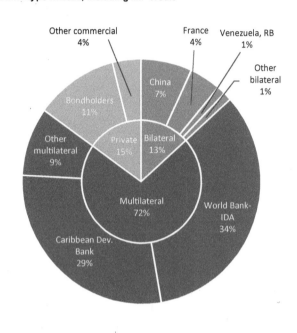

Figure 2 Average terms on new debt commitments from official and private creditors

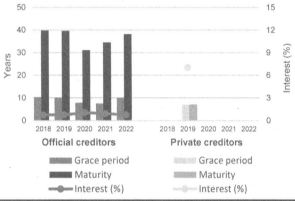

Summary External Debt Data	2010	2018	2019	2020	2021	2022
Total external debt stocks	**271.4**	**278.3**	**277.9**	**329.1**	**378.0**	**400.7**
Long-term external debt stocks	**235.6**	**242.8**	**245.7**	**275.6**	**312.4**	**337.8**
Public and publicly guaranteed debt from:	235.6	242.8	245.7	275.6	312.4	337.8
Official creditors	162.0	187.5	177.7	214.2	254.0	283.8
Multilateral	117.0	123.9	122.1	159.6	197.1	236.4
of which: World Bank	27.8	34.0	35.6	51.4	88.2	121.4
Bilateral	45.0	63.6	55.7	54.6	56.8	47.3
Private creditors	73.6	55.3	67.9	61.4	58.4	54.0
Bondholders	57.1	29.7	45.0	41.5	41.5	40.3
Commercial banks and others	16.5	25.6	23.0	19.9	16.8	13.8
Private nonguaranteed debt from:	..	..	..	..	..	..
Bondholders	..	..	..	..	..	..
Commercial banks and others	..	..	..	..	..	..
Use of IMF credit and SDR allocations	**30.2**	**22.4**	**20.8**	**35.8**	**48.0**	**43.7**
IMF credit	18.2	11.5	9.9	24.5	21.6	18.6
SDR allocations	12.1	10.9	10.8	11.3	26.4	25.1
Short-term external debt stocks	**5.5**	**13.1**	**11.5**	**17.6**	**17.7**	**19.2**
Disbursements, long-term	**29.7**	**5.0**	**22.4**	**39.3**	**47.7**	**50.8**
Public and publicly guaranteed sector	29.7	5.0	22.4	39.3	47.7	50.8
Private sector not guaranteed	..	..	..	..	..	..
Principal repayments, long-term	**9.8**	**23.5**	**18.5**	**19.1**	**10.6**	**19.2**
Public and publicly guaranteed sector	9.8	23.5	18.5	19.1	10.6	19.2
Private sector not guaranteed	..	..	..	..	..	..
Interest payments, long-term	**5.4**	**8.7**	**6.5**	**6.5**	**6.4**	**8.2**
Public and publicly guaranteed sector	5.4	8.7	6.5	6.5	6.4	8.2
Private sector not guaranteed	..	..	..	..	..	..

DOMINICAN REPUBLIC

(US$ million, unless otherwise indicated)

Snapshot	2022
Total external debt stocks	**48,243**
External debt stocks as % of	
Exports	185
GNI	44
Debt service as % of	
Exports	14
GNI	3
Net financial flows, debt and equity	**8,108**
Net debt inflows	4,426
Net equity inflows	3,683
GNI	**109,068**
Population (million)	**11**

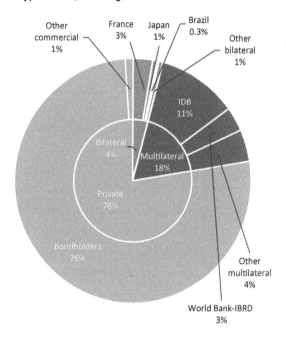

Figure 1 **Public and publicly guaranteed debt, by creditor and creditor type in 2022, including IMF credit**

Figure 2 **Average terms on new debt commitments from official and private creditors**

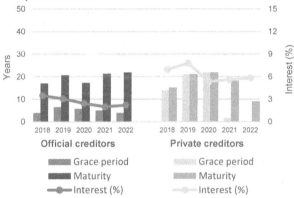

Summary External Debt Data	2010	2018	2019	2020	2021	2022
Total external debt stocks	**13,499**	**31,864**	**35,096**	**40,560**	**43,885**	**48,243**
Long-term external debt stocks	**10,283**	**29,386**	**32,292**	**37,400**	**39,973**	**43,553**
Public and publicly guaranteed debt from:	9,441	21,375	23,006	29,856	32,507	35,559
Official creditors	6,343	5,790	6,068	7,089	7,134	7,491
Multilateral	3,079	4,704	5,086	5,900	5,779	6,042
of which: World Bank	872	923	939	1,183	1,185	1,174
Bilateral	3,264	1,086	982	1,189	1,356	1,448
Private creditors	3,098	15,585	16,938	22,767	25,372	28,069
Bondholders	1,134	14,596	16,229	22,158	24,893	27,671
Commercial banks and others	1,964	989	709	609	479	398
Private nonguaranteed debt from:	843	8,011	9,285	7,544	7,467	7,994
Bondholders	843	1,945	1,395	707	1,007	1,007
Commercial banks and others	0	6,066	7,890	6,837	6,460	6,987
Use of IMF credit and SDR allocations	**1,461**	**290**	**289**	**988**	**1,601**	**1,522**
IMF credit	1,139	0	0	688	668	635
SDR allocations	322	290	289	301	933	887
Short-term external debt stocks	**1,754**	**2,187**	**2,515**	**2,172**	**2,311**	**3,168**
Disbursements, long-term	**2,111**	**4,620**	**2,459**	**9,769**	**3,510**	**4,981**
Public and publicly guaranteed sector	2,111	3,651	2,395	9,769	3,210	4,352
Private sector not guaranteed	..	969	64	..	300	629
Principal repayments, long-term	**799**	**1,422**	**1,867**	**4,531**	**926**	**1,413**
Public and publicly guaranteed sector	798	752	679	2,789	549	1,311
Private sector not guaranteed	0	670	1,188	1,742	377	102
Interest payments, long-term	**444**	**1,440**	**1,744**	**1,662**	**1,870**	**2,086**
Public and publicly guaranteed sector	336	968	1,295	1,415	1,668	1,851
Private sector not guaranteed	108	472	449	247	203	235

ECUADOR

(US$ million, unless otherwise indicated)

Snapshot	2022
Total external debt stocks	**60,685**
External debt stocks as % of	
Exports	168
GNI	54
Debt service as % of	
Exports	14
GNI	5
Net financial flows, debt and equity	**4,407**
Net debt inflows	3,089
Net equity inflows	1,318
GNI	**113,341**
Population (million)	**18**

Figure 2 Average terms on new debt commitments from official and private creditors

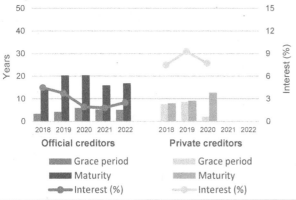

	Official creditors	Private creditors
	Grace period	Grace period
	Maturity	Maturity
	Interest (%)	Interest (%)

Figure 1 Public and publicly guaranteed debt, by creditor and creditor type in 2022, including IMF credit

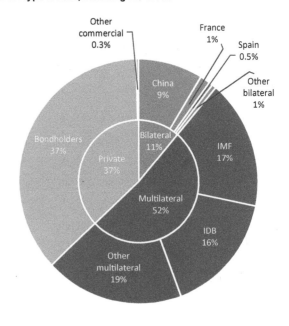

Summary External Debt Data	2010	2018	2019	2020	2021	2022
Total external debt stocks	**15,377**	**44,959**	**51,895**	**56,423**	**58,070**	**60,685**
Long-term external debt stocks	**13,869**	**43,117**	**48,848**	**48,514**	**48,634**	**49,374**
Public and publicly guaranteed debt from:	8,787	35,481	38,391	37,811	38,707	39,484
Official creditors	7,547	17,269	18,119	19,672	20,951	21,891
Multilateral	5,207	9,864	11,081	13,294	14,776	16,569
of which: World Bank	456	617	1,251	2,596	2,897	4,353
Bilateral	2,340	7,405	7,038	6,378	6,175	5,322
Private creditors	1,240	18,211	20,272	18,139	17,756	17,593
Bondholders	1,082	15,250	18,307	17,694	17,494	17,440
Commercial banks and others	159	2,961	1,965	445	262	153
Private nonguaranteed debt from:	5,082	7,636	10,458	10,703	9,928	9,890
Bondholders	..	..	..	..	..	..
Commercial banks and others	5,082	7,636	10,458	10,703	9,928	9,890
Use of IMF credit and SDR allocations	**444**	**765**	**2,114**	**6,781**	**8,183**	**9,387**
IMF credit	0	364	1,716	6,365	6,843	8,113
SDR allocations	444	401	399	415	1,340	1,274
Short-term external debt stocks	**1,064**	**1,077**	**933**	**1,128**	**1,253**	**1,923**
Disbursements, long-term	**2,977**	**10,364**	**12,286**	**7,669**	**4,578**	**4,115**
Public and publicly guaranteed sector	2,307	7,153	6,877	3,689	2,662	2,655
Private sector not guaranteed	670	3,211	5,409	3,981	1,916	1,460
Principal repayments, long-term	**1,259**	**6,443**	**6,505**	**7,548**	**4,441**	**3,297**
Public and publicly guaranteed sector	636	3,202	3,917	3,813	1,750	1,800
Private sector not guaranteed	623	3,241	2,588	3,735	2,691	1,498
Interest payments, long-term	**470**	**2,663**	**2,792**	**1,517**	**1,857**	**1,612**
Public and publicly guaranteed sector	331	2,238	2,385	1,172	1,360	1,336
Private sector not guaranteed	139	425	407	344	497	276

EGYPT, ARAB REPUBLIC OF

(US$ million, unless otherwise indicated)

Snapshot	2022
Total external debt stocks	**163,104**
External debt stocks as % of	
Exports	210
GNI	35
Debt service as % of	
Exports	23
GNI	4
Net financial flows, debt and equity	**30,515**
Net debt inflows	20,501
Net equity inflows	10,014
GNI	**460,985**
Population (million)	**111**

Figure 2 Average terms on new debt commitments from official and private creditors

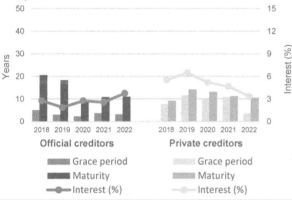

- Grace period
- Maturity
- Interest (%)

Official creditors

- Grace period
- Maturity
- Interest (%)

Private creditors

Figure 1 Public and publicly guaranteed debt, by creditor and creditor type in 2022, including IMF credit

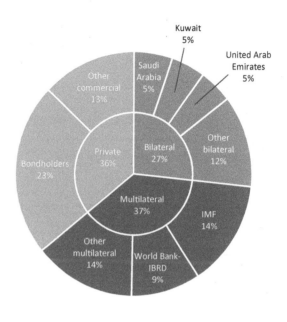

Summary External Debt Data	2010	2018	2019	2020	2021	2022
Total external debt stocks	**36,804**	**99,457**	**114,910**	**132,572**	**145,995**	**163,104**
Long-term external debt stocks	32,271	79,896	90,496	100,252	109,472	111,105
Public and publicly guaranteed debt from:	32,218	79,450	90,136	99,849	108,688	110,206
Official creditors	28,033	56,008	57,944	62,976	62,685	64,049
Multilateral	9,293	20,137	21,569	26,322	28,442	29,967
of which: World Bank	3,881	9,930	11,250	11,993	12,037	12,318
Bilateral	18,741	35,871	36,375	36,654	34,243	34,082
Private creditors	4,184	23,442	32,192	36,873	46,003	46,157
Bondholders	3,333	14,970	22,677	25,940	31,455	29,093
Commercial banks and others	851	8,472	9,515	10,933	14,548	17,064
Private nonguaranteed debt from:	54	446	360	402	784	899
Bondholders	..	..	..	..	100	100
Commercial banks and others	54	446	360	402	684	799
Use of IMF credit and SDR allocations	1,384	9,220	13,130	20,362	23,681	21,753
IMF credit	0	7,971	11,888	19,068	19,691	17,959
SDR allocations	1,384	1,250	1,242	1,294	3,990	3,794
Short-term external debt stocks	3,149	10,341	11,284	11,959	12,842	30,246
Disbursements, long-term	**3,625**	**20,360**	**15,686**	**17,824**	**25,481**	**14,561**
Public and publicly guaranteed sector	3,620	20,234	15,616	17,631	24,771	14,355
Private sector not guaranteed	5	126	71	193	710	206
Principal repayments, long-term	**2,164**	**5,783**	**4,878**	**8,217**	**13,283**	**10,696**
Public and publicly guaranteed sector	2,139	5,696	4,722	8,067	13,054	10,505
Private sector not guaranteed	25	87	156	151	229	191
Interest payments, long-term	**770**	**2,223**	**3,406**	**3,389**	**3,702**	**4,192**
Public and publicly guaranteed sector	769	2,206	3,388	3,378	3,623	4,153
Private sector not guaranteed	1	16	19	12	79	39

EL SALVADOR

(US$ million, unless otherwise indicated)

Snapshot	2022
Total external debt stocks	**21,299**
External debt stocks as % of	
Exports	204
GNI	70
Debt service as % of	
Exports	32
GNI	11
Net financial flows, debt and equity	**134**
Net debt inflows	182
Net equity inflows	-48
GNI	**30,622**
Population (million)	**6**

Figure 1 **Public and publicly guaranteed debt, by creditor and creditor type in 2022, including IMF credit**

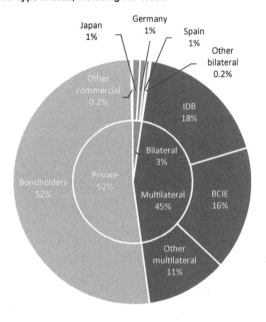

Figure 2 **Average terms on new debt commitments from official and private creditors**

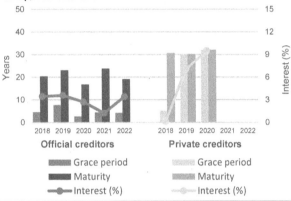

Official creditors	Private creditors
▬ Grace period	▬ Grace period
▬ Maturity	▬ Maturity
▬●▬ Interest (%)	▬○▬ Interest (%)

Summary External Debt Data	2010	2018	2019	2020	2021	2022
Total external debt stocks	**11,496**	**16,725**	**17,398**	**18,479**	**20,326**	**21,299**
Long-term external debt stocks	**10,408**	**14,426**	**14,939**	**15,958**	**17,052**	**17,964**
Public and publicly guaranteed debt from:	6,839	9,505	9,856	10,791	11,544	11,994
Official creditors	4,211	4,368	4,397	4,539	5,335	5,541
Multilateral	3,549	3,996	4,049	4,158	4,987	5,233
of which: World Bank	922	876	831	786	768	879
Bilateral	661	372	348	382	348	308
Private creditors	2,628	5,137	5,459	6,252	6,209	6,452
Bondholders	2,596	5,108	5,422	6,217	6,178	6,424
Commercial banks and others	32	29	37	35	31	28
Private nonguaranteed debt from:	3,569	4,921	5,083	5,167	5,508	5,970
Bondholders	..	38	12	0	0	20
Commercial banks and others	3,569	4,883	5,071	5,167	5,508	5,950
Use of IMF credit and SDR allocations	**252**	**228**	**227**	**650**	**1,016**	**967**
IMF credit	0	0	0	414	402	382
SDR allocations	252	228	227	236	615	584
Short-term external debt stocks	**836**	**2,070**	**2,232**	**1,871**	**2,258**	**2,369**
Disbursements, long-term	**1,455**	**3,211**	**5,283**	**5,297**	**5,683**	**2,170**
Public and publicly guaranteed sector	1,107	588	1,419	1,379	1,232	702
Private sector not guaranteed	348	2,623	3,865	3,918	4,451	1,467
Principal repayments, long-term	**605**	**2,879**	**4,873**	**4,205**	**4,524**	**2,098**
Public and publicly guaranteed sector	456	436	1,179	421	413	1,083
Private sector not guaranteed	149	2,443	3,694	3,785	4,111	1,015
Interest payments, long-term	**495**	**589**	**684**	**927**	**1,241**	**1,185**
Public and publicly guaranteed sector	380	589	684	625	696	736
Private sector not guaranteed	115	..	..	302	545	450

ERITREA

(US$ million, unless otherwise indicated)

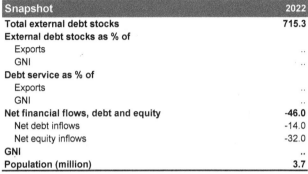

Snapshot	2022
Total external debt stocks	715.3
External debt stocks as % of	
Exports	..
GNI	..
Debt service as % of	
Exports	..
GNI	..
Net financial flows, debt and equity	-46.0
Net debt inflows	-14.0
Net equity inflows	-32.0
GNI	..
Population (million)	3.7

Figure 2 Average terms on new debt commitments from official and private creditors

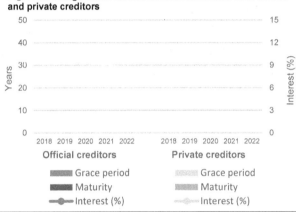

Official creditors
- Grace period
- Maturity
- Interest (%)

Private creditors
- Grace period
- Maturity
- Interest (%)

Figure 1 Public and publicly guaranteed debt, by creditor and creditor type in 2022, including IMF credit

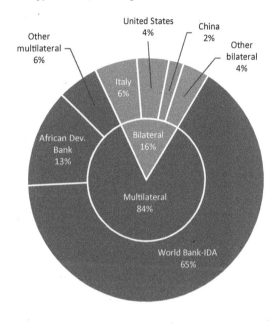

Summary External Debt Data	2010	2018	2019	2020	2021	2022
Total external debt stocks	1,037.3	791.2	771.7	789.7	761.8	715.3
Long-term external debt stocks	998.4	736.1	718.1	730.5	680.4	634.6
Public and publicly guaranteed debt from:	998.4	736.1	718.1	730.5	680.4	634.6
Official creditors	998.4	736.1	718.1	730.5	680.4	634.6
Multilateral	651.4	571.6	567.1	587.8	565.4	533.2
of which: World Bank	467.9	434.5	432.0	449.9	437.2	415.7
Bilateral	347.1	164.5	151.0	142.8	115.0	101.5
Private creditors	..	..	..	..	..	..
Bondholders	..	..	..	..	..	..
Commercial banks and others	..	..	..	..	..	..
Private nonguaranteed debt from:	..	..	..	..	..	..
Bondholders	..	..	..	..	..	..
Commercial banks and others	..	..	..	..	..	..
Use of IMF credit and SDR allocations	23.3	21.1	21.0	21.8	42.5	40.5
IMF credit	0.0	0.0	0.0	0.0	0.0	0.0
SDR allocations	23.3	21.1	21.0	21.8	42.5	40.5
Short-term external debt stocks	15.5	34.0	32.7	37.3	38.9	40.2
Disbursements, long-term	8.6	4.2	4.2	2.8	0.9	0.8
Public and publicly guaranteed sector	8.6	4.2	4.2	2.8	0.9	0.8
Private sector not guaranteed	..	..	..	..	..	..
Principal repayments, long-term	16.9	24.9	18.4	17.8	18.4	14.8
Public and publicly guaranteed sector	16.9	24.9	18.4	17.8	18.4	14.8
Private sector not guaranteed	..	..	..	..	..	..
Interest payments, long-term	10.0	3.1	2.6	2.4	2.2	1.8
Public and publicly guaranteed sector	10.0	3.1	2.6	2.4	2.2	1.8
Private sector not guaranteed	..	..	..	..	..	..

Note: Figure 2 shows no data values because the country did not have new commitments from 2018 to 2022.

ESWATINI

(US$ million, unless otherwise indicated)

Snapshot	2022
Total external debt stocks	**1,211**
External debt stocks as % of	
Exports	54
GNI	27
Debt service as % of	
Exports	6
GNI	3
Net financial flows, debt and equity	**82**
Net debt inflows	64
Net equity inflows	18
GNI	**4,466**
Population (million)	**1**

Figure 2 **Average terms on new debt commitments from official and private creditors**

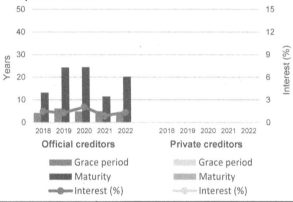

Figure 1 **Public and publicly guaranteed debt, by creditor and creditor type in 2022, including IMF credit**

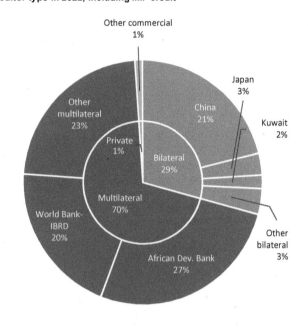

Summary External Debt Data	2010	2018	2019	2020	2021	2022
Total external debt stocks	**1,016**	**766**	**834**	**957**	**1,179**	**1,211**
Long-term external debt stocks	**733**	**685**	**747**	**748**	**857**	**930**
Public and publicly guaranteed debt from:	431	498	540	584	620	758
Official creditors	390	486	529	574	611	749
Multilateral	239	223	245	274	341	497
of which: World Bank	5	40	36	43	87	175
Bilateral	152	263	285	300	270	252
Private creditors	41	12	11	10	9	9
Bondholders	..	..	..	..	..	..
Commercial banks and others	41	12	11	10	9	9
Private nonguaranteed debt from:	302	186	207	164	237	173
Bondholders	..	..	..	..	..	..
Commercial banks and others	302	186	207	164	237	173
Use of IMF credit and SDR allocations	**74**	**67**	**67**	**183**	**283**	**269**
IMF credit	0	0	0	113	110	104
SDR allocations	74	67	67	70	173	164
Short-term external debt stocks	**208**	**14**	**20**	**26**	**40**	**12**
Disbursements, long-term	**320**	**113**	**92**	**78**	**170**	**192**
Public and publicly guaranteed sector	18	113	71	78	97	192
Private sector not guaranteed	302	..	21	..	73	..
Principal repayments, long-term	**34**	**41**	**31**	**82**	**49**	**100**
Public and publicly guaranteed sector	34	32	31	39	49	36
Private sector not guaranteed	..	8	..	43	..	64
Interest payments, long-term	**17**	**15**	**22**	**20**	**15**	**27**
Public and publicly guaranteed sector	17	15	22	20	15	17
Private sector not guaranteed	..	..	..	..	..	10

ETHIOPIA

(US$ million, unless otherwise indicated)

Snapshot	2022
Total external debt stocks	28,610
External debt stocks as % of	
Exports	260
GNI	23
Debt service as % of	
Exports	18
GNI	2
Net financial flows, debt and equity	3,079
Net debt inflows	-591
Net equity inflows	3,670
GNI	126,211
Population (million)	123

Figure 1 **Public and publicly guaranteed debt, by creditor and creditor type in 2022, including IMF credit**

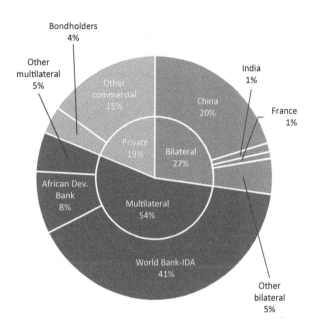

Figure 2 **Average terms on new debt commitments from official and private creditors**

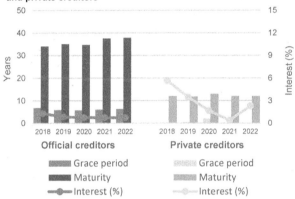

Summary External Debt Data	2010	2018	2019	2020	2021	2022
Total external debt stocks	7,287	27,843	28,377	30,364	29,984	28,610
Long-term external debt stocks	6,500	26,851	27,577	29,016	28,136	27,020
Public and publicly guaranteed debt from:	6,500	26,851	27,577	29,016	28,136	27,020
Official creditors	4,613	19,576	20,619	22,505	22,208	21,778
Multilateral	2,812	11,043	12,200	14,024	14,194	14,244
of which: World Bank	1,804	8,338	9,354	10,991	11,170	11,211
Bilateral	1,800	8,533	8,419	8,482	8,015	7,534
Private creditors	1,887	7,276	6,958	6,511	5,927	5,242
Bondholders	..	1,000	1,000	1,000	1,000	1,000
Commercial banks and others	1,887	6,276	5,958	5,511	4,927	4,242
Private nonguaranteed debt from:	..	..	..	..	..	..
Bondholders	..	..	..	..	..	..
Commercial banks and others	..	..	..	..	..	..
Use of IMF credit and SDR allocations	485	242	318	940	1,317	1,252
IMF credit	288	64	141	755	734	698
SDR allocations	197	178	177	184	582	554
Short-term external debt stocks	302	749	482	408	531	338
Disbursements, long-term	1,763	3,567	2,363	2,194	1,081	1,137
Public and publicly guaranteed sector	1,763	3,567	2,363	2,194	1,081	1,137
Private sector not guaranteed	..	..	..	..	..	..
Principal repayments, long-term	129	1,138	1,431	1,371	1,553	1,535
Public and publicly guaranteed sector	129	1,138	1,431	1,371	1,553	1,535
Private sector not guaranteed	..	..	..	..	..	..
Interest payments, long-term	46	436	670	599	460	459
Public and publicly guaranteed sector	46	436	670	599	460	459
Private sector not guaranteed	..	..	..	..	..	..

FIJI

(US$ million, unless otherwise indicated)

Snapshot	2022
Total external debt stocks	**2,537**
External debt stocks as % of	
Exports	104
GNI	54
Debt service as % of	
Exports	7
GNI	4
Net financial flows, debt and equity	**683**
Net debt inflows	565
Net equity inflows	117
GNI	**4,678**
Population (million)	**1**

Figure 2 Average terms on new debt commitments from official and private creditors

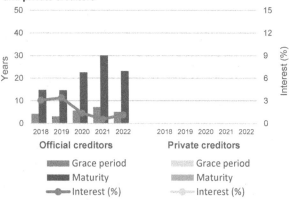

Figure 1 Public and publicly guaranteed debt, by creditor and creditor type in 2022, including IMF credit

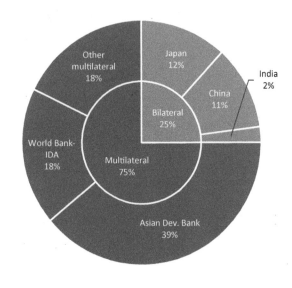

Summary External Debt Data	2010	2018	2019	2020	2021	2022
Total external debt stocks	**1,107**	**1,246**	**1,344**	**1,518**	**2,029**	**2,537**
Long-term external debt stocks	**926**	**1,108**	**1,199**	**1,400**	**1,758**	**2,229**
Public and publicly guaranteed debt from:	426	738	714	904	1,213	1,603
Official creditors	276	538	514	904	1,213	1,603
Multilateral	113	253	263	638	828	1,203
of which: World Bank	..	73	76	142	326	468
Bilateral	162	285	251	265	384	400
Private creditors	150	200	200	0	..	..
Bondholders	150	200	200	0	..	..
Commercial banks and others	..	..	..	..	..	..
Private nonguaranteed debt from:	500	370	485	497	545	626
Bondholders	..	..	..	..	..	..
Commercial banks and others	500	370	485	497	545	626
Use of IMF credit and SDR allocations	**103**	**93**	**93**	**97**	**226**	**215**
IMF credit	0	0	0	0	0	0
SDR allocations	103	93	93	97	226	215
Short-term external debt stocks	**78**	**45**	**53**	**22**	**45**	**93**
Disbursements, long-term	**50**	**86**	**153**	**433**	**399**	**622**
Public and publicly guaranteed sector	38	37	17	403	326	481
Private sector not guaranteed	13	49	136	30	73	141
Principal repayments, long-term	**36**	**75**	**59**	**250**	**39**	**105**
Public and publicly guaranteed sector	9	40	38	231	15	44
Private sector not guaranteed	27	35	21	19	24	60
Interest payments, long-term	**23**	**31**	**150**	**24**	**9**	**62**
Public and publicly guaranteed sector	15	26	146	24	9	59
Private sector not guaranteed	7	5	4	0	0	2

GABON

(US$ million, unless otherwise indicated)

Snapshot	2022
Total external debt stocks	7,954
External debt stocks as % of	
Exports	..
GNI	42
Debt service as % of	
Exports	..
GNI	3
Net financial flows, debt and equity	1,497
Net debt inflows	393
Net equity inflows	1,105
GNI	19,032
Population (million)	2

Figure 1 **Public and publicly guaranteed debt, by creditor and creditor type in 2022, including IMF credit**

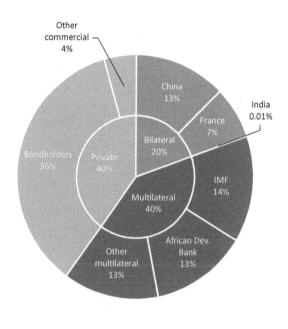

Figure 2 **Average terms on new debt commitments from official and private creditors**

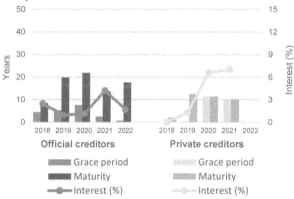

Summary External Debt Data	2010	2018	2019	2020	2021	2022
Total external debt stocks	**2,915**	**6,859**	**7,253**	**7,695**	**7,806**	**7,954**
Long-term external debt stocks	2,519	6,070	6,172	6,557	6,362	6,150
Public and publicly guaranteed debt from:	2,519	6,070	6,172	6,557	6,362	6,150
Official creditors	1,122	3,090	3,451	3,649	3,404	3,284
Multilateral	466	1,697	1,920	2,081	1,935	1,883
of which: World Bank	22	369	581	680	654	649
Bilateral	656	1,394	1,531	1,568	1,469	1,401
Private creditors	1,397	2,980	2,721	2,908	2,958	2,866
Bondholders	879	2,186	2,186	2,436	2,573	2,549
Commercial banks and others	518	794	535	472	384	318
Private nonguaranteed debt from:	..	..	..	..	..	..
Bondholders	..	..	..	..	..	..
Commercial banks and others	..	..	..	..	..	..
Use of IMF credit and SDR allocations	226	601	722	1,063	1,427	1,480
IMF credit	0	397	519	851	932	1,009
SDR allocations	226	204	203	211	495	471
Short-term external debt stocks	170	187	360	76	17	324
Disbursements, long-term	**509**	**857**	**600**	**1,273**	**905**	**268**
Public and publicly guaranteed sector	509	857	600	1,273	905	268
Private sector not guaranteed	..	..	..	..	..	..
Principal repayments, long-term	**313**	**495**	**423**	**1,131**	**902**	**304**
Public and publicly guaranteed sector	313	495	423	1,131	902	304
Private sector not guaranteed	..	..	..	..	..	..
Interest payments, long-term	**137**	**216**	**252**	**274**	**217**	**188**
Public and publicly guaranteed sector	137	216	252	274	217	188
Private sector not guaranteed	..	..	..	..	..	..

GAMBIA, THE

(US$ million, unless otherwise indicated)

Snapshot	2022
Total external debt stocks	**1,130**
External debt stocks as % of	
Exports	431
GNI	51
Debt service as % of	
Exports	14
GNI	2
Net financial flows, debt and equity	**195**
Net debt inflows	86
Net equity inflows	109
GNI	**2,236**
Population (million)	**3**

Figure 2 Average terms on new debt commitments from official and private creditors

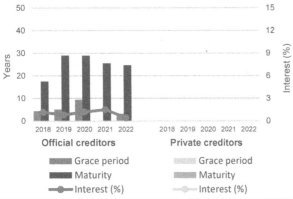

Figure 1 Public and publicly guaranteed debt, by creditor and creditor type in 2022, including IMF credit

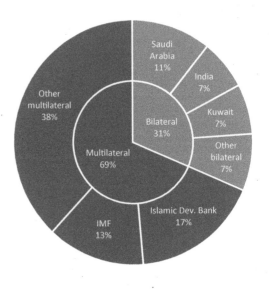

Summary External Debt Data	2010	2018	2019	2020	2021	2022
Total external debt stocks	**544**	**736**	**813**	**929**	**1,081**	**1,130**
Long-term external debt stocks	**422**	**633**	**710**	**797**	**816**	**841**
Public and publicly guaranteed debt from:	422	633	710	797	816	841
Official creditors	416	626	705	794	815	841
Multilateral	296	456	475	528	532	536
of which: World Bank	65	116	118	128	131	126
Bilateral	120	170	230	266	283	305
Private creditors	6	7	5	3	1	0
Bondholders	..	..	..	..	..	..
Commercial banks and others	6	7	5	3	1	..
Private nonguaranteed debt from:	..	..	..	..	..	..
Bondholders	..	..	..	..	..	..
Commercial banks and others	..	..	..	..	..	..
Use of IMF credit and SDR allocations	**77**	**84**	**77**	**103**	**228**	**248**
IMF credit	31	43	36	61	103	129
SDR allocations	46	41	41	43	125	119
Short-term external debt stocks	**45**	**19**	**26**	**29**	**38**	**40**
Disbursements, long-term	**43**	**71**	**109**	**92**	**51**	**74**
Public and publicly guaranteed sector	43	71	109	92	51	74
Private sector not guaranteed	..	..	..	..	..	..
Principal repayments, long-term	**18**	**32**	**30**	**23**	**23**	**22**
Public and publicly guaranteed sector	18	32	30	23	23	22
Private sector not guaranteed	..	..	..	..	..	..
Interest payments, long-term	**7**	**7**	**8**	**8**	**11**	**9**
Public and publicly guaranteed sector	7	7	8	8	11	9
Private sector not guaranteed	..	..	..	..	..	..

GEORGIA

(US$ million, unless otherwise indicated)

Snapshot	2022
Total external debt stocks	**23,982**
External debt stocks as % of	
Exports	163
GNI	104
Debt service as % of	
Exports	22
GNI	14
Net financial flows, debt and equity	**4,316**
Net debt inflows	2,338
Net equity inflows	1,978
GNI	**23,035**
Population (million)	**4**

Figure 2 **Average terms on new debt commitments from official and private creditors**

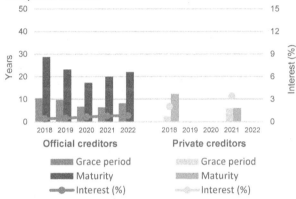

Figure 1 **Public and publicly guaranteed debt, by creditor and creditor type in 2022, including IMF credit**

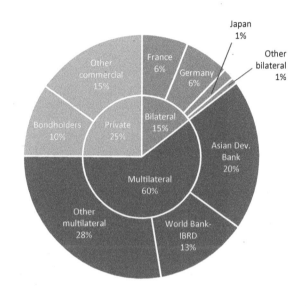

Summary External Debt Data	2010	2018	2019	2020	2021	2022
Total external debt stocks	**8,790**	**17,326**	**18,757**	**20,089**	**22,053**	**23,982**
Long-term external debt stocks	**6,418**	**14,593**	**16,033**	**16,974**	**18,524**	**19,089**
Public and publicly guaranteed debt from:	3,274	6,749	6,993	7,967	9,081	9,723
Official creditors	2,448	4,580	4,880	6,329	6,941	7,146
Multilateral	1,802	3,794	3,934	4,798	5,375	5,624
of which: World Bank	1,359	1,960	1,879	2,054	2,043	2,009
Bilateral	645	786	946	1,531	1,567	1,522
Private creditors	827	2,169	2,113	1,638	2,140	2,577
Bondholders	750	1,250	1,250	750	1,000	1,000
Commercial banks and others	77	919	863	888	1,140	1,577
Private nonguaranteed debt from:	3,143	7,844	9,040	9,007	9,442	9,366
Bondholders	..	1,660	3,320	3,372	3,535	3,381
Commercial banks and others	3,143	6,184	5,720	5,635	5,907	5,985
Use of IMF credit and SDR allocations	**1,272**	**416**	**448**	**792**	**1,158**	**1,084**
IMF credit	1,050	216	249	585	674	624
SDR allocations	222	200	199	207	484	460
Short-term external debt stocks	**1,101**	**2,318**	**2,276**	**2,322**	**2,372**	**3,809**
Disbursements, long-term	**1,026**	**2,468**	**2,983**	**2,508**	**3,792**	**3,382**
Public and publicly guaranteed sector	651	567	616	1,452	2,543	1,319
Private sector not guaranteed	375	1,900	2,367	1,056	1,249	2,062
Principal repayments, long-term	**510**	**1,681**	**1,669**	**1,820**	**2,002**	**2,466**
Public and publicly guaranteed sector	169	300	324	799	1,079	364
Private sector not guaranteed	342	1,381	1,345	1,022	923	2,102
Interest payments, long-term	**247**	**609**	**676**	**587**	**655**	**693**
Public and publicly guaranteed sector	87	167	185	135	100	131
Private sector not guaranteed	160	442	491	452	554	562

GHANA

(US$ million, unless otherwise indicated)

Snapshot	2022
Total external debt stocks	**44,840**
External debt stocks as % of	
Exports	169
GNI	63
Debt service as % of	
Exports	12
GNI	4
Net financial flows, debt and equity	**1,146**
Net debt inflows	-365
Net equity inflows	1,511
GNI	**71,482**
Population (million)	**33**

Figure 1 Public and publicly guaranteed debt, by creditor and creditor type in 2022, including IMF credit

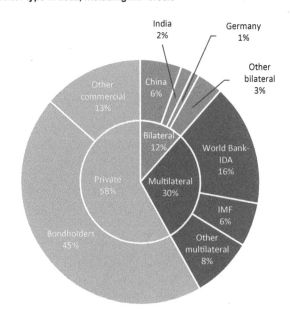

Figure 2 Average terms on new debt commitments from official and private creditors

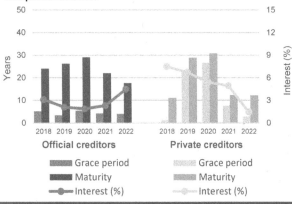

Summary External Debt Data	2010	2018	2019	2020	2021	2022
Total external debt stocks	**17,985**	**35,582**	**32,569**	**40,647**	**44,747**	**44,840**
Long-term external debt stocks	**14,956**	**30,422**	**26,352**	**32,863**	**36,194**	**36,532**
Public and publicly guaranteed debt from:	5,399	17,021	19,574	22,890	26,627	27,647
Official creditors	4,270	8,875	8,831	9,360	9,749	10,560
Multilateral	2,749	5,393	5,513	6,080	6,306	7,142
of which: World Bank	1,868	3,926	3,989	4,477	4,663	4,747
Bilateral	1,521	3,482	3,318	3,280	3,442	3,418
Private creditors	1,130	8,146	10,744	13,530	16,879	17,086
Bondholders	..	4,978	7,695	10,215	13,120	13,104
Commercial banks and others	1,130	3,168	3,049	3,314	3,759	3,982
Private nonguaranteed debt from:	9,556	13,401	6,778	9,973	9,566	8,885
Bondholders	0	1,153	874	1,161	1,103	1,103
Commercial banks and others	9,556	12,248	5,904	8,811	8,463	7,782
Use of IMF credit and SDR allocations	**937**	**1,508**	**1,576**	**2,612**	**3,411**	**3,124**
IMF credit	392	1,016	1,086	2,102	1,926	1,711
SDR allocations	545	492	489	510	1,485	1,412
Short-term external debt stocks	**2,092**	**3,652**	**4,641**	**5,173**	**5,142**	**5,184**
Disbursements, long-term	**4,582**	**4,446**	**4,403**	**7,612**	**5,892**	**2,632**
Public and publicly guaranteed sector	1,321	2,673	3,990	4,417	5,892	2,432
Private sector not guaranteed	3,261	1,773	414	3,195	..	200
Principal repayments, long-term	**171**	**2,801**	**8,406**	**1,534**	**2,157**	**1,837**
Public and publicly guaranteed sector	171	1,760	1,369	1,534	1,751	956
Private sector not guaranteed	0	1,041	7,037	..	407	881
Interest payments, long-term	**96**	**650**	**859**	**921**	**1,202**	**995**
Public and publicly guaranteed sector	96	643	853	915	1,196	989
Private sector not guaranteed	0	6	6	6	6	6

GRENADA

(US$ million, unless otherwise indicated)

Snapshot	2022
Total external debt stocks	**670.0**
External debt stocks as % of	
Exports	80.1
GNI	57.1
Debt service as % of	
Exports	6.2
GNI	4.4
Net financial flows, debt and equity	**111.3**
Net debt inflows	-45.0
Net equity inflows	156.3
GNI	**1,173.6**
Population (thousand)	**125.4**

Figure 2 **Average terms on new debt commitments from official and private creditors**

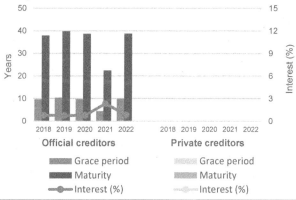

Figure 1 **Public and publicly guaranteed debt, by creditor and creditor type in 2022, including IMF credit**

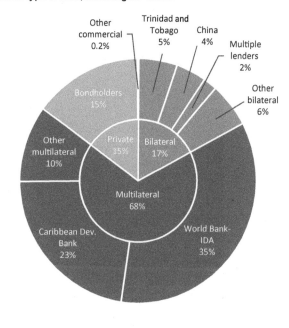

Summary External Debt Data	2010	2018	2019	2020	2021	2022
Total external debt stocks	**560.6**	**554.5**	**525.5**	**658.5**	**725.6**	**670.0**
Long-term external debt stocks	**476.7**	**499.1**	**476.0**	**497.6**	**528.6**	**536.0**
Public and publicly guaranteed debt from:	476.7	499.1	476.0	497.6	528.6	536.0
Official creditors	278.2	370.3	358.4	390.6	432.4	450.5
Multilateral	187.8	278.7	273.6	305.0	329.0	352.5
of which: World Bank	58.2	131.1	131.4	161.4	187.0	211.6
Bilateral	90.4	91.7	84.7	85.6	103.3	98.0
Private creditors	198.5	128.8	117.6	107.0	96.3	85.5
Bondholders	193.2	126.7	115.9	105.4	94.8	84.2
Commercial banks and others	5.3	2.1	1.7	1.6	1.5	1.3
Private nonguaranteed debt from:	..	..	..	..	..	..
Bondholders	..	..	..	..	..	..
Commercial banks and others	..	..	..	..	..	..
Use of IMF credit and SDR allocations	**46.3**	**38.6**	**35.6**	**58.8**	**76.6**	**69.3**
IMF credit	29.1	23.1	20.2	42.7	38.9	33.6
SDR allocations	17.2	15.5	15.4	16.1	37.6	35.8
Short-term external debt stocks	**37.6**	**16.7**	**13.8**	**102.2**	**120.4**	**64.7**
Disbursements, long-term	**21.1**	**38.3**	**12.0**	**44.9**	**65.8**	**46.0**
Public and publicly guaranteed sector	21.1	38.3	12.0	44.9	65.8	46.0
Private sector not guaranteed	..	..	..	..	..	..
Principal repayments, long-term	**15.1**	**33.3**	**34.2**	**28.7**	**30.7**	**31.6**
Public and publicly guaranteed sector	15.1	33.3	34.2	28.7	30.7	31.6
Private sector not guaranteed	..	..	..	..	..	..
Interest payments, long-term	**10.5**	**17.4**	**17.0**	**15.6**	**15.0**	**14.7**
Public and publicly guaranteed sector	10.5	17.4	17.0	15.6	15.0	14.7
Private sector not guaranteed	..	..	..	..	..	..

GUATEMALA

(US$ million, unless otherwise indicated)

Snapshot	2022
Total external debt stocks	**24,992**
External debt stocks as % of	
Exports	130
GNI	27
Debt service as % of	
Exports	27
GNI	6
Net financial flows, debt and equity	**-707**
Net debt inflows	-1,894
Net equity inflows	1,186
GNI	**93,151**
Population (million)	**17**

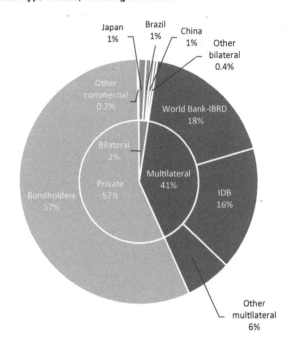

Figure 1 **Public and publicly guaranteed debt, by creditor and creditor type in 2022, including IMF credit**

Figure 2 **Average terms on new debt commitments from official and private creditors**

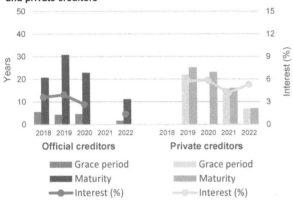

Summary External Debt Data	2010	2018	2019	2020	2021	2022
Total external debt stocks	**15,043**	**24,275**	**25,035**	**24,813**	**26,952**	**24,992**
Long-term external debt stocks	**13,149**	**22,397**	**23,419**	**23,136**	**24,732**	**23,711**
Public and publicly guaranteed debt from:	5,559	8,428	9,843	11,061	11,710	11,701
Official creditors	4,600	5,470	5,188	5,209	4,861	5,052
Multilateral	4,241	4,977	4,686	4,820	4,509	4,754
of which: World Bank	1,372	1,718	1,641	1,758	1,689	2,114
Bilateral	359	493	502	389	352	298
Private creditors	959	2,958	4,655	5,853	6,849	6,649
Bondholders	955	2,930	4,630	5,830	6,830	6,630
Commercial banks and others	4	28	25	23	19	19
Private nonguaranteed debt from:	7,589	13,969	13,576	12,075	13,022	12,009
Bondholders	5	1,650	1,500	700	1,700	3,700
Commercial banks and others	7,584	12,319	12,076	11,375	11,322	8,309
Use of IMF credit and SDR allocations	**309**	**279**	**278**	**289**	**856**	**814**
IMF credit	0	0	0	0	0	0
SDR allocations	309	279	278	289	856	814
Short-term external debt stocks	**1,585**	**1,599**	**1,338**	**1,388**	**1,364**	**467**
Disbursements, long-term	**1,472**	**882**	**2,020**	**1,957**	**2,092**	**3,146**
Public and publicly guaranteed sector	881	406	1,812	1,745	1,061	1,096
Private sector not guaranteed	592	476	208	212	1,030	2,050
Principal repayments, long-term	**949**	**416**	**994**	**2,252**	**476**	**4,143**
Public and publicly guaranteed sector	264	342	394	539	393	1,081
Private sector not guaranteed	685	74	599	1,713	84	3,062
Interest payments, long-term	**636**	**714**	**999**	**1,226**	**1,044**	**1,084**
Public and publicly guaranteed sector	284	267	408	521	496	514
Private sector not guaranteed	352	447	591	705	547	570

100

GUINEA

(US$ million, unless otherwise indicated)

Snapshot	2022
Total external debt stocks	4,929
External debt stocks as % of	
Exports	55
GNI	26
Debt service as % of	
Exports	3
GNI	1
Net financial flows, debt and equity	457
Net debt inflows	457
Net equity inflows	0
GNI	18,904
Population (million)	14

Figure 1 **Public and publicly guaranteed debt, by creditor and creditor type in 2022, including IMF credit**

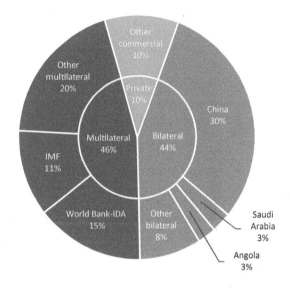

Figure 2 **Average terms on new debt commitments from official and private creditors**

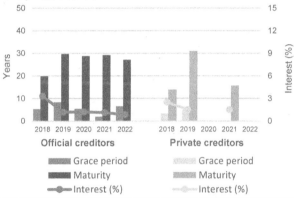

Official creditors	Private creditors
▬ Grace period	▒ Grace period
▬ Maturity	▒ Maturity
●— Interest (%)	●— Interest (%)

Summary External Debt Data	2010	2018	2019	2020	2021	2022
Total external debt stocks	**3,245**	**2,595**	**3,540**	**4,109**	**4,608**	**4,929**
Long-term external debt stocks	**2,925**	**1,989**	**2,865**	**3,291**	**3,498**	**3,791**
Public and publicly guaranteed debt from:	2,925	1,989	2,865	3,291	3,498	3,686
Official creditors	2,900	1,966	2,797	3,063	3,215	3,265
Multilateral	1,875	823	1,028	1,239	1,406	1,431
of which: World Bank	1,248	344	471	572	621	616
Bilateral	1,025	1,142	1,770	1,823	1,809	1,834
Private creditors	25	24	68	228	283	421
Bondholders	..	..	..	..	..	..
Commercial banks and others	25	24	68	228	283	421
Private nonguaranteed debt from:	..	..	..	..	..	105
Bondholders	..	..	..	..	..	..
Commercial banks and others	..	..	..	..	..	105
Use of IMF credit and SDR allocations	**205**	**464**	**481**	**668**	**886**	**884**
IMF credit	48	321	339	520	455	475
SDR allocations	158	143	142	148	431	410
Short-term external debt stocks	**115**	**142**	**193**	**150**	**224**	**254**
Disbursements, long-term	**36**	**239**	**998**	**363**	**325**	**529**
Public and publicly guaranteed sector	36	239	998	363	325	424
Private sector not guaranteed	..	..	..	..	..	105
Principal repayments, long-term	**48**	**82**	**72**	**38**	**63**	**145**
Public and publicly guaranteed sector	48	82	72	38	63	145
Private sector not guaranteed	..	..	..	..	..	..
Interest payments, long-term	**21**	**29**	**30**	**40**	**50**	**48**
Public and publicly guaranteed sector	21	29	30	40	50	48
Private sector not guaranteed	..	..	..	..	..	0

GUINEA-BISSAU

(US$ million, unless otherwise indicated)

Snapshot	2022
Total external debt stocks	**1,021**
External debt stocks as % of	
Exports	406
GNI	62
Debt service as % of	
Exports	27
GNI	4
Net financial flows, debt and equity	**1**
Net debt inflows	-21
Net equity inflows	22
GNI	**1,655**
Population (million)	**2**

Figure 2 **Average terms on new debt commitments from official and private creditors**

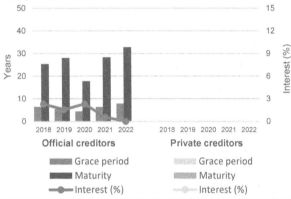

Figure 1 **Public and publicly guaranteed debt, by creditor and creditor type in 2022, including IMF credit**

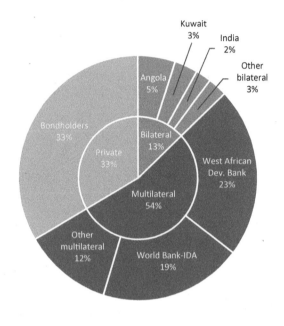

Summary External Debt Data	2010	2018	2019	2020	2021	2022
Total external debt stocks	**1,096**	**547**	**648**	**863**	**1,073**	**1,021**
Long-term external debt stocks	**979**	**481**	**566**	**782**	**930**	**925**
Public and publicly guaranteed debt from:	979	481	566	782	930	925
Official creditors	979	384	440	570	608	603
Multilateral	491	290	344	474	481	478
of which: World Bank	289	111	126	164	182	187
Bilateral	488	95	96	96	127	125
Private creditors	..	97	126	213	322	322
Bondholders	..	97	126	213	322	322
Commercial banks and others	..	..	..	..	..	..
Private nonguaranteed debt from:	..	..	..	..	..	..
Bondholders	..	..	..	..	..	..
Commercial banks and others	..	..	..	..	..	..
Use of IMF credit and SDR allocations	**25**	**53**	**50**	**49**	**103**	**95**
IMF credit	4	34	31	29	46	41
SDR allocations	21	19	19	20	57	54
Short-term external debt stocks	**92**	**14**	**31**	**32**	**40**	**1**
Disbursements, long-term	**9**	**97**	**68**	**111**	**56**	**51**
Public and publicly guaranteed sector	9	97	68	111	56	51
Private sector not guaranteed	..	..	..	..	..	..
Principal repayments, long-term	**6**	**9**	**8**	**11**	**25**	**30**
Public and publicly guaranteed sector	6	9	8	11	25	30
Private sector not guaranteed	..	..	..	..	..	..
Interest payments, long-term	**4**	**6**	**8**	**12**	**19**	**31**
Public and publicly guaranteed sector	4	6	8	12	19	31
Private sector not guaranteed	..	..	..	..	..	..

GUYANA

(US$ million, unless otherwise indicated)

Snapshot	2022
Total external debt stocks	2,387
External debt stocks as % of	
Exports	..
GNI	17
Debt service as % of	
Exports	..
GNI	1
Net financial flows, debt and equity	4,944
Net debt inflows	536
Net equity inflows	4,408
GNI	14,252
Population (million)	1

Figure 2 Average terms on new debt commitments from official and private creditors

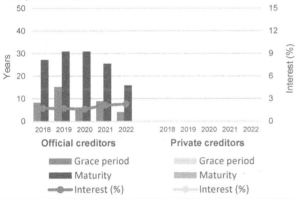

Figure 1 Public and publicly guaranteed debt, by creditor and creditor type in 2022, including IMF credit

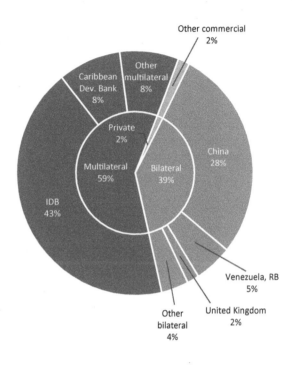

Summary External Debt Data	2010	2018	2019	2020	2021	2022
Total external debt stocks	1,408	1,607	1,530	1,507	1,890	2,387
Long-term external debt stocks	885	1,362	1,361	1,327	1,467	1,985
Public and publicly guaranteed debt from:	885	1,205	1,255	1,271	1,342	1,837
Official creditors	869	1,172	1,223	1,240	1,312	1,807
Multilateral	533	788	815	825	910	1,092
of which: World Bank	9	75	83	90	92	117
Bilateral	336	384	408	415	402	715
Private creditors	16	33	32	31	30	29
Bondholders	0	0	0	0	0	0
Commercial banks and others	16	33	32	31	30	29
Private nonguaranteed debt from:	0	157	106	56	125	148
Bondholders	..	..	..	..	..	..
Commercial banks and others	0	157	106	56	125	148
Use of IMF credit and SDR allocations	190	121	120	125	366	348
IMF credit	56	0	0	0	0	0
SDR allocations	134	121	120	125	366	348
Short-term external debt stocks	333	124	49	54	57	54
Disbursements, long-term	123	138	92	48	218	649
Public and publicly guaranteed sector	123	138	92	48	121	575
Private sector not guaranteed	0	..	..	..	97	74
Principal repayments, long-term	16	106	105	103	85	110
Public and publicly guaranteed sector	16	55	54	52	57	60
Private sector not guaranteed	..	51	51	51	28	50
Interest payments, long-term	11	33	33	30	25	27
Public and publicly guaranteed sector	11	22	23	24	23	24
Private sector not guaranteed	..	11	9	6	3	3

HAITI

(US$ million, unless otherwise indicated)

Snapshot	2022
Total external debt stocks	**2,560**
External debt stocks as % of	
Exports	185
GNI	13
Debt service as % of	
Exports	3
GNI	0
Net financial flows, debt and equity	**48**
Net debt inflows	8
Net equity inflows	39
GNI	**20,277**
Population (million)	**12**

Figure 1 Public and publicly guaranteed debt, by creditor and creditor type in 2022, including IMF credit

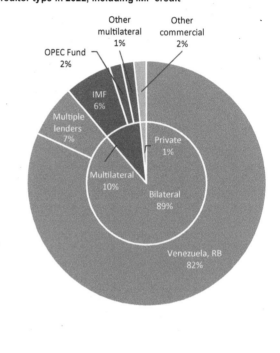

Figure 2 Average terms on new debt commitments from official and private creditors

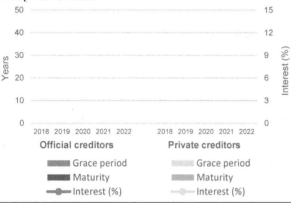

Summary External Debt Data	2010	2018	2019	2020	2021	2022
Total external debt stocks	**959**	**2,220**	**2,214**	**2,318**	**2,604**	**2,560**
Long-term external debt stocks	**824**	**2,019**	**2,012**	**2,027**	**2,102**	**2,115**
Public and publicly guaranteed debt from:	824	2,019	2,012	2,027	2,098	2,110
Official creditors	774	1,973	1,968	1,984	2,057	2,072
Multilateral	557	99	96	92	86	75
of which: World Bank	0	..	..	..	..	..
Bilateral	217	1,874	1,872	1,891	1,971	1,997
Private creditors	50	45	44	43	41	37
Bondholders	..	..	..	..	..	..
Commercial banks and others	50	45	44	43	41	37
Private nonguaranteed debt from:	..	0	0	0	4	6
Bondholders	..	..	..	..	..	..
Commercial banks and others	..	0	0	0	4	6
Use of IMF credit and SDR allocations	**135**	**201**	**185**	**291**	**502**	**445**
IMF credit	13	91	78	181	171	143
SDR allocations	122	110	107	111	332	301
Short-term external debt stocks	**0**	**0**	**16**	**0**	**0**	**0**
Disbursements, long-term	**288**	**40**	**3**	**..**	**87**	**32**
Public and publicly guaranteed sector	288	40	3	..	83	30
Private sector not guaranteed	..	..	..	..	4	2
Principal repayments, long-term	**122**	**5**	**7**	**7**	**12**	**11**
Public and publicly guaranteed sector	122	5	6	7	12	11
Private sector not guaranteed	..	0	0	..	..	..
Interest payments, long-term	**8**	**3**	**3**	**2**	**3**	**19**
Public and publicly guaranteed sector	8	3	3	2	3	19
Private sector not guaranteed	..	0	0	..	..	..

Note: Figure 2 shows no data values because the country did not have new commitments from 2018 to 2022.

HONDURAS

(US$ million, unless otherwise indicated)

Snapshot	2022
Total external debt stocks	**12,609**
External debt stocks as % of	
Exports	133
GNI	43
Debt service as % of	
Exports	16
GNI	5
Net financial flows, debt and equity	**1,185**
Net debt inflows	361
Net equity inflows	824
GNI	**29,212**
Population (million)	**10**

Figure 2 **Average terms on new debt commitments from official and private creditors**

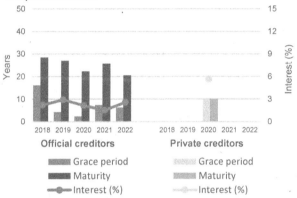

Figure 1 **Public and publicly guaranteed debt, by creditor and creditor type in 2022, including IMF credit**

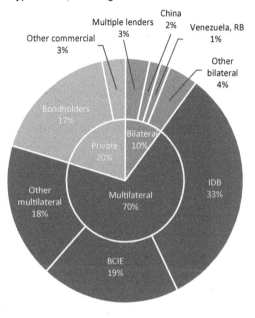

Summary External Debt Data	2010	2018	2019	2020	2021	2022
Total external debt stocks	**4,008**	**9,167**	**9,745**	**11,065**	**12,494**	**12,609**
Long-term external debt stocks	**3,413**	**8,293**	**8,795**	**9,773**	**10,378**	**10,571**
Public and publicly guaranteed debt from:	2,834	7,351	7,751	8,589	8,627	8,998
Official creditors	2,704	5,183	5,620	6,392	6,489	7,052
Multilateral	1,907	4,395	4,564	5,404	5,554	6,076
of which: World Bank	602	937	908	1,034	1,015	936
Bilateral	796	788	1,056	988	935	976
Private creditors	131	2,168	2,131	2,197	2,138	1,946
Bondholders	..	1,700	1,700	1,800	1,800	1,633
Commercial banks and others	131	468	431	397	338	312
Private nonguaranteed debt from:	579	942	1,044	1,184	1,751	1,573
Bondholders	..	..	..	..	300	300
Commercial banks and others	579	942	1,044	1,184	1,451	1,273
Use of IMF credit and SDR allocations	**220**	**172**	**171**	**664**	**1,103**	**1,049**
IMF credit	30	0	0	486	594	565
SDR allocations	191	172	171	178	508	483
Short-term external debt stocks	**374**	**702**	**778**	**628**	**1,013**	**989**
Disbursements, long-term	**906**	**1,013**	**1,079**	**2,098**	**1,351**	**1,502**
Public and publicly guaranteed sector	454	523	693	1,604	389	872
Private sector not guaranteed	452	490	386	494	962	631
Principal repayments, long-term	**453**	**730**	**553**	**1,194**	**876**	**1,117**
Public and publicly guaranteed sector	63	256	276	822	299	442
Private sector not guaranteed	390	474	277	372	576	675
Interest payments, long-term	**56**	**285**	**328**	**321**	**313**	**337**
Public and publicly guaranteed sector	46	267	305	302	247	256
Private sector not guaranteed	10	18	23	19	66	81

INDIA

(US$ million, unless otherwise indicated)

Snapshot	2022
Total external debt stocks	**616,863**
External debt stocks as % of	
Exports	78
GNI	19
Debt service as % of	
Exports	8
GNI	2
Net financial flows, debt and equity	**44,865**
Net debt inflows	14,359
Net equity inflows	30,506
GNI	**3,317,300**
Population (million)	**1,417**

Figure 1 Public and publicly guaranteed debt, by creditor and creditor type in 2022, including IMF credit

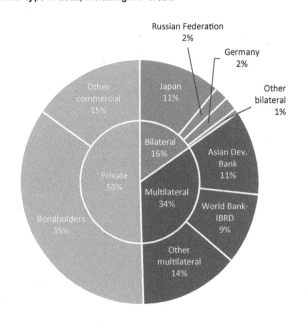

Figure 2 Average terms on new debt commitments from official and private creditors

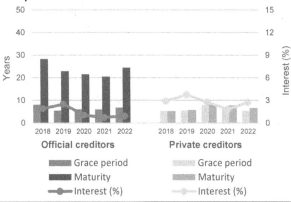

Official creditors	Private creditors
▬ Grace period	▬ Grace period
▬ Maturity	▬ Maturity
▬●▬ Interest (%)	▬●▬ Interest (%)

Summary External Debt Data	2010	2018	2019	2020	2021	2022
Total external debt stocks	**290,428**	**521,176**	**561,017**	**564,979**	**611,987**	**616,863**
Long-term external debt stocks	227,853	411,719	448,737	455,716	474,183	465,673
Public and publicly guaranteed debt from:	100,563	180,540	192,007	192,805	205,282	205,239
Official creditors	72,499	81,146	84,513	96,151	99,657	101,872
Multilateral	46,513	54,310	56,551	64,454	67,713	70,160
of which: World Bank	37,068	36,464	36,809	39,577	39,742	38,257
Bilateral	25,986	26,836	27,962	31,696	31,944	31,711
Private creditors	28,065	99,394	107,495	96,654	105,625	103,367
Bondholders	14,700	73,809	81,351	71,333	75,093	72,077
Commercial banks and others	13,364	25,585	26,144	25,322	30,531	31,291
Private nonguaranteed debt from:	127,290	231,179	256,729	262,911	268,902	260,434
Bondholders	13,217	13,962	19,197	26,822	32,393	33,698
Commercial banks and others	114,073	217,216	237,532	236,089	236,509	226,736
Use of IMF credit and SDR allocations	**6,127**	**5,533**	**5,501**	**5,730**	**23,160**	**22,023**
IMF credit	0	0	0	0	0	0
SDR allocations	6,127	5,533	5,501	5,730	23,160	22,023
Short-term external debt stocks	56,448	103,924	106,780	103,533	114,644	129,168
Disbursements, long-term	**43,406**	**52,174**	**71,710**	**67,698**	**61,278**	**44,214**
Public and publicly guaranteed sector	24,337	19,033	24,617	22,418	30,078	19,360
Private sector not guaranteed	19,069	33,141	47,093	45,280	31,201	24,854
Principal repayments, long-term	**19,018**	**46,229**	**34,762**	**63,444**	**35,724**	**44,379**
Public and publicly guaranteed sector	5,164	21,016	13,220	24,346	13,693	14,347
Private sector not guaranteed	13,854	25,213	21,543	39,098	22,031	30,032
Interest payments, long-term	**4,675**	**13,976**	**12,888**	**11,197**	**12,229**	**15,078**
Public and publicly guaranteed sector	1,063	2,615	3,284	1,655	2,517	3,246
Private sector not guaranteed	3,612	11,361	9,605	9,543	9,712	11,832

(US$ million, unless otherwise indicated)

Snapshot	2022
Total external debt stocks	**395,970**
External debt stocks as % of	
Exports	123
GNI	31
Debt service as % of	
Exports	22
GNI	5
Net financial flows, debt and equity	**22,552**
Net debt inflows	-1,007
Net equity inflows	23,559
GNI	**1,282,834**
Population (million)	**276**

Figure 2 **Average terms on new debt commitments from official and private creditors**

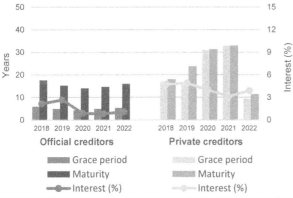

Figure 1 **Public and publicly guaranteed debt, by creditor and creditor type in 2022, including IMF credit**

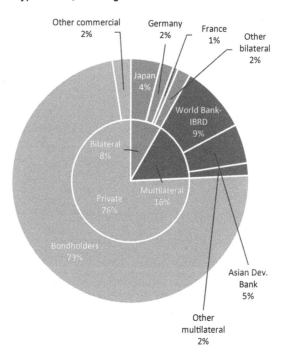

Summary External Debt Data	2010	2018	2019	2020	2021	2022
Total external debt stocks	**198,278**	**379,622**	**402,151**	**416,939**	**411,014**	**395,970**
Long-term external debt stocks	**162,181**	**328,908**	**354,613**	**369,599**	**354,678**	**337,031**
Public and publicly guaranteed debt from:	102,748	215,106	233,572	247,826	235,800	223,805
Official creditors	66,180	53,106	52,323	57,860	54,944	54,256
Multilateral	22,567	30,103	31,452	34,082	34,002	35,478
of which: World Bank	11,367	18,507	19,109	19,669	19,622	20,627
Bilateral	43,613	23,002	20,871	23,778	20,943	18,778
Private creditors	36,568	162,000	181,249	189,966	180,856	169,550
Bondholders	28,698	151,001	173,224	182,704	174,703	163,145
Commercial banks and others	7,870	10,999	8,025	7,261	6,153	6,405
Private nonguaranteed debt from:	59,433	113,802	121,041	121,773	118,878	113,226
Bondholders	8,437	15,038	16,515	18,208	20,214	19,999
Commercial banks and others	50,996	98,764	104,526	103,565	98,664	93,227
Use of IMF credit and SDR allocations	**3,050**	**2,754**	**2,739**	**2,852**	**9,007**	**8,565**
IMF credit	0	0	0	0	0	0
SDR allocations	3,050	2,754	2,739	2,852	9,007	8,565
Short-term external debt stocks	**33,047**	**47,960**	**44,799**	**44,488**	**47,329**	**50,374**
Disbursements, long-term	**34,335**	**72,091**	**94,765**	**65,111**	**50,259**	**53,437**
Public and publicly guaranteed sector	13,695	31,065	31,643	30,273	21,217	18,568
Private sector not guaranteed	20,640	41,026	63,122	34,838	29,042	34,869
Principal repayments, long-term	**26,202**	**42,878**	**68,367**	**52,621**	**61,915**	**57,488**
Public and publicly guaranteed sector	8,072	10,587	13,209	18,513	29,979	27,184
Private sector not guaranteed	18,129	32,291	55,157	34,108	31,935	30,304
Interest payments, long-term	**4,944**	**10,864**	**12,206**	**13,677**	**10,940**	**11,601**
Public and publicly guaranteed sector	3,034	6,928	8,027	9,507	7,911	8,432
Private sector not guaranteed	1,910	3,936	4,179	4,170	3,030	3,169

(US$ million, unless otherwise indicated)

Snapshot	2022
Total external debt stocks	**9,950**
External debt stocks as % of	
Exports	..
GNI	3
Debt service as % of	
Exports	..
GNI	0
Net financial flows, debt and equity	**1,472**
Net debt inflows	-28
Net equity inflows	1,500
GNI	**389,649**
Population (million)	**89**

Figure 1 Public and publicly guaranteed debt, by creditor and creditor type in 2022, including IMF credit

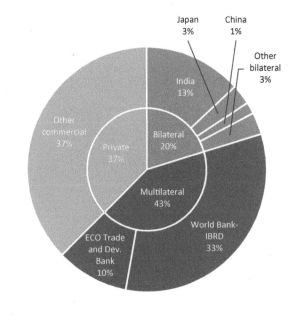

Figure 2 Average terms on new debt commitments from official and private creditors

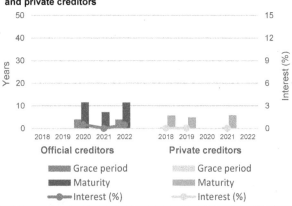

Summary External Debt Data	2010	2018	2019	2020	2021	2022
Total external debt stocks	**19,769**	**5,774**	**4,855**	**5,433**	**10,349**	**9,950**
Long-term external debt stocks	**5,960**	**1,637**	**1,285**	**1,313**	**1,060**	**1,007**
Public and publicly guaranteed debt from:	5,960	437	370	419	332	397
Official creditors	2,068	413	325	300	225	249
Multilateral	833	272	199	190	119	168
of which: World Bank	801	206	141	132	76	129
Bilateral	1,234	141	126	110	106	81
Private creditors	3,892	24	45	118	107	148
Bondholders	..	..	..	..	..	..
Commercial banks and others	3,892	24	45	118	107	148
Private nonguaranteed debt from:	0	1,200	915	894	727	610
Bondholders	..	..	..	..	..	..
Commercial banks and others	0	1,200	915	894	727	610
Use of IMF credit and SDR allocations	**2,196**	**1,983**	**1,972**	**2,054**	**6,781**	**6,448**
IMF credit	0	0	0	0	0	0
SDR allocations	2,196	1,983	1,972	2,054	6,781	6,448
Short-term external debt stocks	**11,613**	**2,154**	**1,599**	**2,067**	**2,508**	**2,496**
Disbursements, long-term	**249**	**0**	**29**	**116**	**21**	**141**
Public and publicly guaranteed sector	249	0	29	116	21	141
Private sector not guaranteed	..	..	..	..	..	..
Principal repayments, long-term	**1,532**	**138**	**256**	**263**	**254**	**169**
Public and publicly guaranteed sector	1,532	138	93	84	88	52
Private sector not guaranteed	..	..	163	178	167	117
Interest payments, long-term	**136**	**18**	**33**	**26**	**46**	**36**
Public and publicly guaranteed sector	136	18	15	15	7	7
Private sector not guaranteed	..	..	18	11	39	29

IRAQ

(US$ million, unless otherwise indicated)

Snapshot	2022
Total external debt stocks	**22,588**
External debt stocks as % of	
Exports	..
GNI	9
Debt service as % of	
Exports	..
GNI	2
Net financial flows, debt and equity	**-3,988**
Net debt inflows	-1,900
Net equity inflows	-2,088
GNI	**263,236**
Population (million)	**44**

Figure 2 **Average terms on new debt commitments from official and private creditors**

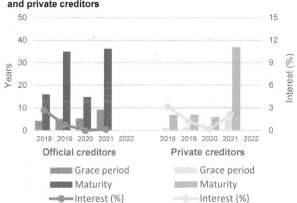

Figure 1 **Public and publicly guaranteed debt, by creditor and creditor type in 2022, including IMF credit**

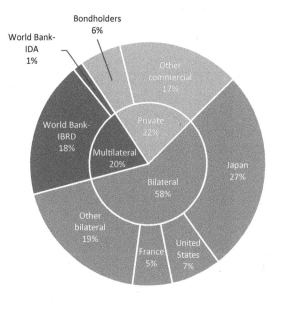

Summary External Debt Data	2010	2018	2019	2020	2021	2022
Total external debt stocks	..	**27,836**	**27,535**	**26,388**	**25,341**	**22,588**
Long-term external debt stocks	..	22,514	22,755	22,864	20,595	17,801
Public and publicly guaranteed debt from:	..	22,514	22,755	22,864	20,595	17,801
Official creditors	..	17,451	17,017	16,891	15,139	13,817
Multilateral	..	3,497	3,568	3,623	3,607	3,462
of which: World Bank	..	3,466	3,550	3,618	3,606	3,460
Bilateral	..	13,955	13,449	13,268	11,531	10,356
Private creditors	..	5,062	5,737	5,973	5,457	3,984
Bondholders	..	2,000	2,000	2,000	2,000	1,000
Commercial banks and others	..	3,062	3,737	3,973	3,457	2,984
Private nonguaranteed debt from:	..	..	..	..	..	..
Bondholders	..	..	..	..	..	..
Commercial banks and others	..	..	..	..	..	..
Use of IMF credit and SDR allocations	..	4,741	4,019	2,944	4,126	3,632
IMF credit	..	3,163	2,450	1,310	307	0
SDR allocations	..	1,578	1,569	1,634	3,820	3,632
Short-term external debt stocks	..	582	762	580	620	1,155
Disbursements, long-term	..	**1,876**	**1,324**	**1,709**	**826**	**1,620**
Public and publicly guaranteed sector	..	1,876	1,324	1,709	826	1,620
Private sector not guaranteed	..	..	..	..	..	..
Principal repayments, long-term	..	**905**	**1,074**	**1,972**	**2,528**	**3,761**
Public and publicly guaranteed sector	..	905	1,074	1,972	2,528	3,761
Private sector not guaranteed	..	..	..	..	..	..
Interest payments, long-term	..	**852**	**845**	**803**	**675**	**591**
Public and publicly guaranteed sector	..	852	845	803	675	591
Private sector not guaranteed	..	..	..	..	..	..

JAMAICA

(US$ million, unless otherwise indicated)

Snapshot	2022
Total external debt stocks	**17,560**
External debt stocks as % of	
Exports	255
GNI	106
Debt service as % of	
Exports	20
GNI	8
Net financial flows, debt and equity	**156**
Net debt inflows	-130
Net equity inflows	286
GNI	**16,607**
Population (million)	**3**

Figure 1 **Public and publicly guaranteed debt, by creditor and creditor type in 2022, including IMF credit**

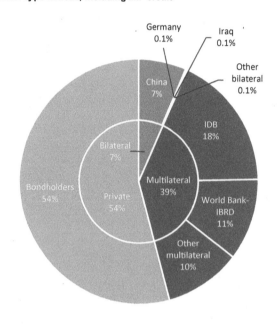

Figure 2 **Average terms on new debt commitments from official and private creditors**

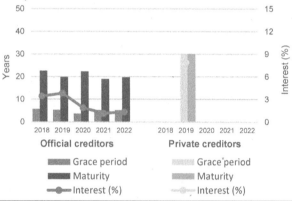

Summary External Debt Data	2010	2018	2019	2020	2021	2022
Total external debt stocks	**14,193**	**16,392**	**16,011**	**15,914**	**17,782**	**17,560**
Long-term external debt stocks	**11,916**	**13,114**	**12,764**	**12,680**	**13,731**	**13,753**
Public and publicly guaranteed debt from:	7,609	9,759	9,407	9,161	9,009	8,749
Official creditors	3,271	3,645	3,585	3,576	3,644	3,605
Multilateral	2,352	2,940	2,915	2,947	3,012	2,969
of which: World Bank	579	865	886	945	1,062	1,032
Bilateral	919	705	670	629	632	636
Private creditors	4,338	6,114	5,822	5,585	5,364	5,144
Bondholders	3,786	6,064	5,810	5,585	5,364	5,144
Commercial banks and others	552	50	12	0	..	..
Private nonguaranteed debt from:	4,307	3,355	3,357	3,519	4,722	5,004
Bondholders	4,290	1,175	1,775	1,750	1,750	1,750
Commercial banks and others	17	2,180	1,582	1,769	2,972	3,254
Use of IMF credit and SDR allocations	**1,188**	**1,074**	**978**	**1,449**	**1,792**	**1,580**
IMF credit	785	710	616	1,072	912	743
SDR allocations	403	364	362	377	880	837
Short-term external debt stocks	**1,089**	**2,205**	**2,269**	**1,785**	**2,259**	**2,228**
Disbursements, long-term	**2,360**	**1,962**	**1,609**	**683**	**1,583**	**532**
Public and publicly guaranteed sector	1,285	294	1,009	270	380	250
Private sector not guaranteed	1,075	1,668	600	413	1,203	281
Principal repayments, long-term	**345**	**498**	**1,953**	**771**	**524**	**503**
Public and publicly guaranteed sector	337	456	1,355	521	524	503
Private sector not guaranteed	9	43	598	250	..	..
Interest payments, long-term	**829**	**673**	**742**	**691**	**647**	**709**
Public and publicly guaranteed sector	489	591	607	552	519	582
Private sector not guaranteed	341	81	135	139	128	128

JORDAN

(US$ million, unless otherwise indicated)

Snapshot	2022
Total external debt stocks	**41,204**
External debt stocks as % of	
Exports	192
GNI	88
Debt service as % of	
Exports	21
GNI	10
Net financial flows, debt and equity	**940**
Net debt inflows	-101
Net equity inflows	1,041
GNI	**46,946**
Population (million)	**11**

Figure 2 **Average terms on new debt commitments from official and private creditors**

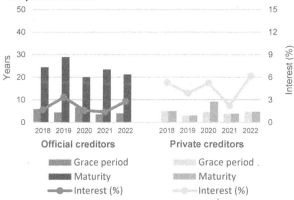

Figure 1 **Public and publicly guaranteed debt, by creditor and creditor type in 2022, including IMF credit**

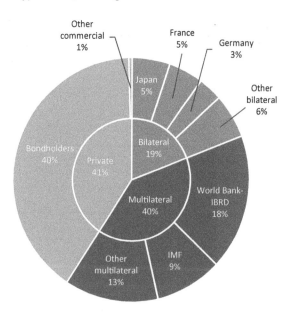

Summary External Debt Data	2010	2018	2019	2020	2021	2022
Total external debt stocks	**16,894**	**31,926**	**33,494**	**38,038**	**41,718**	**41,204**
Long-term external debt stocks	**7,588**	**19,434**	**20,467**	**22,684**	**23,897**	**22,813**
Public and publicly guaranteed debt from:	6,323	16,363	16,853	18,778	19,866	19,231
Official creditors	5,284	7,097	8,215	9,449	10,419	10,584
Multilateral	2,526	3,795	4,731	5,491	6,468	6,526
of which: World Bank	1,040	2,252	2,985	3,329	3,723	3,970
Bilateral	2,757	3,302	3,484	3,958	3,951	4,058
Private creditors	1,040	9,266	8,638	9,330	9,447	8,646
Bondholders	881	9,115	8,500	9,198	9,340	8,550
Commercial banks and others	159	152	138	132	107	96
Private nonguaranteed debt from:	1,265	3,071	3,614	3,905	4,031	3,582
Bondholders	..	..	..	..	..	..
Commercial banks and others	1,265	3,071	3,614	3,905	4,031	3,582
Use of IMF credit and SDR allocations	**257**	**981**	**729**	**1,271**	**2,215**	**2,609**
IMF credit	8	756	505	1,038	1,528	1,955
SDR allocations	250	225	224	233	687	653
Short-term external debt stocks	**9,049**	**11,511**	**12,297**	**14,084**	**15,606**	**15,782**
Disbursements, long-term	**1,508**	**2,782**	**2,824**	**4,052**	**3,820**	**2,641**
Public and publicly guaranteed sector	1,358	2,013	2,049	3,448	3,405	2,641
Private sector not guaranteed	150	769	775	604	415	..
Principal repayments, long-term	**506**	**749**	**1,777**	**2,089**	**2,311**	**3,423**
Public and publicly guaranteed sector	480	591	1,545	1,775	2,022	2,974
Private sector not guaranteed	26	158	231	313	289	449
Interest payments, long-term	**161**	**603**	**742**	**580**	**643**	**774**
Public and publicly guaranteed sector	145	504	589	523	604	639
Private sector not guaranteed	16	99	153	56	39	135

KAZAKHSTAN

(US$ million, unless otherwise indicated)

Snapshot	2022
Total external debt stocks	161,721
External debt stocks as % of	
Exports	167
GNI	83
Debt service as % of	
Exports	46
GNI	23
Net financial flows, debt and equity	7,833
Net debt inflows	1,309
Net equity inflows	6,524
GNI	193,943
Population (million)	20

Figure 1 Public and publicly guaranteed debt, by creditor and creditor type in 2022, including IMF credit

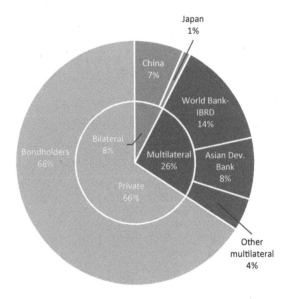

Figure 2 Average terms on new debt commitments from official and private creditors

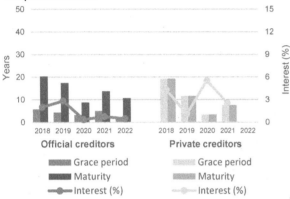

Summary External Debt Data	2010	2018	2019	2020	2021	2022
Total external debt stocks	119,151	157,269	159,282	161,455	160,815	161,721
Long-term external debt stocks	109,757	148,425	149,784	150,959	146,169	143,136
Public and publicly guaranteed debt from:	3,845	24,472	25,006	25,718	27,240	25,572
Official creditors	3,845	8,372	7,634	8,097	8,833	8,738
Multilateral	2,785	6,638	6,010	6,265	6,794	6,771
of which: World Bank	1,830	3,977	3,802	3,615	3,463	3,576
Bilateral	1,060	1,734	1,624	1,833	2,039	1,967
Private creditors	0	16,100	17,372	17,620	18,406	16,834
Bondholders	..	16,100	17,372	17,620	18,406	16,834
Commercial banks and others	0	..	..	..	..	..
Private nonguaranteed debt from:	105,912	123,954	124,779	125,242	118,929	117,564
Bondholders	21,044	7,908	6,684	6,361	5,917	5,220
Commercial banks and others	84,868	116,046	118,094	118,881	113,012	112,345
Use of IMF credit and SDR allocations	529	478	475	495	2,035	1,935
IMF credit	0	0	0	0	0	0
SDR allocations	529	478	475	495	2,035	1,935
Short-term external debt stocks	8,864	8,366	9,022	10,001	12,611	16,650
Disbursements, long-term	45,054	33,912	31,801	34,185	22,818	35,867
Public and publicly guaranteed sector	1,522	3,504	1,975	1,567	2,358	623
Private sector not guaranteed	43,532	30,408	29,826	32,618	20,460	35,245
Principal repayments, long-term	34,639	29,807	29,334	27,125	27,289	38,596
Public and publicly guaranteed sector	278	581	1,433	1,082	461	1,981
Private sector not guaranteed	34,361	29,226	27,901	26,042	26,829	36,615
Interest payments, long-term	4,517	3,530	3,188	3,336	3,652	4,800
Public and publicly guaranteed sector	54	913	1,091	1,005	920	973
Private sector not guaranteed	4,463	2,617	2,098	2,331	2,732	3,827

KENYA

(US$ million, unless otherwise indicated)

Snapshot	2022
Total external debt stocks	**41,563**
External debt stocks as % of	
Exports	299
GNI	37
Debt service as % of	
Exports	24
GNI	3
Net financial flows, debt and equity	**1,925**
Net debt inflows	1,680
Net equity inflows	246
GNI	**111,679**
Population (million)	**54**

Figure 2 Average terms on new debt commitments from official and private creditors

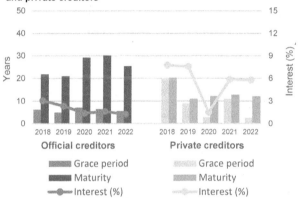

Figure 1 Public and publicly guaranteed debt, by creditor and creditor type in 2022, including IMF credit

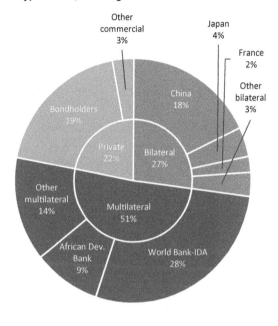

Summary External Debt Data	2010	2018	2019	2020	2021	2022
Total external debt stocks	**8,885**	**31,434**	**34,970**	**38,038**	**41,219**	**41,563**
Long-term external debt stocks	**7,027**	**28,009**	**31,631**	**34,354**	**35,871**	**35,606**
Public and publicly guaranteed debt from:	7,027	26,988	30,814	33,533	35,228	35,037
Official creditors	6,754	20,364	23,721	26,135	26,898	26,839
Multilateral	4,110	10,108	12,709	15,111	15,780	16,720
of which: World Bank	3,238	5,802	7,125	9,334	10,228	11,053
Bilateral	2,644	10,256	11,012	11,024	11,118	10,120
Private creditors	273	6,624	7,093	7,399	8,330	8,198
Bondholders	..	4,750	6,100	6,100	7,100	7,100
Commercial banks and others	273	1,874	993	1,299	1,230	1,098
Private nonguaranteed debt from:	..	1,021	817	821	644	569
Bondholders	..	..	..	..	..	..
Commercial banks and others	..	1,021	817	821	644	569
Use of IMF credit and SDR allocations	**817**	**879**	**720**	**1,391**	**2,913**	**3,389**
IMF credit	417	517	361	1,017	1,821	2,351
SDR allocations	400	361	359	374	1,092	1,038
Short-term external debt stocks	**1,041**	**2,546**	**2,619**	**2,293**	**2,435**	**2,567**
Disbursements, long-term	**532**	**6,622**	**6,722**	**3,417**	**3,406**	**2,958**
Public and publicly guaranteed sector	532	6,248	6,712	3,273	3,406	2,882
Private sector not guaranteed	..	374	10	144	..	76
Principal repayments, long-term	**260**	**1,567**	**3,009**	**1,465**	**1,334**	**2,016**
Public and publicly guaranteed sector	260	1,371	2,799	1,311	1,165	1,872
Private sector not guaranteed	..	196	210	154	169	143
Interest payments, long-term	**90**	**996**	**1,242**	**1,195**	**952**	**1,118**
Public and publicly guaranteed sector	90	941	1,181	1,150	916	1,089
Private sector not guaranteed	..	55	61	45	36	29

KOSOVO

(US$ million, unless otherwise indicated)

Snapshot	2022
Total external debt stocks	**3,639**
External debt stocks as % of	
Exports	92
GNI	38
Debt service as % of	
Exports	8
GNI	3
Net financial flows, debt and equity	**1,091**
Net debt inflows	416
Net equity inflows	675
GNI	**9,524**
Population (million)	**2**

Figure 2 **Average terms on new debt commitments from official and private creditors**

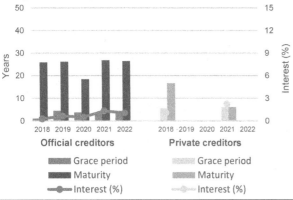

Figure 1 **Public and publicly guaranteed debt, by creditor and creditor type in 2022, including IMF credit**

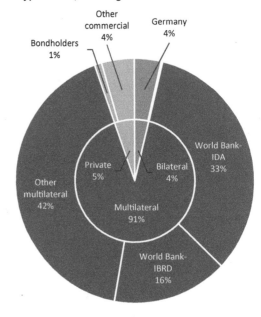

Summary External Debt Data	2010	2018	2019	2020	2021	2022
Total external debt stocks	**1,456**	**2,326**	**2,428**	**3,088**	**3,344**	**3,639**
Long-term external debt stocks	**886**	**1,265**	**1,357**	**1,911**	**1,982**	**2,154**
Public and publicly guaranteed debt from:	319	305	320	517	596	642
Official creditors	319	297	304	488	557	605
Multilateral	319	240	254	441	521	578
of which: World Bank	319	225	220	314	313	342
Bilateral	0	56	50	46	36	26
Private creditors	..	8	16	30	39	37
Bondholders	..	..	..	..	7	7
Commercial banks and others	..	8	16	30	32	31
Private nonguaranteed debt from:	567	961	1,037	1,394	1,386	1,511
Bondholders	..	..	..	..	..	..
Commercial banks and others	567	961	1,037	1,394	1,386	1,511
Use of IMF credit and SDR allocations	**114**	**260**	**225**	**216**	**260**	**234**
IMF credit	29	183	148	136	72	55
SDR allocations	85	77	77	80	188	179
Short-term external debt stocks	**455**	**800**	**846**	**962**	**1,102**	**1,251**
Disbursements, long-term	**169**	**225**	**283**	**567**	**647**	**548**
Public and publicly guaranteed sector	0	25	44	192	152	118
Private sector not guaranteed	169	200	239	375	495	430
Principal repayments, long-term	**76**	**208**	**171**	**251**	**327**	**267**
Public and publicly guaranteed sector	14	21	24	27	33	39
Private sector not guaranteed	61	187	148	224	293	229
Interest payments, long-term	**34**	**55**	**47**	**47**	**18**	**15**
Public and publicly guaranteed sector	11	11	10	11	11	10
Private sector not guaranteed	23	45	37	36	7	5

(US$ million, unless otherwise indicated)

Snapshot	2022
Total external debt stocks	**9,525**
External debt stocks as % of	
Exports	265
GNI	92
Debt service as % of	
Exports	22
GNI	8
Net financial flows, debt and equity	**637**
Net debt inflows	619
Net equity inflows	18
GNI	**10,393**
Population (million)	**7**

Figure 2 Average terms on new debt commitments from official and private creditors

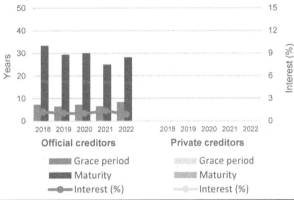

Figure 1 Public and publicly guaranteed debt, by creditor and creditor type in 2022, including IMF credit

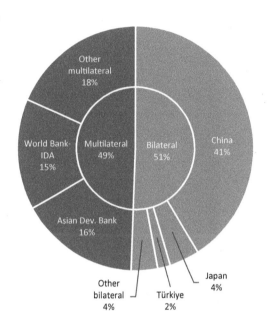

Summary External Debt Data	2010	2018	2019	2020	2021	2022
Total external debt stocks	**4,118**	**8,164**	**8,454**	**8,676**	**9,061**	**9,525**
Long-term external debt stocks	3,616	7,422	7,680	7,653	7,825	7,949
Public and publicly guaranteed debt from:	2,446	3,653	3,712	3,844	3,959	4,031
Official creditors	2,446	3,653	3,712	3,844	3,959	4,031
Multilateral	1,296	1,448	1,462	1,588	1,704	1,839
of which: World Bank	649	660	657	677	653	636
Bilateral	1,150	2,205	2,250	2,255	2,255	2,192
Private creditors	..	..	..	..	..	..
Bondholders	..	..	..	..	..	..
Commercial banks and others	..	..	..	..	..	..
Private nonguaranteed debt from:	1,171	3,769	3,968	3,809	3,866	3,918
Bondholders	..	0	0	0	0	0
Commercial banks and others	1,171	3,768	3,968	3,809	3,866	3,918
Use of IMF credit and SDR allocations	307	285	258	498	697	642
IMF credit	177	167	140	376	340	302
SDR allocations	130	118	117	122	357	339
Short-term external debt stocks	195	457	517	525	539	935
Disbursements, long-term	**672**	**681**	**898**	**391**	**626**	**755**
Public and publicly guaranteed sector	151	144	189	166	289	380
Private sector not guaranteed	521	537	708	224	336	375
Principal repayments, long-term	**462**	**432**	**630**	**509**	**464**	**510**
Public and publicly guaranteed sector	38	101	122	125	117	187
Private sector not guaranteed	424	331	509	384	347	324
Interest payments, long-term	**39**	**199**	**170**	**104**	**93**	**210**
Public and publicly guaranteed sector	23	54	56	55	40	57
Private sector not guaranteed	15	145	114	49	53	153

(US$ million, unless otherwise indicated)

Snapshot	2022
Total external debt stocks	**18,701**
External debt stocks as % of	
Exports	215
GNI	127
Debt service as % of	
Exports	13
GNI	8
Net financial flows, debt and equity	**387**
Net debt inflows	-249
Net equity inflows	636
GNI	**14,767**
Population (million)	**8**

Figure 1 Public and publicly guaranteed debt, by creditor and creditor type in 2022, including IMF credit

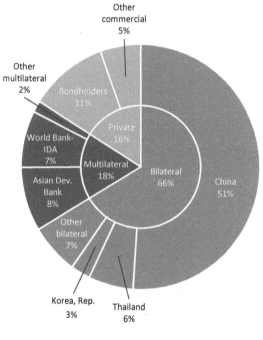

Figure 2 **Average terms on new debt commitments from official and private creditors**

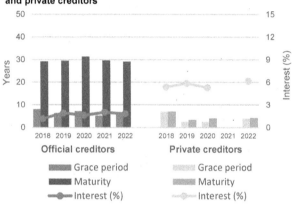

Summary External Debt Data	2010	2018	2019	2020	2021	2022
Total external debt stocks	**6,554**	**15,871**	**18,972**	**20,499**	**19,232**	**18,701**
Long-term external debt stocks	**6,410**	**15,397**	**18,317**	**19,441**	**18,158**	**17,749**
Public and publicly guaranteed debt from:	3,751	9,471	10,199	10,660	10,271	10,131
Official creditors	3,652	7,584	8,082	8,525	8,585	8,501
Multilateral	2,084	1,577	1,707	1,823	1,809	1,773
of which: World Bank	655	588	659	717	740	756
Bilateral	1,569	6,007	6,375	6,701	6,777	6,728
Private creditors	98	1,887	2,117	2,135	1,686	1,629
Bondholders	..	1,596	1,606	1,368	981	1,076
Commercial banks and others	98	291	511	767	705	553
Private nonguaranteed debt from:	2,659	5,926	8,118	8,782	7,886	7,618
Bondholders	..	560	691	692	779	1,041
Commercial banks and others	2,659	5,366	7,426	8,090	7,107	6,577
Use of IMF credit and SDR allocations	**88**	**70**	**70**	**73**	**213**	**202**
IMF credit	10	0	0	0	0	0
SDR allocations	78	70	70	73	213	202
Short-term external debt stocks	**56**	**404**	**585**	**985**	**861**	**750**
Disbursements, long-term	**460**	**1,700**	**3,356**	**1,374**	**551**	**698**
Public and publicly guaranteed sector	267	1,559	1,169	706	356	431
Private sector not guaranteed	193	141	2,186	668	196	268
Principal repayments, long-term	**217**	**417**	**506**	**443**	**1,607**	**836**
Public and publicly guaranteed sector	59	417	504	439	539	306
Private sector not guaranteed	159	..	2	4	1,067	531
Interest payments, long-term	**78**	**334**	**398**	**335**	**267**	**265**
Public and publicly guaranteed sector	28	222	268	201	125	115
Private sector not guaranteed	50	112	130	134	142	150

LEBANON

(US$ million, unless otherwise indicated)

Snapshot	2022
Total external debt stocks	67,109
External debt stocks as % of	
Exports	514
GNI	..
Debt service as % of	
Exports	33
GNI	..
Net financial flows, debt and equity	-1,448
Net debt inflows	-1,680
Net equity inflows	232
GNI	..
Population (million)	5

Figure 1 Public and publicly guaranteed debt, by creditor and creditor type in 2022, including IMF credit

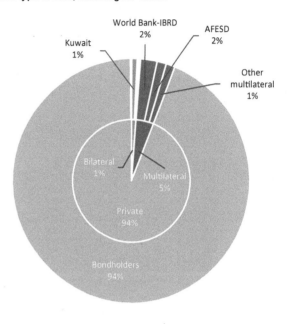

Figure 2 Average terms on new debt commitments from official and private creditors

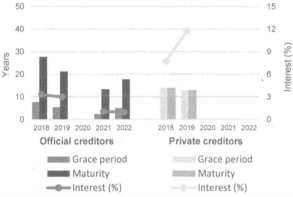

Summary External Debt Data	2010	2018	2019	2020	2021	2022
Total external debt stocks	**47,819**	**79,650**	**73,893**	**68,874**	**66,900**	**67,109**
Long-term external debt stocks	**43,857**	**73,834**	**68,663**	**58,442**	**52,923**	**50,529**
Public and publicly guaranteed debt from:	20,386	33,072	33,319	33,361	33,277	33,376
Official creditors	2,358	1,943	1,875	1,938	1,892	1,994
Multilateral	1,368	1,369	1,373	1,461	1,469	1,604
of which: World Bank	321	510	536	615	663	846
Bilateral	990	574	502	476	423	390
Private creditors	18,028	31,128	31,444	31,423	31,385	31,381
Bondholders	17,422	30,964	31,314	31,314	31,314	31,314
Commercial banks and others	606	164	130	109	71	67
Private nonguaranteed debt from:	23,471	40,763	35,343	25,081	19,646	17,154
Bondholders	500	600	600	600	600	600
Commercial banks and others	22,971	40,163	34,743	24,481	19,046	16,554
Use of IMF credit and SDR allocations	**395**	**269**	**267**	**278**	**1,120**	**1,065**
IMF credit	98	0	0	0	0	0
SDR allocations	298	269	267	278	1,120	1,065
Short-term external debt stocks	**3,567**	**5,547**	**4,963**	**10,154**	**12,857**	**15,515**
Disbursements, long-term	**9,615**	**20,746**	**8,597**	**202**	**145**	**242**
Public and publicly guaranteed sector	2,186	5,716	3,173	202	145	242
Private sector not guaranteed	7,430	15,030	5,424	..	..	..
Principal repayments, long-term	**8,395**	**11,996**	**13,761**	**10,458**	**5,638**	**2,603**
Public and publicly guaranteed sector	2,477	2,589	2,917	196	202	111
Private sector not guaranteed	5,918	9,407	10,844	10,262	5,436	2,492
Interest payments, long-term	**2,735**	**4,275**	**4,597**	**2,287**	**1,561**	**1,221**
Public and publicly guaranteed sector	1,406	2,150	2,142	157	47	32
Private sector not guaranteed	1,328	2,125	2,455	2,130	1,514	1,188

LESOTHO

(US$ million, unless otherwise indicated)

Snapshot	2022
Total external debt stocks	**1,810**
External debt stocks as % of	
Exports	108
GNI	60
Debt service as % of	
Exports	18
GNI	10
Net financial flows, debt and equity	**1**
Net debt inflows	35
Net equity inflows	-34
GNI	**2,999**
Population (million)	**2**

Figure 2 Average terms on new debt commitments from official and private creditors

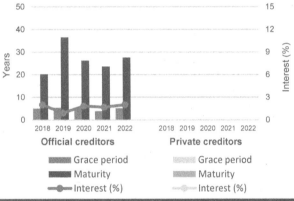

Figure 1 Public and publicly guaranteed debt, by creditor and creditor type in 2022, including IMF credit

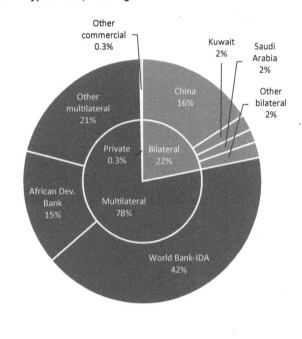

Summary External Debt Data	2010	2018	2019	2020	2021	2022
Total external debt stocks	**788**	**1,463**	**1,583**	**1,738**	**1,833**	**1,810**
Long-term external debt stocks	**709**	**1,369**	**1,504**	**1,616**	**1,633**	**1,614**
Public and publicly guaranteed debt from:	709	809	856	931	978	968
Official creditors	688	805	852	927	974	965
Multilateral	633	697	722	755	760	743
of which: World Bank	330	338	363	400	424	427
Bilateral	55	108	131	171	215	222
Private creditors	21	5	4	4	4	3
Bondholders	..	..	..	..	..	..
Commercial banks and others	21	5	4	4	4	3
Private nonguaranteed debt from:	..	560	648	685	655	645
Bondholders	..	..	..	..	..	..
Commercial banks and others	..	560	648	685	655	645
Use of IMF credit and SDR allocations	**79**	**94**	**79**	**119**	**198**	**182**
IMF credit	28	48	34	72	58	49
SDR allocations	51	46	45	47	140	133
Short-term external debt stocks	**0**	**1**	**0**	**2**	**3**	**14**
Disbursements, long-term	**45**	**43**	**179**	**117**	**106**	**84**
Public and publicly guaranteed sector	45	43	91	79	106	84
Private sector not guaranteed	..	..	88	38	..	..
Principal repayments, long-term	**19**	**51**	**37**	**44**	**66**	**54**
Public and publicly guaranteed sector	19	42	37	44	35	45
Private sector not guaranteed	..	8	..	..	31	9
Interest payments, long-term	**8**	**17**	**24**	**16**	**262**	**238**
Public and publicly guaranteed sector	8	17	24	16	262	238
Private sector not guaranteed	..	..	..	..	..	..

LIBERIA

(US$ million, unless otherwise indicated)

Snapshot	2022
Total external debt stocks	**1,904**
External debt stocks as % of	
Exports	153
GNI	51
Debt service as % of	
Exports	6
GNI	2
Net financial flows, debt and equity	**1,080**
Net debt inflows	132
Net equity inflows	948
GNI	**3,754**
Population (million)	**5**

Figure 2 Average terms on new debt commitments from official and private creditors

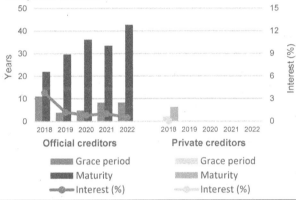

Figure 1 Public and publicly guaranteed debt, by creditor and creditor type in 2022, including IMF credit

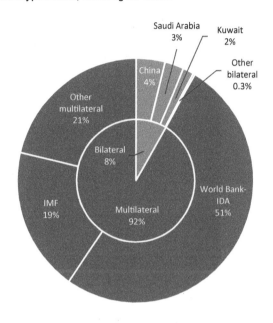

Summary External Debt Data	2010	2018	2019	2020	2021	2022
Total external debt stocks	**419**	**1,158**	**1,267**	**1,462**	**1,849**	**1,904**
Long-term external debt stocks	**183**	**768**	**870**	**989**	**1,050**	**1,147**
Public and publicly guaranteed debt from:	183	713	822	948	1,017	1,110
Official creditors	183	713	822	948	1,017	1,110
Multilateral	63	597	705	828	898	995
of which: World Bank	..	368	455	550	616	703
Bilateral	120	116	117	120	120	114
Private creditors	0	0	..	..	..	..
Bondholders	..	..	..	..	..	..
Commercial banks and others	..	..	..	..	..	..
Private nonguaranteed debt from:	..	55	49	41	33	37
Bondholders	..	..	..	..	..	..
Commercial banks and others	..	55	49	41	33	37
Use of IMF credit and SDR allocations	**235**	**389**	**396**	**473**	**798**	**757**
IMF credit	44	217	225	294	278	263
SDR allocations	191	172	171	179	520	495
Short-term external debt stocks	**0**	**0**	**0**	**0**	**0**	**0**
Disbursements, long-term	**0**	**153**	**120**	**112**	**99**	**170**
Public and publicly guaranteed sector	0	151	119	110	99	148
Private sector not guaranteed	..	2	1	1	..	22
Principal repayments, long-term	**4**	**13**	**14**	**22**	**18**	**37**
Public and publicly guaranteed sector	4	5	6	14	10	19
Private sector not guaranteed	..	8	8	8	8	18
Interest payments, long-term	**1**	**8**	**8**	**11**	**10**	**13**
Public and publicly guaranteed sector	1	7	7	10	9	12
Private sector not guaranteed	..	1	1	1	0	0

MADAGASCAR

(US$ million, unless otherwise indicated)

Snapshot	2022
Total external debt stocks	**5,938**
External debt stocks as % of	
Exports	125
GNI	41
Debt service as % of	
Exports	5
GNI	1
Net financial flows, debt and equity	**892**
Net debt inflows	823
Net equity inflows	69
GNI	**14,531**
Population (million)	**30**

Figure 2 Average terms on new debt commitments from official and private creditors

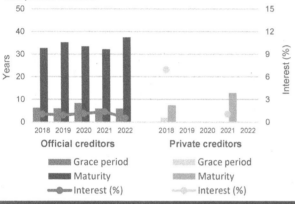

Figure 1 Public and publicly guaranteed debt, by creditor and creditor type in 2022, including IMF credit

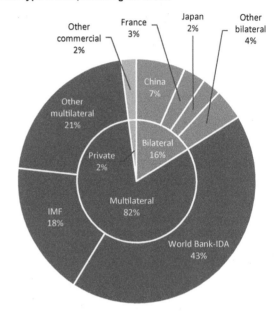

Summary External Debt Data	2010	2018	2019	2020	2021	2022
Total external debt stocks	**2,756**	**3,720**	**4,045**	**4,841**	**5,345**	**5,938**
Long-term external debt stocks	**2,054**	**2,984**	**3,218**	**3,612**	**3,811**	**4,441**
Public and publicly guaranteed debt from:	2,039	2,901	3,117	3,508	3,715	3,934
Official creditors	2,031	2,737	2,963	3,362	3,598	3,835
Multilateral	1,575	2,347	2,488	2,809	2,986	3,059
of which: World Bank	1,161	1,648	1,686	1,874	2,010	2,043
Bilateral	456	390	475	553	612	776
Private creditors	8	164	154	146	118	99
Bondholders	..	..	..	..	..	..
Commercial banks and others	8	164	154	146	118	99
Private nonguaranteed debt from:	15	84	101	104	95	507
Bondholders	..	..	..	..	..	420
Commercial banks and others	15	84	101	104	95	87
Use of IMF credit and SDR allocations	**278**	**465**	**545**	**956**	**1,304**	**1,317**
IMF credit	97	302	383	788	812	850
SDR allocations	180	163	162	169	492	468
Short-term external debt stocks	**425**	**271**	**281**	**273**	**230**	**180**
Disbursements, long-term	**198**	**361**	**327**	**347**	**413**	**905**
Public and publicly guaranteed sector	198	295	300	336	413	485
Private sector not guaranteed	..	66	26	11	..	420
Principal repayments, long-term	**39**	**81**	**76**	**82**	**105**	**109**
Public and publicly guaranteed sector	37	72	67	73	96	100
Private sector not guaranteed	1	9	9	9	9	9
Interest payments, long-term	**16**	**33**	**36**	**37**	**39**	**72**
Public and publicly guaranteed sector	16	29	30	31	32	36
Private sector not guaranteed	0	4	6	6	6	37

MALAWI

(US$ million, unless otherwise indicated)

Snapshot	2022
Total external debt stocks	**3,338**
External debt stocks as % of	
Exports	285
GNI	26
Debt service as % of	
Exports	12
GNI	1
Net financial flows, debt and equity	**462**
Net debt inflows	274
Net equity inflows	189
GNI	**12,925**
Population (million)	**20**

Figure 1 Public and publicly guaranteed debt, by creditor and creditor type in 2022, including IMF credit

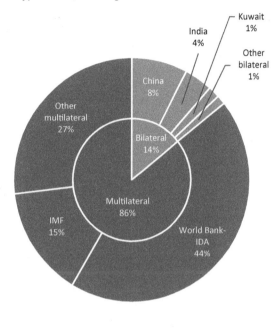

Figure 2 Average terms on new debt commitments from official and private creditors

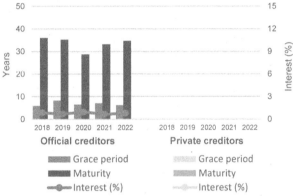

Summary External Debt Data	2010	2018	2019	2020	2021	2022
Total external debt stocks	**1,021**	**2,266**	**2,429**	**2,943**	**3,198**	**3,338**
Long-term external debt stocks	**730**	**1,926**	**2,021**	**2,237**	**2,379**	**2,544**
Public and publicly guaranteed debt from:	730	1,926	2,021	2,237	2,379	2,544
Official creditors	724	1,926	2,021	2,237	2,379	2,544
Multilateral	586	1,487	1,600	1,799	1,929	2,119
of which: World Bank	243	917	969	1,104	1,177	1,319
Bilateral	138	439	421	438	451	425
Private creditors	5	..	..	..	..	..
Bondholders	..	..	..	..	..	..
Commercial banks and others	5	..	..	..	..	..
Private nonguaranteed debt from:	..	..	..	..	..	..
Bondholders	..	..	..	..	..	..
Commercial banks and others	..	..	..	..	..	..
Use of IMF credit and SDR allocations	**248**	**314**	**339**	**528**	**673**	**704**
IMF credit	146	222	248	432	394	438
SDR allocations	102	92	92	96	279	265
Short-term external debt stocks	**43**	**25**	**68**	**178**	**146**	**91**
Disbursements, long-term	**81**	**223**	**168**	**193**	**245**	**340**
Public and publicly guaranteed sector	81	223	168	193	245	340
Private sector not guaranteed	..	..	..	..	..	..
Principal repayments, long-term	**13**	**42**	**62**	**52**	**60**	**77**
Public and publicly guaranteed sector	13	42	62	52	60	77
Private sector not guaranteed	..	..	..	..	..	..
Interest payments, long-term	**7**	**12**	**17**	**21**	**22**	**24**
Public and publicly guaranteed sector	7	12	17	21	22	24
Private sector not guaranteed	..	..	..	..	..	..

(US$ million, unless otherwise indicated)

Snapshot	2022
Total external debt stocks	**4,039**
External debt stocks as % of	
Exports	79
GNI	72
Debt service as % of	
Exports	14
GNI	12
Net financial flows, debt and equity	**665**
Net debt inflows	-57
Net equity inflows	722
GNI	**5,630**
Population (million)	**1**

Figure 1 **Public and publicly guaranteed debt, by creditor and creditor type in 2022, including IMF credit**

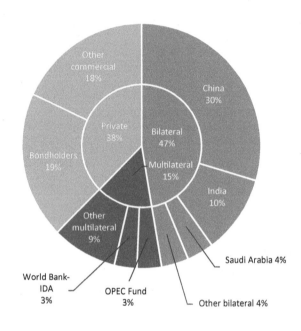

Figure 2 **Average terms on new debt commitments from official and private creditors**

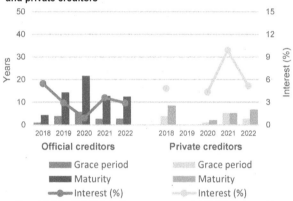

Summary External Debt Data	2010	2018	2019	2020	2021	2022
Total external debt stocks	**917**	**2,323**	**2,679**	**3,703**	**4,163**	**4,039**
Long-term external debt stocks	**743**	**2,073**	**2,332**	**3,212**	**3,546**	**3,476**
Public and publicly guaranteed debt from:	628	2,004	2,228	2,853	3,135	3,067
Official creditors	536	1,294	1,446	1,990	1,824	1,907
Multilateral	301	340	384	413	443	440
of which: World Bank	99	85	92	106	101	95
Bilateral	236	954	1,062	1,576	1,381	1,467
Private creditors	92	710	782	864	1,311	1,161
Bondholders	..	350	350	350	850	600
Commercial banks and others	92	360	432	514	461	561
Private nonguaranteed debt from:	115	69	104	359	411	409
Bondholders	..	..	..	..	..	..
Commercial banks and others	115	69	104	359	411	409
Use of IMF credit and SDR allocations	**28**	**11**	**11**	**42**	**69**	**65**
IMF credit	16	1	0	31	30	28
SDR allocations	12	11	11	11	39	37
Short-term external debt stocks	**146**	**238**	**336**	**449**	**549**	**497**
Disbursements, long-term	**168**	**1,124**	**613**	**1,070**	**1,037**	**501**
Public and publicly guaranteed sector	142	1,124	562	775	934	450
Private sector not guaranteed	26	..	51	295	102	51
Principal repayments, long-term	**60**	**372**	**364**	**231**	**706**	**524**
Public and publicly guaranteed sector	51	334	331	191	656	470
Private sector not guaranteed	9	38	33	40	50	53
Interest payments, long-term	**11**	**57**	**84**	**78**	**91**	**150**
Public and publicly guaranteed sector	9	55	80	74	85	134
Private sector not guaranteed	1	3	3	5	5	16

MALI

(US$ million, unless otherwise indicated)

Snapshot	2022
Total external debt stocks	**6,343**
External debt stocks as % of	
Exports	116
GNI	35
Debt service as % of	
Exports	6
GNI	2
Net financial flows, debt and equity	**487**
Net debt inflows	235
Net equity inflows	253
GNI	**18,068**
Population (million)	**23**

Figure 2 Average terms on new debt commitments from official and private creditors

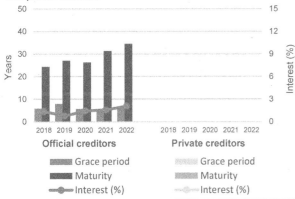

Figure 1 Public and publicly guaranteed debt, by creditor and creditor type in 2022, including IMF credit

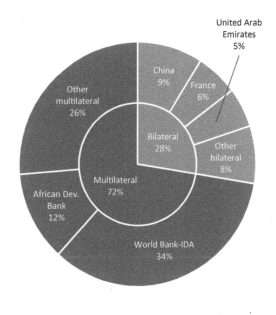

Summary External Debt Data	2010	2018	2019	2020	2021	2022
Total external debt stocks	**2,439**	**4,595**	**4,998**	**5,814**	**6,402**	**6,343**
Long-term external debt stocks	**2,246**	**4,046**	**4,452**	**5,061**	**5,371**	**5,411**
Public and publicly guaranteed debt from:	2,246	4,046	4,452	5,061	5,371	5,411
Official creditors	2,241	4,046	4,452	5,061	5,371	5,411
Multilateral	1,788	3,055	3,391	3,795	3,781	3,776
of which: World Bank	840	1,682	1,970	2,146	2,131	2,033
Bilateral	453	990	1,061	1,266	1,590	1,635
Private creditors	5	0	0	..	..	..
Bondholders	..	..	..	..	..	..
Commercial banks and others	5	0	0	..	..	..
Private nonguaranteed debt from:	..	..	..	..	..	..
Bondholders	..	..	..	..	..	..
Commercial banks and others	..	..	..	..	..	..
Use of IMF credit and SDR allocations	**187**	**441**	**447**	**681**	**946**	**880**
IMF credit	49	316	323	552	571	523
SDR allocations	138	124	124	129	375	357
Short-term external debt stocks	**6**	**109**	**100**	**72**	**85**	**53**
Disbursements, long-term	**310**	**388**	**595**	**555**	**730**	**515**
Public and publicly guaranteed sector	310	388	595	555	730	515
Private sector not guaranteed	..	..	..	..	..	..
Principal repayments, long-term	**47**	**121**	**141**	**196**	**211**	**228**
Public and publicly guaranteed sector	47	121	141	196	211	228
Private sector not guaranteed	..	..	..	..	..	..
Interest payments, long-term	**21**	**40**	**47**	**37**	**59**	**60**
Public and publicly guaranteed sector	21	40	47	37	59	60
Private sector not guaranteed	..	..	..	..	..	..

MAURITANIA

(US$ million, unless otherwise indicated)

Snapshot	2022
Total external debt stocks	**4,604**
External debt stocks as % of	
Exports	108
GNI	45
Debt service as % of	
Exports	8
GNI	3
Net financial flows, debt and equity	**1,312**
Net debt inflows	-89
Net equity inflows	1,402
GNI	**10,219**
Population (million)	**5**

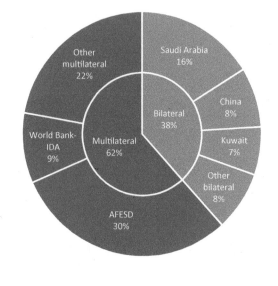

Figure 1 **Public and publicly guaranteed debt, by creditor and creditor type in 2022, including IMF credit**

Figure 2 **Average terms on new debt commitments from official and private creditors**

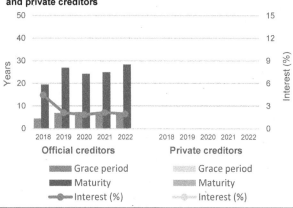

Summary External Debt Data	2010	2018	2019	2020	2021	2022
Total external debt stocks	**3,556**	**5,224**	**5,371**	**5,717**	**4,813**	**4,604**
Long-term external debt stocks	**2,326**	**3,951**	**4,044**	**4,217**	**4,038**	**3,841**
Public and publicly guaranteed debt from:	2,326	3,951	4,044	4,217	4,038	3,841
Official creditors	2,325	3,951	4,044	4,217	4,038	3,841
Multilateral	1,501	2,284	2,386	2,490	2,355	2,251
of which: World Bank	316	382	388	418	415	385
Bilateral	824	1,667	1,658	1,727	1,683	1,590
Private creditors	1	..	..	..	..	..
Bondholders	..	..	..	..	..	..
Commercial banks and others	1	..	..	..	..	..
Private nonguaranteed debt from:	..	..	..	..	..	..
Bondholders	..	..	..	..	..	..
Commercial banks and others	..	..	..	..	..	..
Use of IMF credit and SDR allocations	**145**	**221**	**244**	**424**	**594**	**556**
IMF credit	50	135	159	336	335	310
SDR allocations	95	86	85	89	259	246
Short-term external debt stocks	**1,086**	**1,052**	**1,083**	**1,075**	**180**	**206**
Disbursements, long-term	**412**	**270**	**374**	**232**	**129**	**154**
Public and publicly guaranteed sector	412	270	374	232	129	154
Private sector not guaranteed	..	..	..	..	..	..
Principal repayments, long-term	**77**	**270**	**266**	**210**	**336**	**261**
Public and publicly guaranteed sector	77	270	266	210	336	261
Private sector not guaranteed	..	..	..	..	..	..
Interest payments, long-term	**35**	**92**	**88**	**59**	**57**	**66**
Public and publicly guaranteed sector	35	92	88	59	57	66
Private sector not guaranteed	..	..	..	..	..	..

MAURITIUS

(US$ million, unless otherwise indicated)

Snapshot	2022
Total external debt stocks	**17,365**
External debt stocks as % of	
Exports	146
GNI	132
Debt service as % of	
Exports	8
GNI	7
Net financial flows, debt and equity	**4,313**
Net debt inflows	2,771
Net equity inflows	1,542
GNI	**13,175**
Population (million)	**1**

Figure 1 **Public and publicly guaranteed debt, by creditor and creditor type in 2022, including IMF credit**

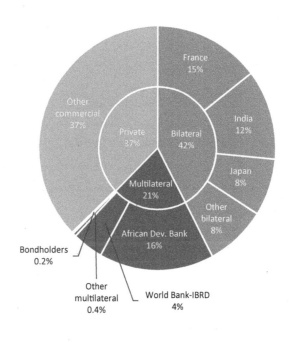

Figure 2 **Average terms on new debt commitments from official and private creditors**

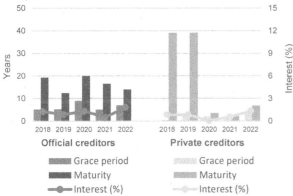

Summary External Debt Data	2010	2018	2019	2020	2021	2022
Total external debt stocks	**7,929**	**11,234**	**12,361**	**12,402**	**14,706**	**17,365**
Long-term external debt stocks	**6,294**	**6,244**	**6,515**	**5,996**	**6,965**	**8,736**
Public and publicly guaranteed debt from:	1,007	1,434	1,386	1,917	2,826	3,100
Official creditors	888	1,411	1,366	1,883	2,004	1,943
Multilateral	501	757	789	790	702	633
of which: World Bank	204	231	207	189	158	131
Bilateral	387	654	577	1,093	1,302	1,310
Private creditors	119	24	20	33	822	1,157
Bondholders	..	5	7	8	9	7
Commercial banks and others	119	19	13	26	814	1,150
Private nonguaranteed debt from:	5,287	4,810	5,130	4,079	4,139	5,636
Bondholders	..	309	468	399	381	666
Commercial banks and others	5,287	4,501	4,661	3,681	3,757	4,970
Use of IMF credit and SDR allocations	**149**	**135**	**134**	**139**	**326**	**310**
IMF credit	0	0	0	0	0	0
SDR allocations	149	135	134	139	326	310
Short-term external debt stocks	**1,485**	**4,855**	**5,712**	**6,267**	**7,414**	**8,318**
Disbursements, long-term	**2,568**	**3,861**	**2,794**	**1,636**	**3,164**	**2,150**
Public and publicly guaranteed sector	356	64	134	784	1,163	522
Private sector not guaranteed	2,212	3,797	2,660	851	2,001	1,628
Principal repayments, long-term	**2,118**	**2,849**	**2,499**	**2,243**	**2,390**	**278**
Public and publicly guaranteed sector	69	150	159	341	164	147
Private sector not guaranteed	2,049	2,699	2,341	1,902	2,227	131
Interest payments, long-term	**73**	**297**	**622**	**314**	**286**	**483**
Public and publicly guaranteed sector	17	28	29	27	20	38
Private sector not guaranteed	56	269	593	287	267	444

(US$ million, unless otherwise indicated)

Snapshot	2022
Total external debt stocks	**600,423**
External debt stocks as % of	
Exports	93
GNI	43
Debt service as % of	
Exports	8
GNI	4
Net financial flows, debt and equity	**45,608**
Net debt inflows	15,940
Net equity inflows	29,668
GNI	**1,384,249**
Population (million)	**128**

Figure 1 **Public and publicly guaranteed debt, by creditor and creditor type in 2022, including IMF credit**

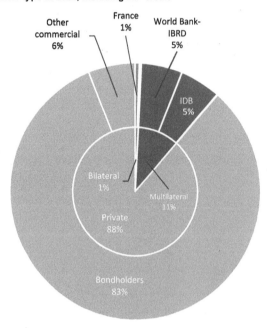

Figure 2 **Average terms on new debt commitments from official and private creditors**

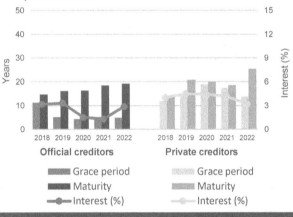

Official creditors / Private creditors

- Grace period
- Maturity
- Interest (%)

Summary External Debt Data	2010	2018	2019	2020	2021	2022
Total external debt stocks	**306,835**	**605,852**	**609,312**	**602,686**	**594,284**	**600,423**
Long-term external debt stocks	259,383	545,751	549,912	552,201	531,296	530,495
Public and publicly guaranteed debt from:	145,925	297,827	306,433	309,061	290,868	293,095
Official creditors	25,389	32,605	33,476	34,877	33,844	33,597
Multilateral	21,433	29,794	30,989	32,215	31,144	31,234
of which: World Bank	12,462	14,611	14,942	15,714	15,237	15,596
Bilateral	3,956	2,811	2,487	2,662	2,699	2,363
Private creditors	120,536	265,222	272,957	274,184	257,024	259,498
Bondholders	97,656	237,163	247,179	250,632	237,190	241,697
Commercial banks and others	22,880	28,059	25,778	23,552	19,835	17,802
Private nonguaranteed debt from:	113,458	247,924	243,479	243,140	240,428	237,400
Bondholders	32,898	90,263	96,452	99,950	97,286	92,214
Commercial banks and others	80,560	157,661	147,027	143,190	143,142	145,186
Use of IMF credit and SDR allocations	4,391	3,965	3,943	4,106	15,946	15,163
IMF credit	0	0	0	0	0	0
SDR allocations	4,391	3,965	3,943	4,106	15,946	15,163
Short-term external debt stocks	43,061	56,135	55,457	46,378	47,041	54,764
Disbursements, long-term	**62,651**	**49,764**	**55,190**	**56,658**	**47,450**	**36,766**
Public and publicly guaranteed sector	41,812	25,731	37,532	33,031	27,421	24,259
Private sector not guaranteed	20,839	24,033	17,658	23,627	20,028	12,507
Principal repayments, long-term	**21,683**	**32,563**	**43,237**	**47,968**	**55,437**	**28,550**
Public and publicly guaranteed sector	13,941	15,051	25,172	25,548	35,863	13,015
Private sector not guaranteed	7,742	17,512	18,065	22,420	19,573	15,535
Interest payments, long-term	**8,658**	**23,584**	**22,982**	**21,676**	**21,555**	**18,377**
Public and publicly guaranteed sector	5,859	15,899	17,120	16,415	16,155	11,509
Private sector not guaranteed	2,799	7,686	5,862	5,261	5,400	6,869

MOLDOVA

(US$ million, unless otherwise indicated)

Snapshot	2022
Total external debt stocks	**9,723**
External debt stocks as % of	
Exports	141
GNI	67
Debt service as % of	
Exports	10
GNI	5
Net financial flows, debt and equity	**1,394**
Net debt inflows	823
Net equity inflows	571
GNI	**14,486**
Population (million)	**3**

Figure 1 Public and publicly guaranteed debt, by creditor and creditor type in 2022, including IMF credit

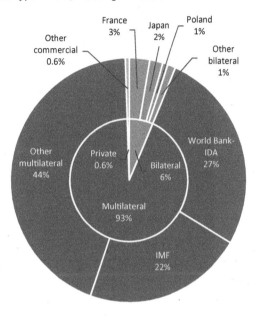

Figure 2 Average terms on new debt commitments from official and private creditors

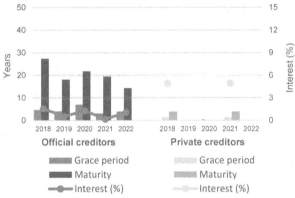

Summary External Debt Data	2010	2018	2019	2020	2021	2022
Total external debt stocks	**4,725**	**7,286**	**7,299**	**7,916**	**9,035**	**9,723**
Long-term external debt stocks	**2,745**	**4,925**	**5,074**	**5,251**	**5,772**	**6,268**
Public and publicly guaranteed debt from:	839	1,450	1,464	1,761	1,819	2,260
Official creditors	816	1,425	1,440	1,736	1,799	2,244
Multilateral	565	1,152	1,226	1,574	1,700	2,058
of which: World Bank	479	712	716	792	813	928
Bilateral	251	273	214	163	99	186
Private creditors	23	25	24	24	20	16
Bondholders	..	..	..	..	..	..
Commercial banks and others	23	25	24	24	20	16
Private nonguaranteed debt from:	1,906	3,476	3,610	3,490	3,953	4,008
Bondholders	..	..	..	..	500	500
Commercial banks and others	1,906	3,476	3,610	3,490	3,453	3,508
Use of IMF credit and SDR allocations	**509**	**496**	**458**	**669**	**912**	**1,008**
IMF credit	327	332	295	499	516	631
SDR allocations	181	164	163	170	396	377
Short-term external debt stocks	**1,471**	**1,865**	**1,768**	**1,996**	**2,350**	**2,448**
Disbursements, long-term	**464**	**551**	**549**	**815**	**1,191**	**1,013**
Public and publicly guaranteed sector	94	138	130	312	305	641
Private sector not guaranteed	370	413	419	503	886	372
Principal repayments, long-term	**306**	**375**	**427**	**544**	**508**	**430**
Public and publicly guaranteed sector	55	89	101	122	140	113
Private sector not guaranteed	251	286	325	422	368	317
Interest payments, long-term	**49**	**67**	**63**	**65**	**110**	**109**
Public and publicly guaranteed sector	16	22	23	20	21	23
Private sector not guaranteed	33	44	40	45	89	86

MONGOLIA

(US$ million, unless otherwise indicated)

Snapshot	2022
Total external debt stocks	**33,765**
External debt stocks as % of	
Exports	298
GNI	229
Debt service as % of	
Exports	29
GNI	22
Net financial flows, debt and equity	**1,739**
Net debt inflows	1,481
Net equity inflows	258
GNI	**14,735**
Population (million)	**3**

Figure 2 **Average terms on new debt commitments from official and private creditors**

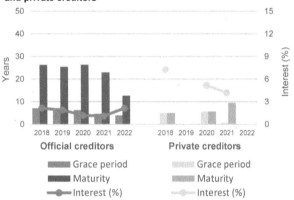

Figure 1 **Public and publicly guaranteed debt, by creditor and creditor type in 2022, including IMF credit**

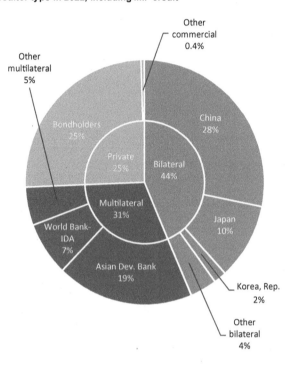

Summary External Debt Data	2010	2018	2019	2020	2021	2022
Total external debt stocks	**5,928**	**29,808**	**31,573**	**32,360**	**34,340**	**33,765**
Long-term external debt stocks	**5,290**	**26,404**	**28,399**	**30,678**	**32,441**	**31,250**
Public and publicly guaranteed debt from:	1,782	8,006	8,348	11,189	11,580	10,433
Official creditors	1,776	4,384	4,787	7,691	7,839	7,687
Multilateral	1,073	1,878	2,099	2,692	2,876	3,011
of which: World Bank	403	570	579	760	809	798
Bilateral	703	2,507	2,688	5,000	4,963	4,676
Private creditors	7	3,622	3,562	3,498	3,741	2,747
Bondholders	0	3,400	3,400	3,432	3,637	2,700
Commercial banks and others	7	222	162	66	104	47
Private nonguaranteed debt from:	3,508	18,398	20,050	19,489	20,861	20,816
Bondholders	..	1,865	2,228	1,318	1,346	771
Commercial banks and others	3,508	16,533	17,822	18,171	19,515	20,046
Use of IMF credit and SDR allocations	**273**	**287**	**285**	**401**	**483**	**436**
IMF credit	198	219	217	331	318	279
SDR allocations	75	68	67	70	165	157
Short-term external debt stocks	**365**	**3,118**	**2,889**	**1,281**	**1,417**	**2,079**
Disbursements, long-term	**2,929**	**8,363**	**12,750**	**3,604**	**3,939**	**3,552**
Public and publicly guaranteed sector	67	1,098	520	1,670	1,568	460
Private sector not guaranteed	2,863	7,265	12,229	1,935	2,370	3,092
Principal repayments, long-term	**139**	**6,614**	**11,137**	**2,193**	**2,223**	**2,710**
Public and publicly guaranteed sector	121	630	171	817	1,019	1,119
Private sector not guaranteed	18	5,984	10,966	1,376	1,204	1,591
Interest payments, long-term	**89**	**1,037**	**504**	**508**	**375**	**407**
Public and publicly guaranteed sector	20	244	309	320	269	276
Private sector not guaranteed	70	793	196	189	105	131

MONTENEGRO

(US$ million, unless otherwise indicated)

Snapshot	2022
Total external debt stocks	**8,815**
External debt stocks as % of	
Exports	247
GNI	142
Debt service as % of	
Exports	28
GNI	16
Net financial flows, debt and equity	**352**
Net debt inflows	-203
Net equity inflows	554
GNI	**6,219**
Population (million)	**1**

Figure 1 Public and publicly guaranteed debt, by creditor and creditor type in 2022, including IMF credit

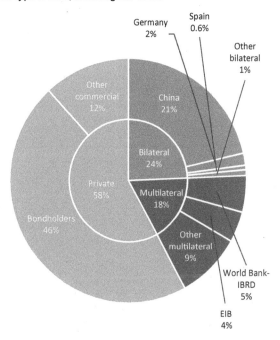

Figure 2 Average terms on new debt commitments from official and private creditors

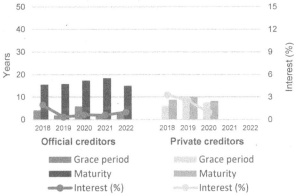

Summary External Debt Data	2010	2018	2019	2020	2021	2022
Total external debt stocks	**4,503**	**7,159**	**7,585**	**9,469**	**9,235**	**8,815**
Long-term external debt stocks	4,277	6,908	7,273	8,933	8,817	8,424
Public and publicly guaranteed debt from:	1,349	3,425	3,709	4,842	4,305	3,965
Official creditors	818	1,442	1,534	1,675	1,669	1,621
Multilateral	546	571	539	654	661	637
of which: World Bank	306	271	243	252	232	208
Bilateral	271	871	995	1,021	1,008	984
Private creditors	531	1,984	2,175	3,168	2,636	2,344
Bondholders	267	1,394	1,740	2,427	1,982	1,867
Commercial banks and others	264	589	435	741	654	477
Private nonguaranteed debt from:	2,928	3,483	3,564	4,091	4,512	4,459
Bondholders	..	..	..	..	..	..
Commercial banks and others	2,928	3,483	3,564	4,091	4,512	4,459
Use of IMF credit and SDR allocations	40	36	36	124	202	192
IMF credit	0	0	0	87	85	81
SDR allocations	40	36	36	37	117	112
Short-term external debt stocks	186	215	277	411	216	199
Disbursements, long-term	**676**	**1,452**	**1,720**	**2,333**	**1,198**	**622**
Public and publicly guaranteed sector	383	1,157	787	1,328	213	164
Private sector not guaranteed	293	295	933	1,004	985	458
Principal repayments, long-term	**59**	**1,421**	**1,292**	**1,009**	**1,009**	**808**
Public and publicly guaranteed sector	59	591	443	517	456	305
Private sector not guaranteed	..	830	849	492	553	503
Interest payments, long-term	**33**	**231**	**207**	**159**	**294**	**189**
Public and publicly guaranteed sector	33	102	105	108	239	97
Private sector not guaranteed	..	129	102	51	55	91

(US$ million, unless otherwise indicated)

Snapshot	2022
Total external debt stocks	**64,713**
External debt stocks as % of	
Exports	109
GNI	49
Debt service as % of	
Exports	10
GNI	5
Net financial flows, debt and equity	**2,746**
Net debt inflows	1,108
Net equity inflows	1,637
GNI	**132,376**
Population (million)	**37**

Figure 2 **Average terms on new debt commitments from official and private creditors**

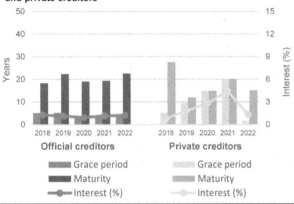

Figure 1 **Public and publicly guaranteed debt, by creditor and creditor type in 2022, including IMF credit**

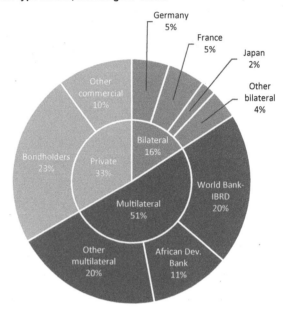

Summary External Debt Data	2010	2018	2019	2020	2021	2022
Total external debt stocks	**27,296**	**50,411**	**55,000**	**65,712**	**65,373**	**64,713**
Long-term external debt stocks	**23,684**	**42,185**	**45,528**	**53,660**	**52,210**	**50,884**
Public and publicly guaranteed debt from:	21,095	33,485	36,493	43,652	42,108	41,064
Official creditors	17,249	23,149	23,625	27,113	25,857	26,800
Multilateral	10,186	15,668	16,669	19,693	19,054	19,907
of which: World Bank	2,518	5,529	6,414	7,886	8,118	8,669
Bilateral	7,063	7,481	6,956	7,419	6,803	6,893
Private creditors	3,846	10,336	12,868	16,539	16,251	14,263
Bondholders	1,336	6,390	7,590	10,912	11,602	9,897
Commercial banks and others	2,510	3,946	5,278	5,627	4,649	4,367
Private nonguaranteed debt from:	2,589	8,700	9,036	10,008	10,102	9,820
Bondholders	..	..	..	..	..	..
Commercial banks and others	2,589	8,700	9,036	10,008	10,102	9,820
Use of IMF credit and SDR allocations	**865**	**781**	**776**	**3,906**	**4,085**	**3,884**
IMF credit	0	0	0	3,098	2,099	1,996
SDR allocations	865	781	776	809	1,986	1,888
Short-term external debt stocks	**2,747**	**7,446**	**8,695**	**8,146**	**9,079**	**9,945**
Disbursements, long-term	**4,999**	**3,274**	**6,737**	**9,296**	**5,332**	**4,593**
Public and publicly guaranteed sector	3,882	1,813	5,483	8,179	4,172	4,187
Private sector not guaranteed	1,116	1,462	1,253	1,117	1,160	407
Principal repayments, long-term	**2,428**	**2,818**	**2,986**	**4,037**	**4,292**	**4,351**
Public and publicly guaranteed sector	1,274	2,135	2,106	3,360	3,502	3,665
Private sector not guaranteed	1,154	682	880	677	790	686
Interest payments, long-term	**850**	**1,090**	**1,060**	**1,040**	**1,156**	**1,097**
Public and publicly guaranteed sector	820	934	954	934	1,015	997
Private sector not guaranteed	31	155	106	106	141	99

MOZAMBIQUE

(US$ million, unless otherwise indicated)

Snapshot	2022
Total external debt stocks	64,028
External debt stocks as % of	
Exports	667
GNI	374
Debt service as % of	
Exports	63
GNI	35
Net financial flows, debt and equity	2,038
Net debt inflows	1,717
Net equity inflows	321
GNI	17,128
Population (million)	33

Figure 1 **Public and publicly guaranteed debt, by creditor and creditor type in 2022, including IMF credit**

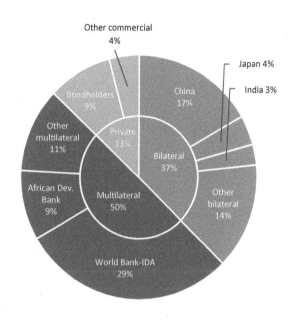

Figure 2 **Average terms on new debt commitments from official and private creditors**

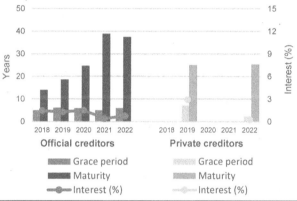

Summary External Debt Data	2010	2018	2019	2020	2021	2022
Total external debt stocks	11,231	49,810	54,212	58,708	62,733	64,028
Long-term external debt stocks	10,263	48,259	52,288	56,282	59,926	62,216
Public and publicly guaranteed debt from:	3,263	10,216	10,384	10,554	10,305	9,630
Official creditors	3,167	8,397	8,607	8,983	8,859	8,306
Multilateral	2,262	4,255	4,455	4,746	4,675	4,475
of which: World Bank	1,491	2,904	3,039	3,224	3,147	2,984
Bilateral	905	4,142	4,152	4,236	4,184	3,832
Private creditors	96	1,819	1,778	1,572	1,446	1,324
Bondholders	..	727	900	900	900	900
Commercial banks and others	96	1,093	878	672	546	424
Private nonguaranteed debt from:	7,001	38,043	41,903	45,727	49,621	52,586
Bondholders	..	..	..	..	..	..
Commercial banks and others	7,001	38,043	41,903	45,727	49,621	52,586
Use of IMF credit and SDR allocations	357	303	375	689	947	1,027
IMF credit	190	152	225	532	490	592
SDR allocations	168	151	151	157	457	435
Short-term external debt stocks	610	1,248	1,549	1,738	1,860	785
Disbursements, long-term	3,810	4,238	4,364	4,139	10,104	6,156
Public and publicly guaranteed sector	419	632	503	315	366	218
Private sector not guaranteed	3,391	3,606	3,861	3,824	9,738	5,938
Principal repayments, long-term	39	327	480	473	6,264	3,484
Public and publicly guaranteed sector	39	327	480	473	420	511
Private sector not guaranteed	..	..	..	..	5,844	2,973
Interest payments, long-term	149	1,611	1,359	733	798	2,516
Public and publicly guaranteed sector	47	136	138	158	133	158
Private sector not guaranteed	102	1,474	1,220	575	665	2,358

MYANMAR

(US$ million, unless otherwise indicated)

Snapshot	2022
Total external debt stocks	**12,530**
External debt stocks as % of	
Exports	95
GNI	22
Debt service as % of	
Exports	7
GNI	2
Net financial flows, debt and equity	**1,030**
Net debt inflows	-219
Net equity inflows	1,250
GNI	**58,080**
Population (million)	**54**

Figure 1 Public and publicly guaranteed debt, by creditor and creditor type in 2022, including IMF credit

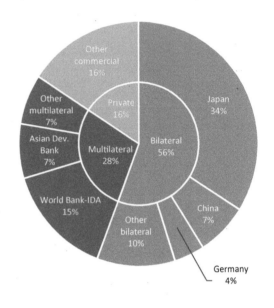

Figure 2 Average terms on new debt commitments from official and private creditors

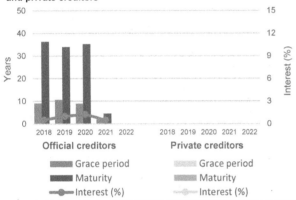

Summary External Debt Data	2010	2018	2019	2020	2021	2022
Total external debt stocks	**9,990**	**10,729**	**11,178**	**13,399**	**13,750**	**12,530**
Long-term external debt stocks	**8,433**	**10,283**	**10,772**	**12,605**	**11,958**	**10,824**
Public and publicly guaranteed debt from:	8,433	10,268	10,744	12,570	11,796	10,450
Official creditors	7,482	7,662	8,365	10,141	9,669	8,694
Multilateral	1,447	1,859	2,081	2,629	2,676	2,485
of which: World Bank	799	1,266	1,468	1,804	1,769	1,641
Bilateral	6,035	5,804	6,283	7,512	6,994	6,209
Private creditors	952	2,606	2,380	2,429	2,127	1,755
Bondholders	..	..	..	..	..	..
Commercial banks and others	952	2,606	2,380	2,429	2,127	1,755
Private nonguaranteed debt from:	..	14	28	35	162	374
Bondholders	..	..	..	..	..	..
Commercial banks and others	..	14	28	35	162	374
Use of IMF credit and SDR allocations	**378**	**342**	**340**	**726**	**1,761**	**1,674**
IMF credit	0	0	0	372	723	688
SDR allocations	378	342	340	354	1,037	986
Short-term external debt stocks	**1,179**	**105**	**66**	**68**	**32**	**32**
Disbursements, long-term	**714**	**793**	**1,040**	**1,671**	**697**	**533**
Public and publicly guaranteed sector	714	793	976	1,589	498	311
Private sector not guaranteed	..	..	65	81	199	222
Principal repayments, long-term	**201**	**546**	**506**	**488**	**721**	**753**
Public and publicly guaranteed sector	201	532	454	414	637	743
Private sector not guaranteed	..	14	51	74	84	10
Interest payments, long-term	**40**	**287**	**186**	**112**	**157**	**172**
Public and publicly guaranteed sector	40	287	176	97	149	156
Private sector not guaranteed	..	..	10	15	7	15

NEPAL

(US$ million, unless otherwise indicated)

Snapshot	2022
Total external debt stocks	**9,140**
External debt stocks as % of	
Exports	277
GNI	22
Debt service as % of	
Exports	11
GNI	1
Net financial flows, debt and equity	**806**
Net debt inflows	740
Net equity inflows	65
GNI	**41,067**
Population (million)	**31**

Figure 2 Average terms on new debt commitments from official and private creditors

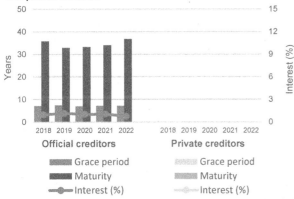

Figure 1 Public and publicly guaranteed debt, by creditor and creditor type in 2022, including IMF credit

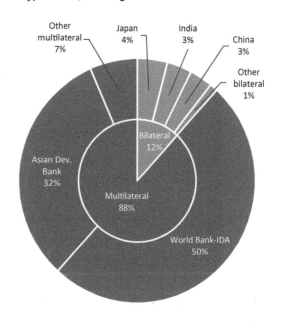

Summary External Debt Data	2010	2018	2019	2020	2021	2022
Total external debt stocks	**3,787**	**5,511**	**6,516**	**7,906**	**8,821**	**9,140**
Long-term external debt stocks	**3,507**	**5,103**	**5,966**	**7,175**	**7,925**	**8,186**
Public and publicly guaranteed debt from:	3,507	4,974	5,847	7,057	7,759	7,957
Official creditors	3,504	4,974	5,847	7,057	7,759	7,957
Multilateral	3,130	4,458	5,083	6,157	6,758	6,981
of which: World Bank	1,426	2,477	2,877	3,469	3,966	4,155
Bilateral	374	516	765	900	1,002	976
Private creditors	3	0	0	0	0	0
Bondholders	..	..	..	..	..	..
Commercial banks and others	3	0	0	0	0	0
Private nonguaranteed debt from:	..	129	118	118	166	229
Bondholders	..	..	..	..	..	..
Commercial banks and others	..	129	118	118	166	229
Use of IMF credit and SDR allocations	**219**	**156**	**147**	**370**	**560**	**633**
IMF credit	114	61	53	272	255	342
SDR allocations	105	95	94	98	306	291
Short-term external debt stocks	**61**	**252**	**403**	**361**	**335**	**322**
Disbursements, long-term	**126**	**1,017**	**1,098**	**1,158**	**1,170**	**921**
Public and publicly guaranteed sector	126	955	1,098	1,158	1,122	835
Private sector not guaranteed	..	63	..	..	48	86
Principal repayments, long-term	**148**	**181**	**205**	**205**	**213**	**268**
Public and publicly guaranteed sector	148	174	194	205	213	244
Private sector not guaranteed	..	8	11	..	..	24
Interest payments, long-term	**32**	**45**	**57**	**60**	**66**	**68**
Public and publicly guaranteed sector	32	41	52	54	63	65
Private sector not guaranteed	..	4	6	6	2	3

(US$ million, unless otherwise indicated)

Snapshot	2022
Total external debt stocks	**14,867**
External debt stocks as % of	
Exports	186
GNI	102
Debt service as % of	
Exports	30
GNI	17
Net financial flows, debt and equity	**1,613**
Net debt inflows	358
Net equity inflows	1,255
GNI	**14,543**
Population (million)	**7**

Figure 2 **Average terms on new debt commitments from official and private creditors**

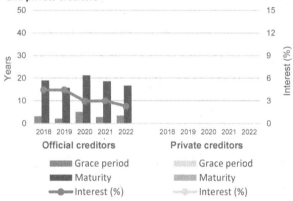

Figure 1 **Public and publicly guaranteed debt, by creditor and creditor type in 2022, including IMF credit**

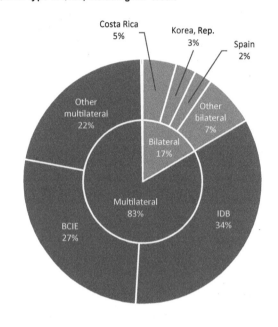

Summary External Debt Data	2010	2018	2019	2020	2021	2022
Total external debt stocks	**7,017**	**13,003**	**13,610**	**13,760**	**14,583**	**14,867**
Long-term external debt stocks	**5,256**	**11,432**	**12,224**	**12,350**	**12,798**	**13,053**
Public and publicly guaranteed debt from:	2,704	5,108	5,428	5,903	6,407	6,719
Official creditors	2,694	5,083	5,402	5,879	6,386	6,701
Multilateral	1,661	3,914	4,215	4,653	5,193	5,550
of which: World Bank	447	624	692	771	872	886
Bilateral	1,033	1,170	1,187	1,225	1,193	1,151
Private creditors	11	24	26	25	21	18
Bondholders	..	..	..	..	..	..
Commercial banks and others	11	24	26	25	21	18
Private nonguaranteed debt from:	2,552	6,324	6,796	6,446	6,391	6,335
Bondholders	..	..	..	..	..	..
Commercial banks and others	2,552	6,324	6,796	6,446	6,391	6,335
Use of IMF credit and SDR allocations	**359**	**195**	**181**	**369**	**705**	**670**
IMF credit	167	22	9	190	182	173
SDR allocations	192	173	172	179	523	497
Short-term external debt stocks	**1,402**	**1,376**	**1,205**	**1,042**	**1,080**	**1,143**
Disbursements, long-term	**1,181**	**2,286**	**2,206**	**1,482**	**2,220**	**2,486**
Public and publicly guaranteed sector	267	572	509	652	811	660
Private sector not guaranteed	914	1,714	1,697	830	1,409	1,827
Principal repayments, long-term	**459**	**1,868**	**1,430**	**1,491**	**1,634**	**2,164**
Public and publicly guaranteed sector	56	135	176	230	257	295
Private sector not guaranteed	403	1,733	1,254	1,261	1,377	1,869
Interest payments, long-term	**103**	**276**	**322**	**289**	**197**	**230**
Public and publicly guaranteed sector	34	94	119	117	112	133
Private sector not guaranteed	70	183	203	171	85	97

NIGER

(US$ million, unless otherwise indicated)

Snapshot	2022
Total external debt stocks	5,416
External debt stocks as % of	
Exports	349
GNI	39
Debt service as % of	
Exports	18
GNI	2
Net financial flows, debt and equity	1,278
Net debt inflows	697
Net equity inflows	581
GNI	14,059
Population (million)	26

Figure 1 **Public and publicly guaranteed debt, by creditor and creditor type in 2022, including IMF credit**

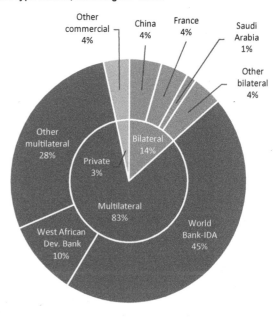

Figure 2 **Average terms on new debt commitments from official and private creditors**

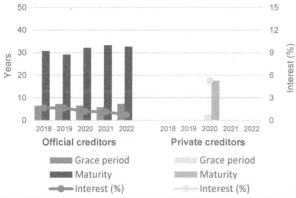

Summary External Debt Data	2010	2018	2019	2020	2021	2022
Total external debt stocks	1,534	3,177	3,585	4,553	4,967	5,416
Long-term external debt stocks	1,206	2,805	3,155	4,006	4,238	4,636
Public and publicly guaranteed debt from:	1,206	2,805	3,155	4,006	4,238	4,636
Official creditors	1,205	2,805	3,155	3,787	4,036	4,453
Multilateral	664	2,081	2,452	3,058	3,312	3,756
of which: World Bank	275	1,044	1,347	1,694	1,863	2,310
Bilateral	541	724	703	729	724	698
Private creditors	1	..	..	219	202	183
Bondholders	..	..	..	..	..	..
Commercial banks and others	1	..	..	219	202	183
Private nonguaranteed debt from:	0	..	..	..	..	..
Bondholders	..	..	..	..	..	..
Commercial banks and others	0	..	..	..	..	..
Use of IMF credit and SDR allocations	158	311	346	498	687	737
IMF credit	61	224	259	407	423	486
SDR allocations	97	88	87	91	265	252
Short-term external debt stocks	170	61	84	48	42	43
Disbursements, long-term	279	278	422	745	556	801
Public and publicly guaranteed sector	279	278	422	745	556	801
Private sector not guaranteed	..	..	..	..	..	..
Principal repayments, long-term	16	72	94	122	129	189
Public and publicly guaranteed sector	9	72	94	122	129	189
Private sector not guaranteed	7	..	..	..	..	..
Interest payments, long-term	8	44	35	50	64	65
Public and publicly guaranteed sector	8	44	35	50	64	65
Private sector not guaranteed	0	..	..	..	..	..

NIGERIA

(US$ million, unless otherwise indicated)

Snapshot	2022
Total external debt stocks	**98,335**
External debt stocks as % of	
Exports	139
GNI	21
Debt service as % of	
Exports	11
GNI	2
Net financial flows, debt and equity	**8,654**
Net debt inflows	8,588
Net equity inflows	66
GNI	**460,252**
Population (million)	**219**

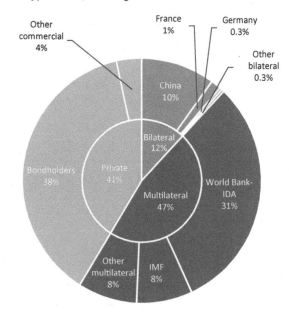

Figure 1 **Public and publicly guaranteed debt, by creditor and creditor type in 2022, including IMF credit**

Figure 2 **Average terms on new debt commitments from official and private creditors**

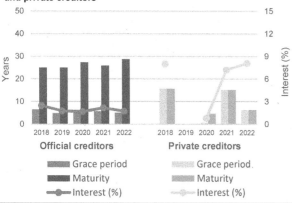

Summary External Debt Data	2010	2018	2019	2020	2021	2022
Total external debt stocks	**28,262**	**66,566**	**77,709**	**82,833**	**90,887**	**98,335**
Long-term external debt stocks	**16,241**	**50,437**	**54,534**	**58,461**	**63,240**	**67,830**
Public and publicly guaranteed debt from:	4,686	25,290	27,612	32,113	36,205	40,004
Official creditors	4,686	14,122	16,443	18,573	19,775	22,161
Multilateral	4,304	10,972	12,565	14,328	15,261	16,992
of which: World Bank	3,705	8,557	9,959	11,415	12,310	13,996
Bilateral	381	3,150	3,878	4,246	4,514	5,169
Private creditors	0	11,168	11,168	13,540	16,430	17,843
Bondholders	..	11,168	11,168	11,168	14,668	16,365
Commercial banks and others	..	..	..	2,371	1,762	1,478
Private nonguaranteed debt from:	11,556	25,147	26,922	26,349	27,035	27,826
Bondholders	..	6,017	6,367	5,817	5,900	4,550
Commercial banks and others	11,556	19,130	20,555	20,531	21,135	23,276
Use of IMF credit and SDR allocations	**2,580**	**2,330**	**2,317**	**5,948**	**9,073**	**8,627**
IMF credit	0	0	0	3,535	3,435	3,267
SDR allocations	2,580	2,330	2,317	2,413	5,637	5,361
Short-term external debt stocks	**9,441**	**13,798**	**20,858**	**18,424**	**18,574**	**21,879**
Disbursements, long-term	**1,111**	**12,663**	**9,212**	**7,621**	**11,098**	**10,333**
Public and publicly guaranteed sector	1,051	7,386	2,695	4,402	6,093	5,924
Private sector not guaranteed	60	5,277	6,517	3,219	5,005	4,409
Principal repayments, long-term	**1,189**	**4,942**	**5,037**	**4,243**	**5,846**	**5,049**
Public and publicly guaranteed sector	248	735	295	451	1,527	1,431
Private sector not guaranteed	942	4,207	4,742	3,792	4,319	3,618
Interest payments, long-term	**59**	**1,412**	**1,813**	**1,811**	**1,721**	**1,944**
Public and publicly guaranteed sector	59	699	1,096	1,115	1,118	1,485
Private sector not guaranteed	..	713	717	696	603	459

(US$ million, unless otherwise indicated)

Snapshot	2022
Total external debt stocks	**11,572**
External debt stocks as % of	
Exports	112
GNI	89
Debt service as % of	
Exports	9
GNI	7
Net financial flows, debt and equity	**1,369**
Net debt inflows	1,052
Net equity inflows	317
GNI	**12,976**
Population (million)	**2**

Figure 2 Average terms on new debt commitments from official and private creditors

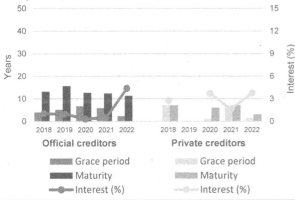

Figure 1 Public and publicly guaranteed debt, by creditor and creditor type in 2022, including IMF credit

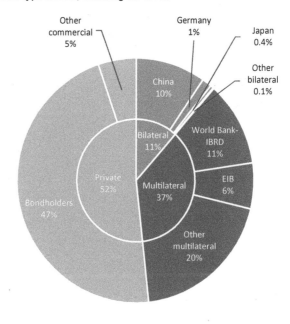

Summary External Debt Data	2010	2018	2019	2020	2021	2022
Total external debt stocks	**5,159**	**8,667**	**9,000**	**10,324**	**10,644**	**11,572**
Long-term external debt stocks	**3,840**	**7,238**	**7,506**	**8,738**	**8,721**	**9,042**
Public and publicly guaranteed debt from:	1,880	4,061	4,163	5,102	5,092	5,094
Official creditors	1,369	1,865	2,051	2,390	2,391	2,307
Multilateral	1,127	1,245	1,387	1,735	1,770	1,690
of which: World Bank	681	614	732	856	799	761
Bilateral	242	620	665	655	621	617
Private creditors	512	2,196	2,112	2,712	2,701	2,787
Bondholders	434	1,864	1,829	2,638	2,662	2,507
Commercial banks and others	77	332	283	74	39	280
Private nonguaranteed debt from:	1,959	3,177	3,343	3,637	3,629	3,948
Bondholders	..	1	7	8	7	7
Commercial banks and others	1,959	3,176	3,336	3,629	3,622	3,941
Use of IMF credit and SDR allocations	**101**	**91**	**91**	**297**	**476**	**565**
IMF credit	0	0	0	202	196	299
SDR allocations	101	91	91	95	280	266
Short-term external debt stocks	**1,218**	**1,339**	**1,403**	**1,289**	**1,447**	**1,965**
Disbursements, long-term	**596**	**1,401**	**827**	**1,803**	**1,752**	**1,129**
Public and publicly guaranteed sector	197	794	383	1,202	1,178	502
Private sector not guaranteed	399	607	444	601	574	626
Principal repayments, long-term	**443**	**1,077**	**513**	**948**	**1,241**	**680**
Public and publicly guaranteed sector	98	406	219	625	829	238
Private sector not guaranteed	344	671	293	323	412	442
Interest payments, long-term	**128**	**159**	**151**	**149**	**191**	**150**
Public and publicly guaranteed sector	56	105	115	112	129	107
Private sector not guaranteed	71	54	36	36	62	43

PAKISTAN

(US$ million, unless otherwise indicated)

Snapshot	2022
Total external debt stocks	**126,942**
External debt stocks as % of	
Exports	320
GNI	34
Debt service as % of	
Exports	42
GNI	4
Net financial flows, debt and equity	**740**
Net debt inflows	-536
Net equity inflows	1,276
GNI	**371,237**
Population (million)	**236**

Figure 1 **Public and publicly guaranteed debt, by creditor and creditor type in 2022, including IMF credit**

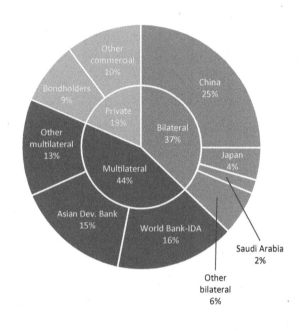

Figure 2 **Average terms on new debt commitments from official and private creditors**

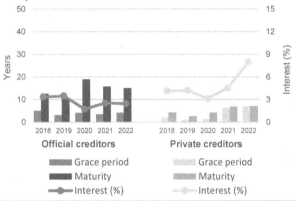

Summary External Debt Data	2010	2018	2019	2020	2021	2022
Total external debt stocks	**63,483**	**100,199**	**110,178**	**118,049**	**130,873**	**126,942**
Long-term external debt stocks	**48,558**	**84,835**	**92,825**	**101,917**	**110,958**	**106,652**
Public and publicly guaranteed debt from:	44,085	73,149	78,396	87,009	95,413	91,520
Official creditors	42,434	56,664	62,467	69,004	73,194	73,050
Multilateral	24,670	27,880	30,141	33,340	34,323	36,144
of which: World Bank	11,806	15,162	15,305	17,176	18,262	18,071
Bilateral	17,764	28,784	32,326	35,664	38,871	36,907
Private creditors	1,651	16,485	15,930	18,004	22,219	18,469
Bondholders	1,550	7,300	5,300	5,300	8,300	8,300
Commercial banks and others	101	9,185	10,630	12,704	13,919	10,169
Private nonguaranteed debt from:	4,473	11,687	14,428	14,909	15,545	15,133
Bondholders	250	12	12	12	0	..
Commercial banks and others	4,223	11,675	14,416	14,897	15,545	15,133
Use of IMF credit and SDR allocations	**10,258**	**7,276**	**8,097**	**8,902**	**10,841**	**11,522**
IMF credit	8,736	5,901	6,730	7,479	6,733	7,615
SDR allocations	1,522	1,375	1,367	1,424	4,108	3,906
Short-term external debt stocks	**4,667**	**8,088**	**9,256**	**7,230**	**9,074**	**8,768**
Disbursements, long-term	**3,960**	**12,052**	**14,401**	**14,441**	**18,992**	**10,719**
Public and publicly guaranteed sector	1,869	9,853	11,042	13,066	17,477	10,067
Private sector not guaranteed	2,091	2,199	3,358	1,375	1,515	652
Principal repayments, long-term	**3,046**	**3,327**	**7,500**	**7,190**	**8,867**	**12,169**
Public and publicly guaranteed sector	2,163	2,888	6,884	6,295	7,989	11,105
Private sector not guaranteed	883	439	616	895	879	1,064
Interest payments, long-term	**891**	**2,274**	**2,705**	**2,258**	**2,179**	**3,197**
Public and publicly guaranteed sector	791	1,840	2,166	1,701	1,741	2,660
Private sector not guaranteed	100	434	539	557	437	536

PAPUA NEW GUINEA

(US$ million, unless otherwise indicated)

Snapshot	2022
Total external debt stocks	18,700
External debt stocks as % of	
Exports	128
GNI	64
Debt service as % of	
Exports	31
GNI	15
Net financial flows, debt and equity	**-899**
Net debt inflows	-1,225
Net equity inflows	327
GNI	29,417
Population (million)	10

Figure 1 **Public and publicly guaranteed debt, by creditor and creditor type in 2022, including IMF credit**

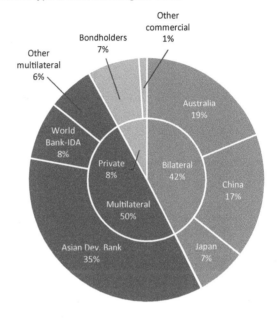

Figure 2 **Average terms on new debt commitments from official and private creditors**

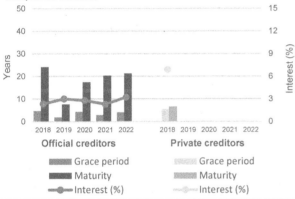

Summary External Debt Data	2010	2018	2019	2020	2021	2022
Total external debt stocks	**5,987**	**17,724**	**18,745**	**18,047**	**19,710**	**18,700**
Long-term external debt stocks	5,380	17,085	17,914	17,088	15,903	14,799
Public and publicly guaranteed debt from:	1,042	3,411	4,313	5,142	6,046	6,747
Official creditors	1,009	2,374	3,161	4,210	5,452	6,167
Multilateral	712	1,633	1,853	2,565	2,923	3,159
of which: World Bank	225	446	446	480	562	545
Bilateral	297	741	1,307	1,646	2,529	3,008
Private creditors	33	1,037	1,152	931	594	580
Bondholders	..	500	500	500	500	500
Commercial banks and others	33	537	652	431	94	80
Private nonguaranteed debt from:	4,337	13,674	13,601	11,947	9,858	8,052
Bondholders	..	..	..	..	..	..
Commercial banks and others	4,337	13,674	13,601	11,947	9,858	8,052
Use of IMF credit and SDR allocations	193	175	174	560	897	853
IMF credit	0	0	0	379	368	350
SDR allocations	193	175	174	181	529	503
Short-term external debt stocks	414	464	657	399	2,910	3,047
Disbursements, long-term	**3,153**	**3,046**	**1,501**	**1,538**	**2,552**	**2,860**
Public and publicly guaranteed sector	37	1,234	1,201	1,538	1,539	1,192
Private sector not guaranteed	3,116	1,812	300	..	1,013	1,668
Principal repayments, long-term	**758**	**2,029**	**1,568**	**1,095**	**3,716**	**3,927**
Public and publicly guaranteed sector	67	93	281	845	538	240
Private sector not guaranteed	691	1,937	1,286	250	3,178	3,688
Interest payments, long-term	**50**	**741**	**772**	**201**	**332**	**516**
Public and publicly guaranteed sector	16	88	149	143	107	130
Private sector not guaranteed	33	653	623	58	226	386

PARAGUAY

(US$ million, unless otherwise indicated)

Snapshot	2022
Total external debt stocks	**24,515**
External debt stocks as % of	
Exports	162
GNI	60
Debt service as % of	
Exports	14
GNI	5
Net financial flows, debt and equity	**1,967**
Net debt inflows	1,508
Net equity inflows	459
GNI	**40,576**
Population (million)	**7**

Figure 2 Average terms on new debt commitments from official and private creditors

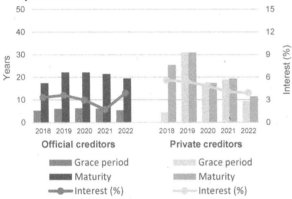

Figure 1 Public and publicly guaranteed debt, by creditor and creditor type in 2022, including IMF credit

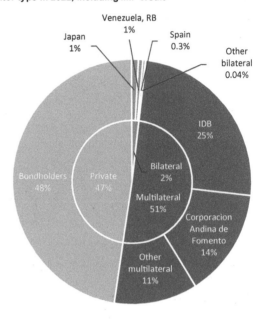

Summary External Debt Data	2010	2018	2019	2020	2021	2022
Total external debt stocks	**16,123**	**17,183**	**17,640**	**20,727**	**22,193**	**24,515**
Long-term external debt stocks	**14,951**	**14,761**	**15,240**	**18,672**	**19,918**	**21,815**
Public and publicly guaranteed debt from:	2,390	6,401	7,182	10,257	11,346	12,774
Official creditors	2,123	2,978	3,272	4,897	5,490	6,703
Multilateral	1,510	2,790	3,062	4,653	5,230	6,460
of which: World Bank	270	636	619	852	882	887
Bilateral	613	188	210	244	259	243
Private creditors	267	3,423	3,910	5,360	5,856	6,071
Bondholders	..	3,410	3,910	5,360	5,856	6,071
Commercial banks and others	267	13	0	0	0	0
Private nonguaranteed debt from:	12,561	8,359	8,058	8,415	8,572	9,041
Bondholders	..	600	600	1,150	1,450	1,150
Commercial banks and others	12,561	7,759	7,458	7,265	7,122	7,891
Use of IMF credit and SDR allocations	**147**	**132**	**132**	**137**	**403**	**384**
IMF credit	0	0	0	0	0	0
SDR allocations	147	132	132	137	403	384
Short-term external debt stocks	**1,025**	**2,290**	**2,268**	**1,918**	**1,872**	**2,316**
Disbursements, long-term	**2,076**	**1,535**	**1,453**	**4,334**	**2,013**	**2,424**
Public and publicly guaranteed sector	308	1,003	994	3,281	1,669	1,988
Private sector not guaranteed	1,769	533	459	1,053	344	436
Principal repayments, long-term	**314**	**1,717**	**961**	**667**	**740**	**1,360**
Public and publicly guaranteed sector	240	208	207	218	552	535
Private sector not guaranteed	75	1,510	754	449	188	825
Interest payments, long-term	**183**	**698**	**497**	**460**	**492**	**674**
Public and publicly guaranteed sector	65	254	330	359	365	469
Private sector not guaranteed	118	444	167	101	127	206

PERU

(US$ million, unless otherwise indicated)

Snapshot	2022
Total external debt stocks	**88,084**
External debt stocks as % of	
Exports	120
GNI	39
Debt service as % of	
Exports	10
GNI	3
Net financial flows, debt and equity	**11,702**
Net debt inflows	2,094
Net equity inflows	9,609
GNI	**227,006**
Population (million)	**34**

Figure 2 Average terms on new debt commitments from official and private creditors

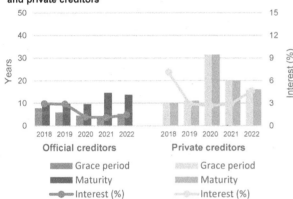

Official creditors — Private creditors

- ▨ Grace period — ▨ Grace period
- ▨ Maturity — ▨ Maturity
- ●Interest (%) — ○Interest (%)

Figure 1 Public and publicly guaranteed debt, by creditor and creditor type in 2022, including IMF credit

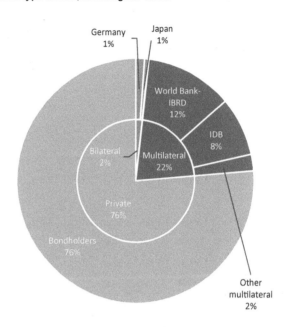

Summary External Debt Data	2010	2018	2019	2020	2021	2022
Total external debt stocks	**42,154**	**66,769**	**64,247**	**73,549**	**86,461**	**88,084**
Long-term external debt stocks	**34,822**	**55,923**	**54,837**	**62,387**	**73,532**	**75,043**
Public and publicly guaranteed debt from:	20,009	18,145	18,606	28,027	39,854	40,699
Official creditors	10,672	4,447	4,916	7,174	9,131	9,635
Multilateral	7,870	3,426	3,843	6,123	8,271	8,917
of which: World Bank	2,965	1,145	1,564	3,441	4,685	4,860
Bilateral	2,802	1,021	1,074	1,051	860	718
Private creditors	9,337	13,698	13,690	20,853	30,722	31,064
Bondholders	9,311	13,698	13,690	20,853	30,722	31,064
Commercial banks and others	26	..	..	..	..	..
Private nonguaranteed debt from:	14,813	37,778	36,231	34,360	33,679	34,345
Bondholders	727	15,510	16,285	17,800	18,345	17,415
Commercial banks and others	14,086	22,268	19,946	16,560	15,334	16,930
Use of IMF credit and SDR allocations	**939**	**848**	**843**	**878**	**2,644**	**2,514**
IMF credit	0	0	0	0	0	0
SDR allocations	939	848	843	878	2,644	2,514
Short-term external debt stocks	**6,393**	**9,998**	**8,567**	**10,284**	**10,285**	**10,527**
Disbursements, long-term	**5,425**	**3,513**	**3,291**	**11,457**	**15,597**	**5,698**
Public and publicly guaranteed sector	3,862	569	1,866	9,427	12,592	2,046
Private sector not guaranteed	1,563	2,945	1,425	2,030	3,005	3,652
Principal repayments, long-term	**4,060**	**4,583**	**4,327**	**4,191**	**2,779**	**3,847**
Public and publicly guaranteed sector	3,490	1,263	1,356	290	396	861
Private sector not guaranteed	570	3,320	2,972	3,901	2,382	2,986
Interest payments, long-term	**2,550**	**2,328**	**2,103**	**2,049**	**2,293**	**3,070**
Public and publicly guaranteed sector	1,096	982	979	919	1,109	1,404
Private sector not guaranteed	1,454	1,346	1,124	1,130	1,184	1,666

PHILIPPINES

(US$ million, unless otherwise indicated)

Snapshot	2022
Total external debt stocks	**111,217**
External debt stocks as % of	
Exports	99
GNI	26
Debt service as % of	
Exports	8
GNI	2
Net financial flows, debt and equity	**11,119**
Net debt inflows	8,679
Net equity inflows	2,440
GNI	**428,117**
Population (million)	**116**

Figure 1 Public and publicly guaranteed debt, by creditor and creditor type in 2022, including IMF credit

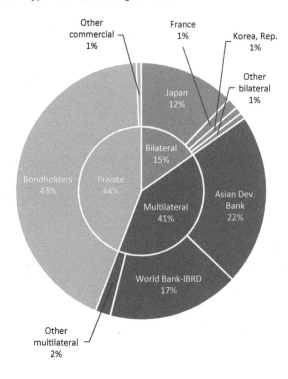

Figure 2 Average terms on new debt commitments from official and private creditors

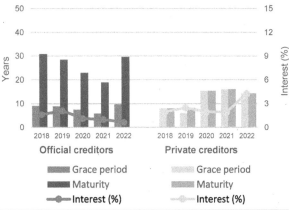

Summary External Debt Data	2010	2018	2019	2020	2021	2022
Total external debt stocks	**65,346**	**78,990**	**83,644**	**98,498**	**106,448**	**111,217**
Long-term external debt stocks	**53,544**	**61,756**	**65,277**	**83,083**	**87,445**	**90,877**
Public and publicly guaranteed debt from:	45,082	38,377	41,753	56,499	59,710	62,610
Official creditors	23,209	20,076	21,554	29,416	32,801	35,059
Multilateral	8,372	12,058	13,180	19,672	22,930	25,395
of which: World Bank	2,738	5,842	6,456	8,100	9,740	10,649
Bilateral	14,837	8,018	8,375	9,744	9,871	9,664
Private creditors	21,873	18,301	20,199	27,083	26,909	27,551
Bondholders	20,590	17,636	19,081	26,062	26,256	27,158
Commercial banks and others	1,283	665	1,118	1,021	652	393
Private nonguaranteed debt from:	8,462	23,379	23,524	26,584	27,735	28,266
Bondholders	1,651	5,187	7,041	9,551	10,242	9,867
Commercial banks and others	6,811	18,192	16,483	17,033	17,493	18,399
Use of IMF credit and SDR allocations	**1,290**	**1,165**	**1,159**	**1,207**	**3,913**	**3,721**
IMF credit	0	0	0	0	0	0
SDR allocations	1,290	1,165	1,159	1,207	3,913	3,721
Short-term external debt stocks	**10,512**	**16,068**	**17,208**	**14,209**	**15,090**	**16,619**
Disbursements, long-term	**10,928**	**9,887**	**11,355**	**21,033**	**16,721**	**12,820**
Public and publicly guaranteed sector	8,251	5,011	7,035	15,043	11,937	9,582
Private sector not guaranteed	2,677	4,876	4,320	5,990	4,784	3,238
Principal repayments, long-term	**8,341**	**6,237**	**7,368**	**6,297**	**9,279**	**5,671**
Public and publicly guaranteed sector	6,813	2,382	4,109	3,356	5,651	3,167
Private sector not guaranteed	1,527	3,855	3,259	2,941	3,629	2,504
Interest payments, long-term	**3,112**	**2,564**	**3,212**	**2,975**	**2,858**	**3,278**
Public and publicly guaranteed sector	2,977	2,300	2,417	2,296	2,105	2,340
Private sector not guaranteed	135	264	795	679	752	938

142

RUSSIAN FEDERATION

(US$ million, unless otherwise indicated)

Snapshot	2022
Total external debt stocks	376,117
External debt stocks as % of	
Exports	55
GNI	17
Debt service as % of	
Exports	15
GNI	5
Net financial flows, debt and equity	-125,199
Net debt inflows	-94,296
Net equity inflows	-30,904
GNI	2,196,713
Population (million)	144

Figure 1 **Public and publicly guaranteed debt, by creditor and creditor type in 2022, including IMF credit**

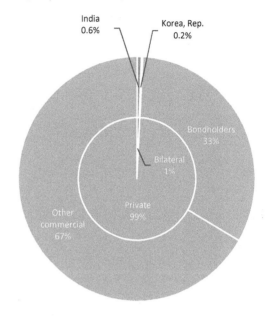

Figure 2 **Average terms on new debt commitments from official and private creditors**

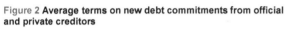
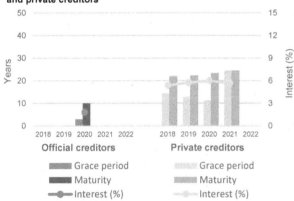

Summary External Debt Data	2010	2018	2019	2020	2021	2022
Total external debt stocks	**417,886**	**477,785**	**485,793**	**460,934**	**472,158**	**376,117**
Long-term external debt stocks	**348,938**	**415,696**	**409,644**	**390,911**	**369,952**	**286,543**
Public and publicly guaranteed debt from:	165,665	195,226	201,325	193,502	176,769	136,086
Official creditors	7,637	966	772	800	1,084	997
Multilateral	3,087	476	353	261	194	10
of which: World Bank	2,618	428	315	236	178	..
Bilateral	4,550	489	420	539	890	987
Private creditors	158,028	194,260	200,553	192,702	175,685	135,089
Bondholders	25,510	64,594	82,772	79,082	73,922	44,443
Commercial banks and others	132,518	129,666	117,781	113,620	101,763	90,646
Private nonguaranteed debt from:	183,273	220,470	208,319	197,409	193,184	150,458
Bondholders	2,100	19,890	27,126	29,324	25,451	23,470
Commercial banks and others	181,173	200,580	181,193	168,085	167,733	126,988
Use of IMF credit and SDR allocations	**8,735**	**7,888**	**7,843**	**8,169**	**25,248**	**24,008**
IMF credit	0	0	0	0	0	0
SDR allocations	8,735	7,888	7,843	8,169	25,248	24,008
Short-term external debt stocks	**60,214**	**54,201**	**68,306**	**61,854**	**76,958**	**65,566**
Disbursements, long-term	**70,301**	**51,285**	**72,025**	**72,350**	**58,603**	**2,751**
Public and publicly guaranteed sector	49,805	32,406	39,084	43,569	10,262	235
Private sector not guaranteed	20,496	18,878	32,941	28,780	48,341	2,517
Principal repayments, long-term	**42,974**	**90,548**	**78,405**	**92,298**	**79,085**	**85,655**
Public and publicly guaranteed sector	30,001	53,051	32,975	52,263	26,363	40,338
Private sector not guaranteed	12,973	37,497	45,430	40,035	52,722	45,317
Interest payments, long-term	**12,291**	**19,051**	**17,259**	**17,324**	**16,264**	**11,610**
Public and publicly guaranteed sector	1,707	8,930	7,306	8,182	7,725	5,076
Private sector not guaranteed	10,584	10,121	9,953	9,142	8,539	6,533

RWANDA

(US$ million, unless otherwise indicated)

Snapshot	2022
Total external debt stocks	**9,690**
External debt stocks as % of	
Exports	321
GNI	74
Debt service as % of	
Exports	12
GNI	3
Net financial flows, debt and equity	**931**
Net debt inflows	629
Net equity inflows	302
GNI	**13,033**
Population (million)	**14**

Figure 2 Average terms on new debt commitments from official and private creditors

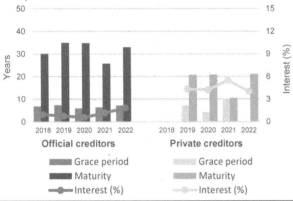

Official creditors — Private creditors

- Grace period / Grace period
- Maturity / Maturity
- Interest (%) / Interest (%)

Figure 1 Public and publicly guaranteed debt, by creditor and creditor type in 2022, including IMF credit

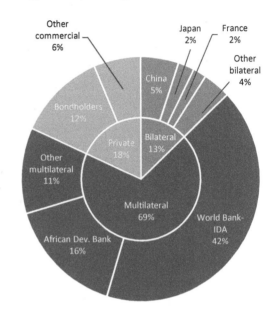

Summary External Debt Data	2010	2018	2019	2020	2021	2022
Total external debt stocks	**1,233**	**5,681**	**6,515**	**8,194**	**9,318**	**9,690**
Long-term external debt stocks	**1,086**	**5,019**	**5,866**	**7,295**	**8,226**	**8,701**
Public and publicly guaranteed debt from:	759	3,249	3,929	5,122	5,794	6,145
Official creditors	759	2,849	3,465	4,377	4,739	4,970
Multilateral	639	2,467	2,979	3,737	3,924	4,135
of which: World Bank	259	1,610	1,897	2,432	2,575	2,696
Bilateral	120	382	486	640	815	835
Private creditors	..	400	464	745	1,055	1,174
Bondholders	..	400	421	475	775	765
Commercial banks and others	..	..	43	270	280	410
Private nonguaranteed debt from:	327	1,769	1,937	2,173	2,432	2,556
Bondholders	..	..	..	..	..	..
Commercial banks and others	327	1,769	1,937	2,173	2,432	2,556
Use of IMF credit and SDR allocations	**133**	**308**	**306**	**520**	**678**	**613**
IMF credit	15	201	199	410	356	306
SDR allocations	118	107	106	111	322	307
Short-term external debt stocks	**14**	**354**	**343**	**378**	**414**	**376**
Disbursements, long-term	**182**	**852**	**1,044**	**1,368**	**1,483**	**822**
Public and publicly guaranteed sector	63	497	727	1,086	1,207	659
Private sector not guaranteed	119	355	318	282	276	163
Principal repayments, long-term	**41**	**155**	**185**	**102**	**424**	**124**
Public and publicly guaranteed sector	8	29	31	52	406	85
Private sector not guaranteed	33	126	154	50	18	39
Interest payments, long-term	**10**	**101**	**133**	**148**	**148**	**183**
Public and publicly guaranteed sector	6	51	56	61	55	81
Private sector not guaranteed	4	50	78	87	93	102

SAMOA

(US$ million, unless otherwise indicated)

Snapshot	2022
Total external debt stocks	459.3
External debt stocks as % of	
Exports	245.0
GNI	56.8
Debt service as % of	
Exports	20.5
GNI	4.7
Net financial flows, debt and equity	2.2
Net debt inflows	-4.3
Net equity inflows	6.5
GNI	808.5
Population (thousand)	222.4

Figure 1 **Public and publicly guaranteed debt, by creditor and creditor type in 2022, including IMF credit**

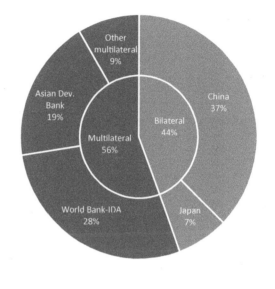

Figure 2 **Average terms on new debt commitments from official and private creditors**

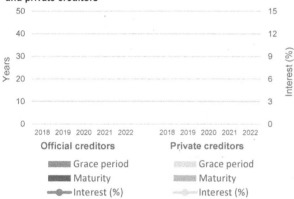

Summary External Debt Data	2010	2018	2019	2020	2021	2022
Total external debt stocks	**325.1**	**446.5**	**434.9**	**477.2**	**493.3**	**459.3**
Long-term external debt stocks	**299.1**	**406.0**	**389.6**	**395.8**	**382.2**	**330.2**
Public and publicly guaranteed debt from:	299.1	403.2	387.6	393.8	380.9	328.8
Official creditors	299.1	403.2	387.6	393.8	380.9	328.8
Multilateral	219.2	208.1	205.8	206.1	189.2	173.1
of which: World Bank	99.3	104.9	110.3	114.6	107.8	99.1
Bilateral	79.9	195.1	181.8	187.8	191.7	155.7
Private creditors	..	..	..	..	..	..
Bondholders	..	..	..	..	..	..
Commercial banks and others	..	..	..	..	..	..
Private nonguaranteed debt from:	..	2.8	2.0	2.0	1.3	1.4
Bondholders	..	..	..	..	..	..
Commercial banks and others	..	2.8	2.0	2.0	1.3	1.4
Use of IMF credit and SDR allocations	**26.0**	**24.3**	**21.0**	**43.5**	**62.4**	**57.8**
IMF credit	8.9	8.9	5.6	27.5	25.1	22.3
SDR allocations	17.1	15.4	15.3	16.0	37.3	35.4
Short-term external debt stocks	**0.0**	**16.3**	**24.3**	**37.9**	**48.7**	**71.3**
Disbursements, long-term	**78.9**	**24.7**	**9.3**	**3.1**	**0.0**	**3.5**
Public and publicly guaranteed sector	78.9	22.0	9.3	3.1	0.0	3.4
Private sector not guaranteed	..	2.8	..	0.0	..	0.1
Principal repayments, long-term	**7.2**	**21.9**	**22.1**	**18.1**	**12.0**	**28.8**
Public and publicly guaranteed sector	7.2	21.9	21.3	18.1	11.3	28.8
Private sector not guaranteed	..	..	0.8	..	0.7	..
Interest payments, long-term	**3.3**	**6.9**	**6.0**	**3.9**	**2.7**	**5.2**
Public and publicly guaranteed sector	3.3	6.1	5.6	3.8	2.6	5.2
Private sector not guaranteed	..	0.8	0.4	0.1	0.0	0.0

Note: Figure 2 shows no data values because the country did not have new commitments from 2018 to 2022.

SÃO TOMÉ AND PRÍNCIPE

(US$ million, unless otherwise indicated)

Snapshot	2022
Total external debt stocks	**391.5**
External debt stocks as % of	
Exports	352.4
GNI	71.1
Debt service as % of	
Exports	7.2
GNI	1.5
Net financial flows, debt and equity	**1.3**
Net debt inflows	1.3
Net equity inflows	..
GNI	**550.7**
Population (thousand)	**227.4**

Figure 1 Public and publicly guaranteed debt, by creditor and creditor type in 2022, including IMF credit

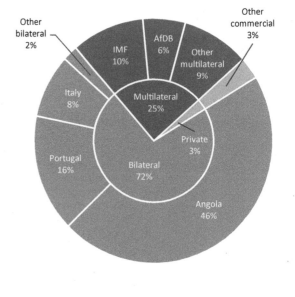

Figure 2 Average terms on new debt commitments from official and private creditors

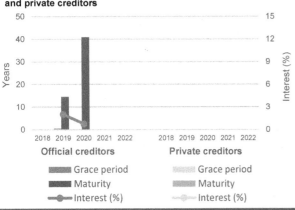

Summary External Debt Data	2010	2018	2019	2020	2021	2022
Total external debt stocks	**181.1**	**248.8**	**277.1**	**316.7**	**331.3**	**391.5**
Long-term external debt stocks	**145.3**	**223.3**	**240.7**	**256.4**	**249.4**	**309.1**
Public and publicly guaranteed debt from:	145.3	223.3	240.7	256.4	249.4	309.1
Official creditors	145.3	213.3	230.7	246.4	239.4	299.1
Multilateral	37.3	46.9	48.9	55.9	54.0	51.1
of which: World Bank	14.2	11.5	11.1	11.3	10.7	9.9
Bilateral	108.0	166.4	181.8	190.6	185.4	248.0
Private creditors	..	10.0	10.0	10.0	10.0	10.0
Bondholders	..	..	..	..	..	..
Commercial banks and others	..	10.0	10.0	10.0	10.0	10.0
Private nonguaranteed debt from:	..	..	..	..	..	..
Bondholders	..	..	..	..	..	..
Commercial banks and others	..	..	..	..	..	..
Use of IMF credit and SDR allocations	**15.9**	**16.8**	**18.8**	**37.0**	**60.5**	**62.0**
IMF credit	4.9	6.9	9.0	26.8	30.7	33.6
SDR allocations	10.9	9.9	9.8	10.2	29.8	28.3
Short-term external debt stocks	**19.9**	**8.8**	**17.6**	**23.3**	**21.4**	**20.5**
Disbursements, long-term	**19.8**	**5.6**	**7.3**	**5.9**	**2.3**	**2.6**
Public and publicly guaranteed sector	19.8	5.6	7.3	5.9	2.3	2.6
Private sector not guaranteed	..	..	..	..	..	..
Principal repayments, long-term	**1.2**	**2.7**	**4.8**	**1.3**	**2.0**	**4.9**
Public and publicly guaranteed sector	1.2	2.7	4.8	1.3	2.0	4.9
Private sector not guaranteed	..	..	..	..	..	..
Interest payments, long-term	**0.3**	**1.3**	**3.4**	**1.2**	**0.6**	**2.2**
Public and publicly guaranteed sector	0.3	1.3	3.4	1.2	0.6	2.2
Private sector not guaranteed	..	..	..	..	..	..

SENEGAL

(US$ million, unless otherwise indicated)

Snapshot	2022
Total external debt stocks	**32,126**
External debt stocks as % of	
Exports	467
GNI	119
Debt service as % of	
Exports	28
GNI	7
Net financial flows, debt and equity	**6,438**
Net debt inflows	3,851
Net equity inflows	2,586
GNI	**26,944**
Population (million)	**17**

Figure 2 **Average terms on new debt commitments from official and private creditors**

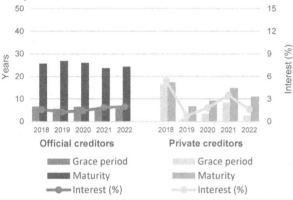

Figure 1 **Public and publicly guaranteed debt, by creditor and creditor type in 2022, including IMF credit**

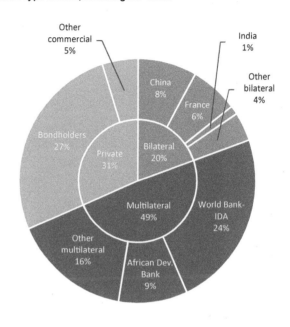

Summary External Debt Data	2010	2018	2019	2020	2021	2022
Total external debt stocks	**4,650**	**18,982**	**19,243**	**23,286**	**28,513**	**32,126**
Long-term external debt stocks	**4,198**	**16,549**	**17,293**	**20,976**	**24,437**	**26,915**
Public and publicly guaranteed debt from:	3,151	11,146	12,267	14,025	14,434	14,524
Official creditors	2,951	6,670	7,815	9,360	9,514	9,648
Multilateral	1,973	3,761	4,845	5,932	6,185	6,617
of which: World Bank	1,023	2,070	2,657	3,102	3,257	3,661
Bilateral	978	2,909	2,970	3,428	3,330	3,031
Private creditors	200	4,476	4,452	4,665	4,920	4,876
Bondholders	200	4,151	4,122	4,158	4,235	4,118
Commercial banks and others	..	325	330	506	685	758
Private nonguaranteed debt from:	1,048	5,403	5,026	6,952	10,004	12,391
Bondholders	..	..	..	..	..	..
Commercial banks and others	1,048	5,403	5,026	6,952	10,004	12,391
Use of IMF credit and SDR allocations	**451**	**242**	**219**	**689**	**1,285**	**1,609**
IMF credit	213	27	4	466	634	990
SDR allocations	238	215	214	223	651	619
Short-term external debt stocks	**0**	**2,191**	**1,731**	**1,621**	**2,791**	**3,602**
Disbursements, long-term	**1,045**	**4,807**	**1,650**	**3,430**	**5,130**	**3,277**
Public and publicly guaranteed sector	355	3,338	1,650	1,504	2,078	1,304
Private sector not guaranteed	690	1,469	..	1,926	3,052	1,973
Principal repayments, long-term	**84**	**307**	**806**	**423**	**1,067**	**626**
Public and publicly guaranteed sector	84	307	429	423	1,067	626
Private sector not guaranteed	..	..	377	..	..	..
Interest payments, long-term	**101**	**433**	**497**	**565**	**979**	**1,133**
Public and publicly guaranteed sector	64	293	367	384	379	390
Private sector not guaranteed	37	140	131	181	600	743

SERBIA

(US$ million, unless otherwise indicated)

Snapshot	2022
Total external debt stocks	**44,160**
External debt stocks as % of	
Exports	109
GNI	73
Debt service as % of	
Exports	14
GNI	9
Net financial flows, debt and equity	**7,051**
Net debt inflows	4,046
Net equity inflows	3,005
GNI	**60,332**
Population (million)	**7**

Figure 2 Average terms on new debt commitments from official and private creditors

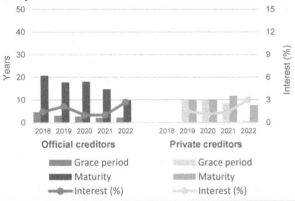

Figure 1 Public and publicly guaranteed debt, by creditor and creditor type in 2022, including IMF credit

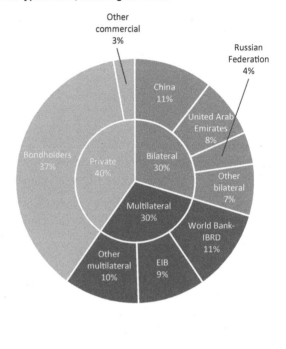

Summary External Debt Data	2010	2018	2019	2020	2021	2022
Total external debt stocks	**32,907**	**31,054**	**32,109**	**38,041**	**41,166**	**44,160**
Long-term external debt stocks	**27,389**	**28,802**	**29,332**	**35,497**	**37,671**	**39,127**
Public and publicly guaranteed debt from:	9,477	15,089	15,341	18,370	20,619	21,852
Official creditors	8,011	11,566	11,768	12,046	12,043	13,062
Multilateral	4,848	5,861	5,743	6,064	5,776	5,540
of which: World Bank	2,499	2,799	2,708	2,891	2,655	2,440
Bilateral	3,163	5,704	6,025	5,982	6,267	7,522
Private creditors	1,466	3,523	3,573	6,324	8,575	8,790
Bondholders	..	3,500	3,552	6,303	8,287	8,166
Commercial banks and others	1,466	23	21	21	289	624
Private nonguaranteed debt from:	17,912	13,713	13,990	17,127	17,053	17,274
Bondholders	165	..	..	..	..	..
Commercial banks and others	17,747	13,713	13,990	17,127	17,053	17,274
Use of IMF credit and SDR allocations	**2,720**	**619**	**615**	**641**	**1,501**	**2,473**
IMF credit	2,034	0	0	0	0	1,046
SDR allocations	685	619	615	641	1,501	1,428
Short-term external debt stocks	**2,798**	**1,633**	**2,162**	**1,902**	**1,993**	**2,561**
Disbursements, long-term	**4,594**	**4,709**	**7,846**	**8,248**	**8,274**	**7,294**
Public and publicly guaranteed sector	1,365	1,502	3,125	4,205	5,105	3,248
Private sector not guaranteed	3,230	3,207	4,721	4,043	3,169	4,046
Principal repayments, long-term	**3,431**	**4,813**	**6,150**	**4,411**	**4,956**	**4,917**
Public and publicly guaranteed sector	351	2,501	2,745	2,219	1,713	1,093
Private sector not guaranteed	3,081	2,312	3,406	2,193	3,243	3,825
Interest payments, long-term	**759**	**734**	**718**	**593**	**694**	**773**
Public and publicly guaranteed sector	321	546	515	479	404	422
Private sector not guaranteed	438	188	203	114	289	350

SIERRA LEONE

(US$ million, unless otherwise indicated)

Snapshot	2022
Total external debt stocks	2,331
External debt stocks as % of	
Exports	185
GNI	60
Debt service as % of	
Exports	9
GNI	3
Net financial flows, debt and equity	220
Net debt inflows	-30
Net equity inflows	250
GNI	3,913
Population (million)	9

Figure 2 **Average terms on new debt commitments from official and private creditors**

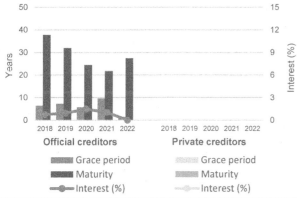

Figure 1 **Public and publicly guaranteed debt, by creditor and creditor type in 2022, including IMF credit**

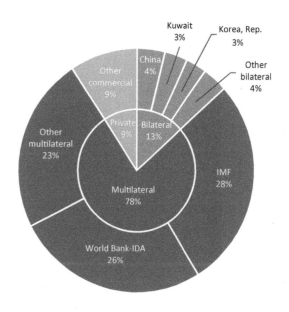

Summary External Debt Data	2010	2018	2019	2020	2021	2022
Total external debt stocks	931	1,757	1,856	2,109	2,451	2,331
Long-term external debt stocks	661	1,068	1,166	1,273	1,310	1,278
Public and publicly guaranteed debt from:	661	1,068	1,166	1,273	1,310	1,278
Official creditors	450	874	979	1,094	1,142	1,113
Multilateral	371	687	759	856	893	878
of which: World Bank	155	284	348	432	464	466
Bilateral	78	187	221	238	250	235
Private creditors	211	193	187	179	168	165
Bondholders	..	..	..	..	..	..
Commercial banks and others	211	193	187	179	168	165
Private nonguaranteed debt from:	..	..	..	..	..	..
Bondholders	..	..	..	..	..	..
Commercial banks and others	..	..	..	..	..	..
Use of IMF credit and SDR allocations	266	501	503	652	959	892
IMF credit	113	363	365	509	541	495
SDR allocations	153	138	138	143	417	397
Short-term external debt stocks	4	189	187	184	181	162
Disbursements, long-term	66	61	142	129	100	50
Public and publicly guaranteed sector	66	61	142	129	100	50
Private sector not guaranteed	..	..	..	..	..	..
Principal repayments, long-term	5	29	40	45	45	53
Public and publicly guaranteed sector	5	29	40	45	45	53
Private sector not guaranteed	..	..	..	..	..	..
Interest payments, long-term	4	7	10	6	7	9
Public and publicly guaranteed sector	4	7	10	6	7	9
Private sector not guaranteed	..	..	..	..	..	..

SOLOMON ISLANDS

(US$ million, unless otherwise indicated)

Snapshot	2022
Total external debt stocks	**503.0**
External debt stocks as % of	
Exports	105.1
GNI	31.3
Debt service as % of	
Exports	2.5
GNI	0.7
Net financial flows, debt and equity	**69.8**
Net debt inflows	39.3
Net equity inflows	30.5
GNI	**1,607.1**
Population (million)	**0.7**

Figure 1 Public and publicly guaranteed debt, by creditor and creditor type in 2022, including IMF credit

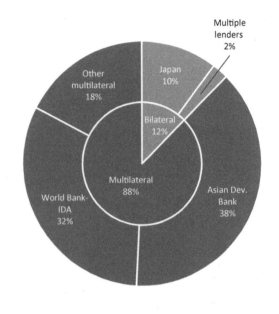

Figure 2 Average terms on new debt commitments from official and private creditors

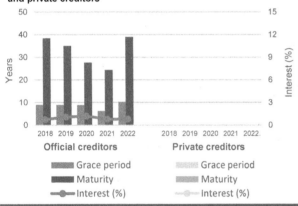

Summary External Debt Data	2010	2018	2019	2020	2021	2022
Total external debt stocks	**230.8**	**323.5**	**350.5**	**428.9**	**483.2**	**503.0**
Long-term external debt stocks	**201.9**	**263.4**	**299.3**	**376.8**	**359.8**	**377.8**
Public and publicly guaranteed debt from:	125.3	96.0	98.1	124.0	140.8	154.8
Official creditors	125.2	96.0	98.1	124.0	140.8	154.8
Multilateral	105.6	87.5	90.7	117.8	113.8	132.0
of which: World Bank	41.7	36.6	38.5	47.8	46.7	58.0
Bilateral	19.6	8.5	7.4	6.3	27.0	22.8
Private creditors	0.1	..	..	..	..	..
Bondholders	..	..	..	..	..	..
Commercial banks and others	0.1	..	..	..	..	..
Private nonguaranteed debt from:	76.6	167.4	201.3	252.8	219.0	223.0
Bondholders	..	..	..	..	..	..
Commercial banks and others	76.6	167.4	201.3	252.8	219.0	223.0
Use of IMF credit and SDR allocations	**24.9**	**17.1**	**15.0**	**25.3**	**71.7**	**67.9**
IMF credit	9.6	3.3	1.3	11.1	29.9	28.2
SDR allocations	15.3	13.8	13.7	14.3	41.8	39.7
Short-term external debt stocks	**4.0**	**43.0**	**36.2**	**26.8**	**51.7**	**57.3**
Disbursements, long-term	**36.8**	**36.8**	**18.0**	**95.3**	**28.7**	**41.2**
Public and publicly guaranteed sector	0.0	6.1	7.6	27.4	25.9	26.1
Private sector not guaranteed	36.8	30.7	10.4	67.9	2.8	15.1
Principal repayments, long-term	**17.5**	**29.5**	**9.8**	**5.7**	**9.1**	**7.3**
Public and publicly guaranteed sector	8.6	4.8	5.1	5.2	5.1	4.9
Private sector not guaranteed	8.9	24.7	4.7	0.5	4.0	2.4
Interest payments, long-term	**3.2**	**6.0**	**3.2**	**2.6**	**2.1**	**2.0**
Public and publicly guaranteed sector	1.7	1.1	1.1	1.1	1.4	1.2
Private sector not guaranteed	1.5	4.9	2.1	1.5	0.7	0.8

SOMALIA

(US$ million, unless otherwise indicated)

Snapshot	2022
Total external debt stocks	4,164
External debt stocks as % of	
Exports	231
GNI	52
Debt service as % of	
Exports	1
GNI	0
Net financial flows, debt and equity	650
Net debt inflows	14
Net equity inflows	636
GNI	8,081
Population (million)	18

Figure 1 **Public and publicly guaranteed debt, by creditor and creditor type in 2022, including IMF credit**

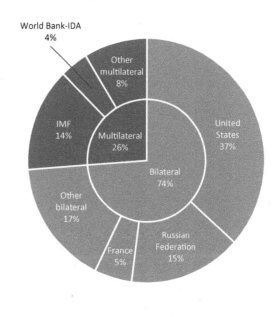

Figure 2 **Average terms on new debt commitments from official and private creditors**

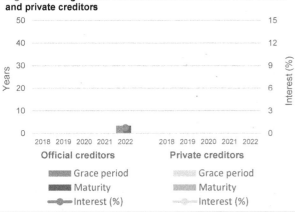

Summary External Debt Data	2010	2018	2019	2020	2021	2022
Total external debt stocks	2,934	5,558	5,621	4,658	4,211	4,164
Long-term external debt stocks	1,879	2,080	2,077	2,637	2,341	2,339
Public and publicly guaranteed debt from:	1,879	2,080	2,077	2,637	2,341	2,339
Official creditors	1,879	2,080	2,077	2,637	2,341	2,339
Multilateral	773	716	714	373	366	338
of which: World Bank	443	413	411	138	122	105
Bilateral	1,106	1,363	1,363	2,264	1,976	2,001
Private creditors	..	..	..	..	..	..
Bondholders	..	..	..	..	..	..
Commercial banks and others	..	..	..	..	..	..
Private nonguaranteed debt from:	..	..	..	..	..	..
Bondholders	..	..	..	..	..	..
Commercial banks and others	..	..	..	..	..	..
Use of IMF credit and SDR allocations	244	220	219	444	650	646
IMF credit	172	155	154	371	360	371
SDR allocations	72	65	64	73	290	276
Short-term external debt stocks	811	3,259	3,325	1,578	1,220	1,178
Disbursements, long-term	0	0	0	0	0	0
Public and publicly guaranteed sector	0	0	0	0	0	0
Private sector not guaranteed	..	..	..	..	..	..
Principal repayments, long-term	0	0	0	350	15	14
Public and publicly guaranteed sector	0	0	0	350	15	14
Private sector not guaranteed	..	..	..	..	..	..
Interest payments, long-term	0	0	0	131	1	1
Public and publicly guaranteed sector	0	0	0	131	1	1
Private sector not guaranteed	..	..	..	..	..	..

SOUTH AFRICA

(US$ million, unless otherwise indicated)

Snapshot	2022
Total external debt stocks	**172,133**
External debt stocks as % of	
Exports	117
GNI	43
Debt service as % of	
Exports	18
GNI	7
Net financial flows, debt and equity	**15,030**
Net debt inflows	5,893
Net equity inflows	9,137
GNI	**397,439**
Population (million)	**60**

Figure 1 **Public and publicly guaranteed debt, by creditor and creditor type in 2022, including IMF credit**

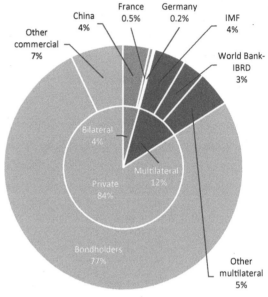

Figure 2 **Average terms on new debt commitments from official and private creditors**

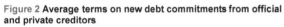
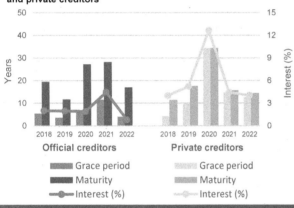

Summary External Debt Data	2010	2018	2019	2020	2021	2022
Total external debt stocks	**115,322**	**180,184**	**190,738**	**175,417**	**169,438**	**172,133**
Long-term external debt stocks	**80,499**	**129,833**	**143,773**	**131,374**	**122,284**	**118,855**
Public and publicly guaranteed debt from:	36,329	88,667	102,054	99,435	95,178	91,617
Official creditors	1,237	6,797	7,708	9,263	10,358	11,424
Multilateral	1,139	4,866	4,870	5,859	6,646	7,290
of which: World Bank	384	2,277	2,239	2,082	1,853	2,787
Bilateral	99	1,931	2,839	3,404	3,712	4,135
Private creditors	35,092	81,870	94,345	90,172	84,820	80,192
Bondholders	30,676	70,911	84,762	81,186	77,723	73,359
Commercial banks and others	4,416	10,958	9,584	8,986	7,097	6,833
Private nonguaranteed debt from:	44,170	41,166	41,719	31,939	27,106	27,239
Bondholders	8,786	4,521	4,737	2,700	2,870	2,823
Commercial banks and others	35,384	36,645	36,982	29,239	24,236	24,416
Use of IMF credit and SDR allocations	**2,750**	**2,483**	**2,469**	**6,966**	**10,862**	**10,329**
IMF credit	0	0	0	4,395	4,270	4,061
SDR allocations	2,750	2,483	2,469	2,571	6,592	6,268
Short-term external debt stocks	**32,073**	**47,868**	**44,496**	**37,077**	**36,292**	**42,949**
Disbursements, long-term	**12,113**	**18,267**	**21,690**	**12,830**	**11,103**	**19,690**
Public and publicly guaranteed sector	8,889	12,237	14,551	3,809	3,198	6,017
Private sector not guaranteed	3,224	6,029	7,138	9,020	7,905	13,673
Principal repayments, long-term	**3,474**	**21,654**	**13,796**	**20,614**	**19,847**	**20,453**
Public and publicly guaranteed sector	1,682	11,393	3,392	6,450	7,014	9,196
Private sector not guaranteed	1,792	10,261	10,403	14,163	12,833	11,258
Interest payments, long-term	**2,177**	**6,241**	**6,563**	**6,243**	**5,904**	**5,588**
Public and publicly guaranteed sector	1,559	4,308	4,281	4,664	4,317	4,101
Private sector not guaranteed	618	1,933	2,282	1,579	1,587	1,487

SRI LANKA

(US$ million, unless otherwise indicated)

Snapshot	2022
Total external debt stocks	58,713
External debt stocks as % of	
Exports	358
GNI	81
Debt service as % of	
Exports	19
GNI	4
Net financial flows, debt and equity	810
Net debt inflows	384
Net equity inflows	426
GNI	72,489
Population (million)	22

Figure 2 Average terms on new debt commitments from official and private creditors

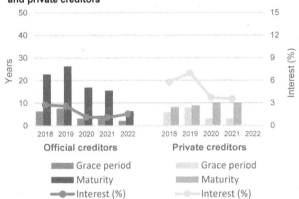

Figure 1 Public and publicly guaranteed debt, by creditor and creditor type in 2022, including IMF credit

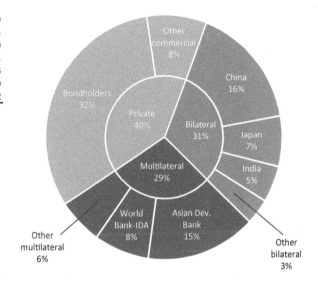

Summary External Debt Data	2010	2018	2019	2020	2021	2022
Total external debt stocks	21,684	52,920	56,118	56,874	58,733	58,713
Long-term external debt stocks	17,349	43,194	45,812	46,552	47,513	47,795
Public and publicly guaranteed debt from:	16,430	34,355	36,986	37,568	38,482	38,481
Official creditors	13,400	18,952	19,396	20,742	22,143	22,663
Multilateral	6,089	8,060	8,254	9,135	9,750	10,273
of which: World Bank	2,531	3,210	3,226	3,492	3,740	3,837
Bilateral	7,311	10,892	11,142	11,607	12,393	12,390
Private creditors	3,029	15,403	17,590	16,826	16,339	15,817
Bondholders	2,000	12,400	15,050	14,050	13,050	12,550
Commercial banks and others	1,029	3,003	2,540	2,776	3,289	3,267
Private nonguaranteed debt from:	919	8,839	8,826	8,984	9,032	9,314
Bondholders	0	262	175	175	175	175
Commercial banks and others	919	8,577	8,651	8,809	8,857	9,139
Use of IMF credit and SDR allocations	1,920	1,545	1,864	1,927	2,593	2,326
IMF credit	1,311	995	1,317	1,357	1,263	1,062
SDR allocations	609	550	547	570	1,330	1,265
Short-term external debt stocks	2,416	8,181	8,442	8,396	8,626	8,591
Disbursements, long-term	3,091	7,256	7,071	3,392	4,529	3,332
Public and publicly guaranteed sector	2,994	5,097	6,235	2,856	4,246	2,506
Private sector not guaranteed	97	2,158	836	536	283	826
Principal repayments, long-term	727	5,523	4,431	3,323	3,043	2,018
Public and publicly guaranteed sector	582	3,190	3,582	2,861	2,808	1,475
Private sector not guaranteed	145	2,333	849	461	235	543
Interest payments, long-term	616	1,546	1,542	1,590	1,522	787
Public and publicly guaranteed sector	596	1,247	1,384	1,492	1,337	540
Private sector not guaranteed	20	300	159	97	185	248

(US$ million, unless otherwise indicated)

Snapshot	2022
Total external debt stocks	**909.3**
External debt stocks as % of	
Exports	72.0
GNI	45.7
Debt service as % of	
Exports	4.1
GNI	2.6
Net financial flows, debt and equity	**71.7**
Net debt inflows	13.4
Net equity inflows	58.2
GNI	**1,989.9**
Population (thousand)	**179.9**

Figure 2 Average terms on new debt commitments from official and private creditors

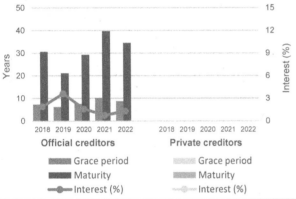

Figure 1 Public and publicly guaranteed debt, by creditor and creditor type in 2022, including IMF credit

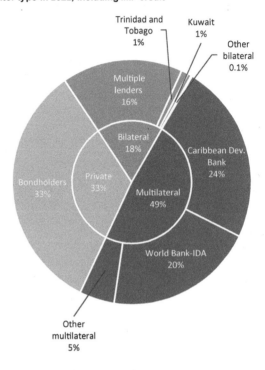

Summary External Debt Data	2010	2018	2019	2020	2021	2022
Total external debt stocks	**584.8**	**615.5**	**638.9**	**733.8**	**892.7**	**909.3**
Long-term external debt stocks	**326.4**	**499.5**	**542.2**	**603.6**	**721.7**	**736.6**
Public and publicly guaranteed debt from:	326.4	499.5	542.2	603.6	721.7	736.6
Official creditors	263.2	242.6	270.7	351.2	478.1	481.4
Multilateral	242.5	211.3	222.7	277.9	340.9	344.4
of which: World Bank	80.3	85.6	86.6	108.3	150.2	156.7
Bilateral	20.7	31.3	48.0	73.4	137.2	137.1
Private creditors	63.2	256.9	271.5	252.4	243.6	255.2
Bondholders	63.2	256.9	271.5	252.4	243.6	255.2
Commercial banks and others	..	..	..	..	..	..
Private nonguaranteed debt from:	..	..	..	..	..	..
Bondholders	..	..	..	..	..	..
Commercial banks and others	..	..	..	..	..	..
Use of IMF credit and SDR allocations	**33.0**	**24.8**	**21.7**	**52.4**	**79.0**	**75.2**
IMF credit	10.6	4.6	1.6	31.4	30.0	28.5
SDR allocations	22.4	20.3	20.1	21.0	49.1	46.7
Short-term external debt stocks	**225.3**	**91.1**	**75.0**	**77.9**	**92.0**	**97.5**
Disbursements, long-term	**36.4**	**10.8**	**48.2**	**94.3**	**148.0**	**28.6**
Public and publicly guaranteed sector	36.4	10.8	48.2	94.3	148.0	28.6
Private sector not guaranteed	..	..	..	..	..	..
Principal repayments, long-term	**30.5**	**19.1**	**19.8**	**17.7**	**18.7**	**20.6**
Public and publicly guaranteed sector	30.5	19.1	19.8	17.7	18.7	20.6
Private sector not guaranteed	..	..	..	..	..	..
Interest payments, long-term	**10.8**	**24.9**	**26.1**	**24.7**	**25.0**	**28.1**
Public and publicly guaranteed sector	10.8	24.9	26.1	24.7	25.0	28.1
Private sector not guaranteed	..	..	..	..	..	..

(US$ million, unless otherwise indicated)

Snapshot	2022
Total external debt stocks	**581.0**
External debt stocks as % of	
Exports	217.5
GNI	62.7
Debt service as % of	
Exports	13.5
GNI	3.9
Net financial flows, debt and equity	**140.1**
Net debt inflows	59.4
Net equity inflows	80.8
GNI	**926.7**
Population (thousand)	**103.9**

Figure 2 **Average terms on new debt commitments from official and private creditors**

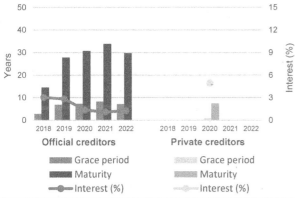

Figure 1 **Public and publicly guaranteed debt, by creditor and creditor type in 2022, including IMF credit**

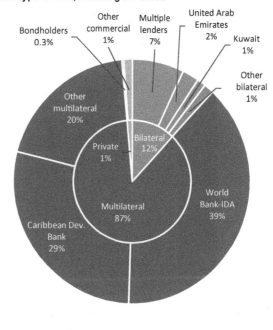

Summary External Debt Data	2010	2018	2019	2020	2021	2022
Total external debt stocks	**295.9**	**323.3**	**351.3**	**414.6**	**529.2**	**581.0**
Long-term external debt stocks	**278.0**	**305.4**	**335.9**	**383.3**	**472.8**	**528.0**
Public and publicly guaranteed debt from:	278.0	305.4	335.9	383.3	472.8	528.0
Official creditors	229.2	286.6	320.3	372.2	462.3	520.1
Multilateral	211.0	241.1	270.8	321.7	411.1	453.9
of which: World Bank	26.5	31.8	69.1	117.1	202.0	214.3
Bilateral	18.2	45.5	49.5	50.5	51.3	66.1
Private creditors	48.7	18.8	15.6	11.1	10.5	8.0
Bondholders	..	9.1	7.9	4.0	2.7	1.5
Commercial banks and others	48.7	9.6	7.7	7.1	7.7	6.4
Private nonguaranteed debt from:	..	..	..	..	..	..
Bondholders	..	..	..	..	..	..
Commercial banks and others	..	..	..	..	..	..
Use of IMF credit and SDR allocations	**17.9**	**18.0**	**15.4**	**31.3**	**56.3**	**53.0**
IMF credit	5.8	7.0	4.4	19.9	29.6	27.6
SDR allocations	12.2	11.0	10.9	11.4	26.8	25.5
Short-term external debt stocks	**0.0**	**0.0**	**0.0**	**0.0**	**0.0**	**0.0**
Disbursements, long-term	**78.1**	**23.3**	**58.6**	**69.2**	**114.4**	**87.3**
Public and publicly guaranteed sector	78.1	23.3	58.6	69.2	114.4	87.3
Private sector not guaranteed	..	..	..	..	..	..
Principal repayments, long-term	**26.2**	**30.3**	**27.9**	**24.4**	**23.1**	**27.4**
Public and publicly guaranteed sector	26.2	30.3	27.9	24.4	23.1	27.4
Private sector not guaranteed	..	..	..	..	..	..
Interest payments, long-term	**10.0**	**7.1**	**8.2**	**7.3**	**6.7**	**7.9**
Public and publicly guaranteed sector	10.0	7.1	8.2	7.3	6.7	7.9
Private sector not guaranteed	..	..	..	..	..	..

SUDAN

(US$ million, unless otherwise indicated)

Snapshot	2022
Total external debt stocks	**22,433**
External debt stocks as % of	
Exports	352
GNI	44
Debt service as % of	
Exports	3
GNI	0
Net financial flows, debt and equity	**446**
Net debt inflows	-128
Net equity inflows	574
GNI	**50,808**
Population (million)	**47**

Figure 1 Public and publicly guaranteed debt, by creditor and creditor type in 2022, including IMF credit

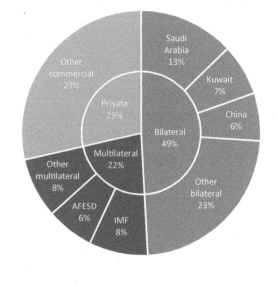

Figure 2 Average terms on new debt commitments from official and private creditors

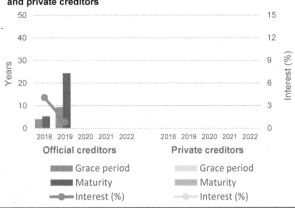

Summary External Debt Data	2010	2018	2019	2020	2021	2022
Total external debt stocks	**22,593**	**21,805**	**22,844**	**23,811**	**22,968**	**22,433**
Long-term external debt stocks	**14,638**	**15,762**	**16,794**	**17,084**	**15,611**	**15,253**
Public and publicly guaranteed debt from:	14,638	15,762	16,794	17,084	15,611	15,253
Official creditors	11,992	11,166	12,164	12,258	10,860	10,526
Multilateral	3,378	3,411	3,672	3,747	2,521	2,375
of which: World Bank	1,290	1,206	1,201	1,234	346	294
Bilateral	8,614	7,755	8,492	8,512	8,339	8,151
Private creditors	2,645	4,596	4,630	4,826	4,751	4,727
Bondholders	..	..	..	..	..	..
Commercial banks and others	2,645	4,596	4,630	4,826	4,751	4,727
Private nonguaranteed debt from:	..	..	..	..	..	..
Bondholders	..	..	..	..	..	..
Commercial banks and others	..	..	..	..	..	..
Use of IMF credit and SDR allocations	**664**	**542**	**528**	**548**	**2,505**	**2,382**
IMF credit	390	294	282	291	1,388	1,320
SDR allocations	274	248	246	256	1,117	1,062
Short-term external debt stocks	**7,292**	**5,500**	**5,522**	**6,179**	**4,852**	**4,798**
Disbursements, long-term	**935**	**65**	**1,152**	**8**	**4**	**0**
Public and publicly guaranteed sector	935	65	1,152	8	4	0
Private sector not guaranteed	..	..	..	..	..	..
Principal repayments, long-term	**400**	**159**	**139**	**111**	**1,238**	**147**
Public and publicly guaranteed sector	400	159	139	111	1,238	147
Private sector not guaranteed	..	..	..	..	..	..
Interest payments, long-term	**84**	**50**	**39**	**30**	**449**	**23**
Public and publicly guaranteed sector	84	50	39	30	449	23
Private sector not guaranteed	..	..	..	..	..	..

SURINAME

(US$ million, unless otherwise indicated)

Snapshot	2022
Total external debt stocks	**4,209**
External debt stocks as % of	
Exports	161
GNI	127
Debt service as % of	
Exports	13
GNI	11
Net financial flows, debt and equity	**53**
Net debt inflows	118
Net equity inflows	-64
GNI	**3,304**
Population (million)	**1**

Figure 2 **Average terms on new debt commitments from official and private creditors**

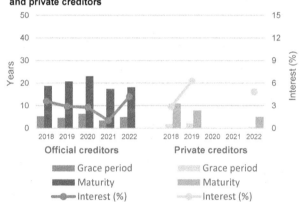

Figure 1 **Public and publicly guaranteed debt, by creditor and creditor type in 2022, including IMF credit**

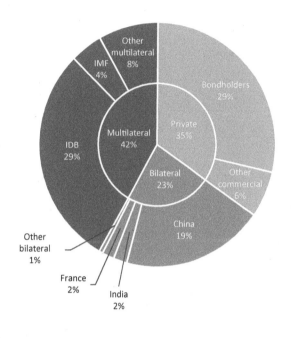

Summary External Debt Data	2010	2018	2019	2020	2021	2022
Total external debt stocks	..	**3,540**	**3,928**	**3,886**	**4,154**	**4,209**
Long-term external debt stocks	..	**3,016**	**3,386**	**3,385**	**3,295**	**3,442**
Public and publicly guaranteed debt from:	..	1,717	1,987	2,059	2,045	2,259
Official creditors	..	1,032	1,158	1,213	1,208	1,440
Multilateral	..	619	636	656	647	886
of which: World Bank	..	..	0	5	5	6
Bilateral	..	412	522	557	561	555
Private creditors	..	686	829	846	837	819
Bondholders	..	550	675	675	675	675
Commercial banks and others	..	136	154	171	162	144
Private nonguaranteed debt from:	..	1,298	1,399	1,326	1,250	1,183
Bondholders	..	..	..	2	2	2
Commercial banks and others	..	1,298	1,399	1,324	1,248	1,181
Use of IMF credit and SDR allocations	..	**203**	**182**	**148**	**351**	**387**
IMF credit	..	81	60	21	55	105
SDR allocations	..	123	122	127	296	282
Short-term external debt stocks	..	**321**	**359**	**353**	**508**	**381**
Disbursements, long-term	..	**781**	**738**	**266**	**304**	**501**
Public and publicly guaranteed sector	..	143	359	80	49	301
Private sector not guaranteed	..	638	379	186	255	200
Principal repayments, long-term	..	**351**	**360**	**306**	**310**	**291**
Public and publicly guaranteed sector	..	94	82	42	59	56
Private sector not guaranteed	..	257	279	264	251	236
Interest payments, long-term	..	**136**	**153**	**107**	**50**	**46**
Public and publicly guaranteed sector	..	86	101	58	24	25
Private sector not guaranteed	..	49	52	49	26	22

(US$ million, unless otherwise indicated)

Snapshot	2022
Total external debt stocks	**4,848**
External debt stocks as % of	
Exports	..
GNI	..
Debt service as % of	
Exports	..
GNI	..
Net financial flows, debt and equity	**10**
Net debt inflows	10
Net equity inflows	..
GNI	**..**
Population (million)	**22**

Figure 1 Public and publicly guaranteed debt, by creditor and creditor type in 2022, including IMF credit

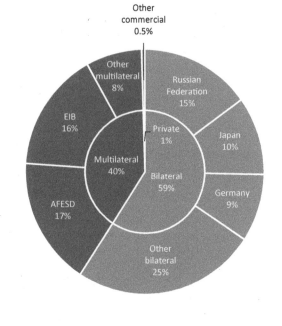

Figure 2 Average terms on new debt commitments from official and private creditors

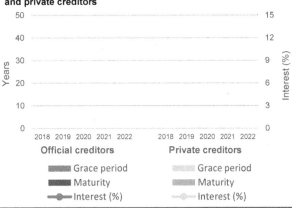

Summary External Debt Data	2010	2018	2019	2020	2021	2022
Total external debt stocks	**5,277**	**4,584**	**4,590**	**4,763**	**5,029**	**4,848**
Long-term external debt stocks	**4,284**	**3,647**	**3,635**	**3,751**	**3,632**	**3,498**
Public and publicly guaranteed debt from:	4,284	3,647	3,635	3,751	3,632	3,498
Official creditors	4,261	3,630	3,619	3,734	3,616	3,482
Multilateral	1,698	1,472	1,459	1,529	1,467	1,412
of which: World Bank	15	14	14	14	14	14
Bilateral	2,563	2,158	2,160	2,205	2,149	2,070
Private creditors	23	17	16	17	16	16
Bondholders	..	..	..	..	..	..
Commercial banks and others	23	17	16	17	16	16
Private nonguaranteed debt from:	..	..	..	..	..	..
Bondholders	..	..	..	..	..	..
Commercial banks and others	..	..	..	..	..	..
Use of IMF credit and SDR allocations	**430**	**388**	**386**	**402**	**785**	**746**
IMF credit	0	0	0	0	0	0
SDR allocations	430	388	386	402	785	746
Short-term external debt stocks	**562**	**548**	**569**	**610**	**612**	**604**
Disbursements, long-term	**286**	**60**	**0**	**0**	**0**	**0**
Public and publicly guaranteed sector	286	60	0	0	0	0
Private sector not guaranteed	..	..	..	..	..	..
Principal repayments, long-term	**509**	**19**	**1**	**0**	**0**	**0**
Public and publicly guaranteed sector	509	19	1	0	0	0
Private sector not guaranteed	..	..	..	..	..	..
Interest payments, long-term	**111**	**1**	**0**	**0**	**0**	**0**
Public and publicly guaranteed sector	111	1	0	0	0	0
Private sector not guaranteed	..	..	..	..	..	..

Note: Figure 2 shows no data values because the country did not have new commitments from 2018 to 2022.

TAJIKISTAN

(US$ million, unless otherwise indicated)

Snapshot	2022
Total external debt stocks	6,745
External debt stocks as % of	
Exports	121
GNI	55
Debt service as % of	
Exports	9
GNI	4
Net financial flows, debt and equity	21
Net debt inflows	-127
Net equity inflows	148
GNI	12,191
Population (million)	10

Figure 2 Average terms on new debt commitments from official and private creditors

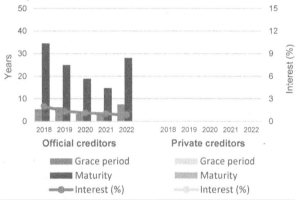

Figure 1 Public and publicly guaranteed debt, by creditor and creditor type in 2022, including IMF credit

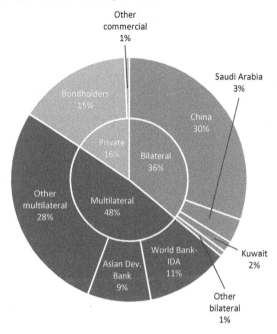

Summary External Debt Data	2010	2018	2019	2020	2021	2022
Total external debt stocks	3,561	6,087	6,633	6,904	6,970	6,745
Long-term external debt stocks	2,733	5,034	5,125	5,451	5,536	5,510
Public and publicly guaranteed debt from:	1,806	2,845	2,827	3,065	3,140	3,073
Official creditors	1,800	2,322	2,304	2,540	2,618	2,552
Multilateral	943	1,012	1,035	1,229	1,332	1,389
of which: World Bank	377	333	342	356	358	369
Bilateral	856	1,309	1,269	1,311	1,286	1,163
Private creditors	6	523	522	525	523	521
Bondholders	..	500	500	500	500	500
Commercial banks and others	6	23	22	25	23	21
Private nonguaranteed debt from:	927	2,190	2,298	2,387	2,396	2,437
Bondholders	..	..	..	..	..	..
Commercial banks and others	927	2,190	2,298	2,387	2,396	2,437
Use of IMF credit and SDR allocations	227	170	144	330	545	516
IMF credit	101	56	31	212	197	185
SDR allocations	126	114	114	118	348	331
Short-term external debt stocks	601	882	1,364	1,122	889	718
Disbursements, long-term	924	538	454	484	513	396
Public and publicly guaranteed sector	251	182	121	275	243	193
Private sector not guaranteed	673	356	332	209	271	204
Principal repayments, long-term	631	402	383	228	375	351
Public and publicly guaranteed sector	37	128	129	103	144	188
Private sector not guaranteed	593	274	254	124	230	162
Interest payments, long-term	54	121	109	91	113	119
Public and publicly guaranteed sector	23	72	75	61	77	79
Private sector not guaranteed	31	49	33	30	37	41

TANZANIA

(US$ million, unless otherwise indicated)

Snapshot	2022
Total external debt stocks	**30,170**
External debt stocks as % of	
Exports	248
GNI	41
Debt service as % of	
Exports	16
GNI	3
Net financial flows, debt and equity	**3,359**
Net debt inflows	2,095
Net equity inflows	1,265
GNI	**74,427**
Population (million)	**65**

Figure 1 Public and publicly guaranteed debt, by creditor and creditor type in 2022, including IMF credit

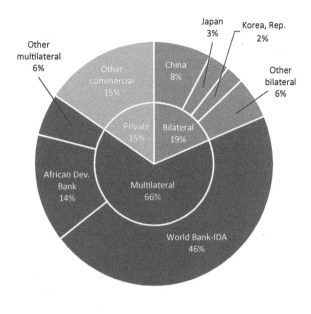

Figure 2 Average terms on new debt commitments from official and private creditors

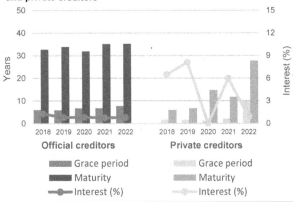

Summary External Debt Data	2010	2018	2019	2020	2021	2022
Total external debt stocks	**8,937**	**22,363**	**24,174**	**25,546**	**28,506**	**30,170**
Long-term external debt stocks	**6,922**	**19,416**	**21,081**	**22,121**	**23,586**	**24,436**
Public and publicly guaranteed debt from:	5,698	15,311	16,853	17,630	18,935	19,455
Official creditors	5,563	13,645	14,285	15,305	15,488	16,322
Multilateral	4,412	9,385	10,088	11,176	11,452	12,556
of which: World Bank	3,248	6,815	7,341	8,148	8,290	9,228
Bilateral	1,152	4,259	4,197	4,129	4,036	3,766
Private creditors	135	1,667	2,569	2,325	3,446	3,133
Bondholders	..	..	..	..	..	..
Commercial banks and others	135	1,667	2,569	2,325	3,446	3,133
Private nonguaranteed debt from:	1,224	4,105	4,228	4,491	4,651	4,981
Bondholders	..	..	..	..	..	..
Commercial banks and others	1,224	4,105	4,228	4,491	4,651	4,981
Use of IMF credit and SDR allocations	**647**	**364**	**301**	**274**	**1,357**	**1,444**
IMF credit	354	99	37	0	557	683
SDR allocations	293	265	263	274	800	761
Short-term external debt stocks	**1,368**	**2,582**	**2,792**	**3,151**	**3,563**	**4,290**
Disbursements, long-term	**1,347**	**1,783**	**2,502**	**1,448**	**3,031**	**2,971**
Public and publicly guaranteed sector	1,131	1,601	2,360	1,169	2,847	2,288
Private sector not guaranteed	216	183	143	279	184	683
Principal repayments, long-term	**132**	**640**	**784**	**866**	**1,243**	**1,534**
Public and publicly guaranteed sector	52	620	764	851	1,219	1,180
Private sector not guaranteed	79	20	20	15	25	353
Interest payments, long-term	**51**	**309**	**381**	**350**	**324**	**417**
Public and publicly guaranteed sector	33	301	375	348	321	365
Private sector not guaranteed	17	8	6	2	4	52

THAILAND

(US$ million, unless otherwise indicated)

Snapshot	2022
Total external debt stocks	**192,078**
External debt stocks as % of	
Exports	57
GNI	40
Debt service as % of	
Exports	13
GNI	9
Net financial flows, debt and equity	**3,501**
Net debt inflows	-13,013
Net equity inflows	16,513
GNI	**481,000**
Population (million)	**72**

Figure 2 Average terms on new debt commitments from official and private creditors

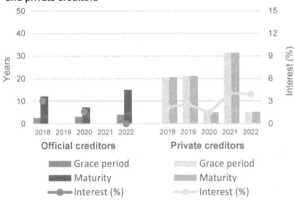

Official creditors — Private creditors

- ▬ Grace period (Official)   ▬ Grace period (Private)
- ▬ Maturity (Official)   ▬ Maturity (Private)
- —●— Interest (%) (Official)   —●— Interest (%) (Private)

Figure 1 Public and publicly guaranteed debt, by creditor and creditor type in 2022, including IMF credit

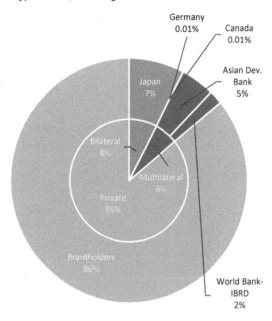

Germany 0.01%
Canada 0.01%
Asian Dev. Bank 5%
Japan 7%
Bilateral 8%
Multilateral 6%
Private 86%
Bondholders 86%
World Bank-IBRD 2%

Summary External Debt Data	2010	2018	2019	2020	2021	2022
Total external debt stocks	**107,166**	**181,636**	**177,871**	**197,234**	**205,810**	**192,078**
Long-term external debt stocks	**55,015**	**116,882**	**116,747**	**121,022**	**125,394**	**108,081**
Public and publicly guaranteed debt from:	16,737	37,509	41,187	36,127	36,817	35,979
Official creditors	6,881	5,094	4,445	4,428	5,359	5,048
Multilateral	187	1,313	1,191	1,068	2,440	2,316
of which: World Bank	128	1,018	927	837	750	666
Bilateral	6,693	3,781	3,254	3,359	2,918	2,732
Private creditors	9,856	32,414	36,742	31,699	31,458	30,931
Bondholders	8,812	32,414	36,742	31,699	31,458	30,931
Commercial banks and others	1,045	..	..	..	..	..
Private nonguaranteed debt from:	38,278	79,373	75,560	84,895	88,577	72,101
Bondholders	4,265	12,723	13,193	15,840	17,747	17,080
Commercial banks and others	34,012	66,650	62,367	69,055	70,830	55,022
Use of IMF credit and SDR allocations	**1,494**	**1,349**	**1,342**	**1,397**	**5,667**	**5,388**
IMF credit	0	0	0	0	0	0
SDR allocations	1,494	1,349	1,342	1,397	5,667	5,388
Short-term external debt stocks	**50,657**	**63,405**	**59,782**	**74,814**	**74,749**	**78,609**
Disbursements, long-term	**17,539**	**40,800**	**28,608**	**24,053**	**24,072**	**22,136**
Public and publicly guaranteed sector	5,941	7,452	4,560	542	2,430	882
Private sector not guaranteed	11,597	33,348	24,049	23,512	21,642	21,254
Principal repayments, long-term	**9,386**	**16,891**	**28,803**	**19,995**	**16,351**	**39,010**
Public and publicly guaranteed sector	803	913	941	5,772	1,435	1,312
Private sector not guaranteed	8,582	15,979	27,862	14,223	14,917	37,698
Interest payments, long-term	**1,079**	**1,227**	**1,695**	**1,648**	**791**	**1,085**
Public and publicly guaranteed sector	202	760	1,114	1,077	109	293
Private sector not guaranteed	877	467	581	571	682	792

161

TIMOR-LESTE

(US$ million, unless otherwise indicated)

Snapshot	2022
Total external debt stocks	**289.7**
External debt stocks as % of	
Exports	12.0
GNI	9.2
Debt service as % of	
Exports	0.6
GNI	0.5
Net financial flows, debt and equity	**282.3**
Net debt inflows	19.9
Net equity inflows	262.5
GNI	**3,133.5**
Population (million)	**1.3**

Figure 1 **Public and publicly guaranteed debt, by creditor and creditor type in 2022, including IMF credit**

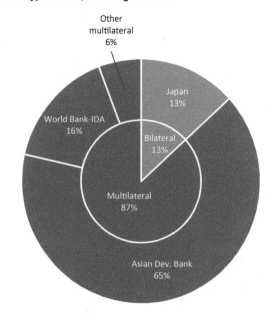

Figure 2 **Average terms on new debt commitments from official and private creditors**

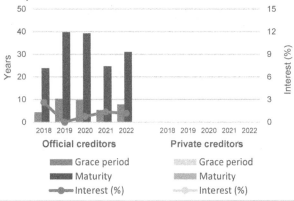

Summary External Debt Data	2010	2018	2019	2020	2021	2022
Total external debt stocks	..	**158.1**	**203.4**	**231.8**	**278.6**	**289.7**
Long-term external debt stocks	..	**144.7**	**191.2**	**220.2**	**232.4**	**246.4**
Public and publicly guaranteed debt from:	..	144.7	191.2	220.2	232.4	246.4
Official creditors	..	144.7	191.2	220.2	232.4	246.4
Multilateral	..	131.5	166.3	189.4	200.6	214.0
of which: World Bank	..	33.5	43.2	47.6	50.7	53.0
Bilateral	..	13.2	24.9	30.9	31.8	32.5
Private creditors	..	..	..	..	..	..
Bondholders	..	..	..	..	..	..
Commercial banks and others	..	..	..	..	..	..
Private nonguaranteed debt from:	..	..	..	..	..	..
Bondholders	..	..	..	..	..	..
Commercial banks and others	..	..	..	..	..	..
Use of IMF credit and SDR allocations	..	**10.7**	**10.7**	**11.1**	**45.2**	**42.9**
IMF credit	..	0.0	0.0	0.0	0.0	0.0
SDR allocations	..	10.7	10.7	11.1	45.2	42.9
Short-term external debt stocks	..	**2.6**	**1.5**	**0.4**	**1.1**	**0.3**
Disbursements, long-term	..	**40.0**	**49.7**	**30.1**	**22.6**	**31.0**
Public and publicly guaranteed sector	..	40.0	49.7	30.1	22.6	31.0
Private sector not guaranteed	..	..	..	..	..	..
Principal repayments, long-term	..	**0.7**	**3.3**	**3.9**	**6.4**	**10.5**
Public and publicly guaranteed sector	..	0.7	3.3	3.9	6.4	10.5
Private sector not guaranteed	..	..	..	..	..	..
Interest payments, long-term	..	**2.5**	**3.8**	**4.1**	**3.2**	**4.0**
Public and publicly guaranteed sector	..	2.5	3.8	4.1	3.2	4.0
Private sector not guaranteed	..	..	..	..	..	..

TOGO

(US$ million, unless otherwise indicated)

Snapshot	2022
Total external debt stocks	3,118
External debt stocks as % of	
Exports	156
GNI	38
Debt service as % of	
Exports	12
GNI	3
Net financial flows, debt and equity	**-409**
Net debt inflows	-182
Net equity inflows	-227
GNI	**8,148**
Population (million)	**9**

Figure 2 **Average terms on new debt commitments from official and private creditors**

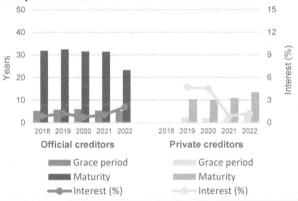

Figure 1 **Public and publicly guaranteed debt, by creditor and creditor type in 2022, including IMF credit**

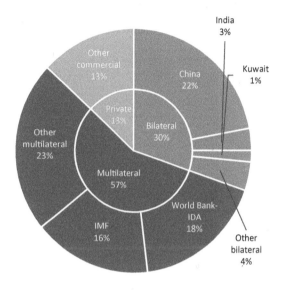

Summary External Debt Data	2010	2018	2019	2020	2021	2022
Total external debt stocks	**1,279**	**1,701**	**1,990**	**2,508**	**3,413**	**3,118**
Long-term external debt stocks	999	1,156	1,347	1,729	2,369	2,341
Public and publicly guaranteed debt from:	999	1,156	1,347	1,729	1,719	1,691
Official creditors	999	1,153	1,230	1,420	1,433	1,426
Multilateral	852	533	626	785	776	816
of which: World Bank	554	66	165	265	288	360
Bilateral	147	620	604	635	657	610
Private creditors	..	4	116	309	286	265
Bondholders	..	..	..	..	..	..
Commercial banks and others	..	4	116	309	286	265
Private nonguaranteed debt from:	..	..	..	..	650	650
Bondholders	..	..	..	..	650	650
Commercial banks and others	..	..	..	..	..	..
Use of IMF credit and SDR allocations	241	266	319	459	642	607
IMF credit	133	168	222	358	347	326
SDR allocations	108	98	97	101	295	281
Short-term external debt stocks	39	278	324	320	402	170
Disbursements, long-term	**91**	**110**	**263**	**338**	**770**	**193**
Public and publicly guaranteed sector	91	110	263	338	120	193
Private sector not guaranteed	..	..	..	..	650	..
Principal repayments, long-term	**28**	**55**	**60**	**53**	**71**	**140**
Public and publicly guaranteed sector	28	55	60	53	71	140
Private sector not guaranteed	..	..	..	..	..	..
Interest payments, long-term	**8**	**27**	**26**	**33**	**89**	**89**
Public and publicly guaranteed sector	8	27	26	33	37	37
Private sector not guaranteed	..	..	..	..	52	52

(US$ million, unless otherwise indicated)

Snapshot	2022
Total external debt stocks	**209.9**
External debt stocks as % of	
Exports	214.7
GNI	..
Debt service as % of	
Exports	11.3
GNI	..
Net financial flows, debt and equity	**5.0**
Net debt inflows	1.5
Net equity inflows	3.5
GNI	..
Population (thousand)	**106.9**

Figure 1 Public and publicly guaranteed debt, by creditor and creditor type in 2022, including IMF credit

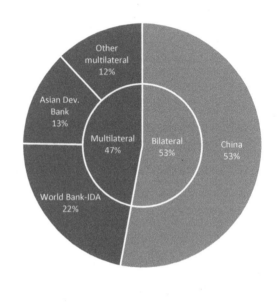

Figure 2 Average terms on new debt commitments from official and private creditors

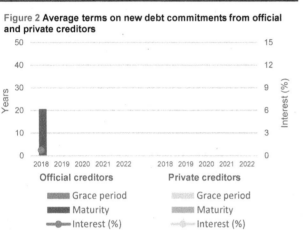

Summary External Debt Data	2010	2018	2019	2020	2021	2022
Total external debt stocks	**153.7**	**187.0**	**186.6**	**194.6**	**223.6**	**209.9**
Long-term external debt stocks	**143.5**	**177.8**	**177.5**	**185.1**	**186.2**	**165.2**
Public and publicly guaranteed debt from:	143.5	177.8	177.5	185.1	186.2	165.2
Official creditors	142.4	177.8	177.5	185.1	186.2	165.2
Multilateral	70.8	74.2	75.9	77.5	73.7	67.8
of which: World Bank	23.6	39.1	42.9	45.0	43.6	40.8
Bilateral	71.7	103.6	101.6	107.6	112.6	97.4
Private creditors	1.1	..	..	..	..	..
Bondholders	..	..	..	..	..	..
Commercial banks and others	1.1	..	..	..	..	..
Private nonguaranteed debt from:	..	..	..	..	..	..
Bondholders	..	..	..	..	..	..
Commercial banks and others	..	..	..	..	..	..
Use of IMF credit and SDR allocations	**10.1**	**9.2**	**9.1**	**9.5**	**37.4**	**44.7**
IMF credit	0.0	0.0	0.0	0.0	9.7	18.4
SDR allocations	10.1	9.2	9.1	9.5	27.7	26.4
Short-term external debt stocks	**0.0**	**0.0**	**0.0**	**0.0**	**0.0**	**0.0**
Disbursements, long-term	**40.9**	**7.5**	**4.9**	**1.3**	**1.0**	**0.3**
Public and publicly guaranteed sector	40.9	7.5	4.9	1.3	1.0	0.3
Private sector not guaranteed	..	..	..	..	..	..
Principal repayments, long-term	**2.7**	**6.2**	**2.7**	**4.7**	**2.7**	**8.1**
Public and publicly guaranteed sector	2.7	6.2	2.7	4.7	2.7	8.1
Private sector not guaranteed	..	..	..	..	..	..
Interest payments, long-term	**2.4**	**3.3**	**2.7**	**1.3**	**2.1**	**2.7**
Public and publicly guaranteed sector	2.4	3.3	2.7	1.3	2.1	2.7
Private sector not guaranteed	..	..	..	..	..	..

TUNISIA

(US$ million, unless otherwise indicated)

Snapshot	2022
Total external debt stocks	**39,652**
External debt stocks as % of	
Exports	170
GNI	87
Debt service as % of	
Exports	18
GNI	9
Net financial flows, debt and equity	**20**
Net debt inflows	-694
Net equity inflows	713
GNI	**45,435**
Population (million)	**12**

Figure 1 **Public and publicly guaranteed debt, by creditor and creditor type in 2022, including IMF credit**

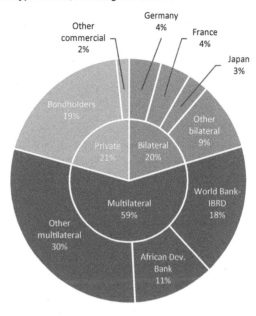

Figure 2 **Average terms on new debt commitments from official and private creditors**

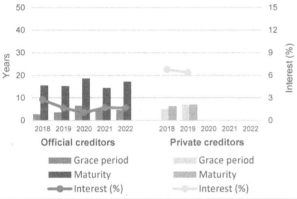

Summary External Debt Data	2010	2018	2019	2020	2021	2022
Total external debt stocks	**22,666**	**35,052**	**39,445**	**41,117**	**41,668**	**39,652**
Long-term external debt stocks	**17,267**	**24,679**	**25,882**	**27,661**	**24,783**	**22,860**
Public and publicly guaranteed debt from:	14,865	22,597	23,815	25,773	23,125	21,522
Official creditors	10,389	14,626	15,888	18,269	17,338	16,624
Multilateral	6,985	10,998	11,338	12,825	12,119	11,799
of which: World Bank	1,399	3,515	3,489	4,196	4,063	4,136
Bilateral	3,404	3,628	4,550	5,444	5,219	4,825
Private creditors	4,476	7,971	7,926	7,504	5,787	4,897
Bondholders	3,819	7,239	7,278	6,877	5,275	4,485
Commercial banks and others	657	732	648	626	512	412
Private nonguaranteed debt from:	2,402	2,082	2,067	1,888	1,658	1,338
Bondholders	..	..	..	..	..	..
Commercial banks and others	2,402	2,082	2,067	1,888	1,658	1,338
Use of IMF credit and SDR allocations	**420**	**2,280**	**2,132**	**2,824**	**3,396**	**3,109**
IMF credit	0	1,901	1,755	2,431	2,283	2,050
SDR allocations	420	379	377	393	1,113	1,058
Short-term external debt stocks	**4,979**	**8,093**	**11,431**	**10,632**	**13,489**	**13,683**
Disbursements, long-term	**1,671**	**2,619**	**3,788**	**2,436**	**1,791**	**1,975**
Public and publicly guaranteed sector	1,574	2,377	3,366	2,305	1,744	1,924
Private sector not guaranteed	97	242	422	130	47	50
Principal repayments, long-term	**1,631**	**1,700**	**1,931**	**2,160**	**3,409**	**2,742**
Public and publicly guaranteed sector	1,411	1,381	1,931	1,814	2,908	2,294
Private sector not guaranteed	220	319	..	346	501	448
Interest payments, long-term	**672**	**603**	**666**	**659**	**622**	**586**
Public and publicly guaranteed sector	548	550	573	583	557	528
Private sector not guaranteed	124	53	94	76	65	58

TÜRKIYE

(US$ million, unless otherwise indicated)

Snapshot	2022
Total external debt stocks	**458,699**
External debt stocks as % of	
Exports	130
GNI	51
Debt service as % of	
Exports	20
GNI	8
Net financial flows, debt and equity	**37,404**
Net debt inflows	29,245
Net equity inflows	8,159
GNI	**897,467**
Population (million)	**85**

Figure 2 Average terms on new debt commitments from official and private creditors

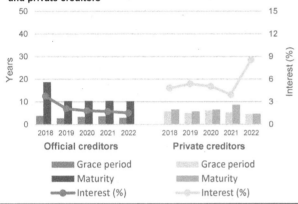

Figure 1 Public and publicly guaranteed debt, by creditor and creditor type in 2022, including IMF credit

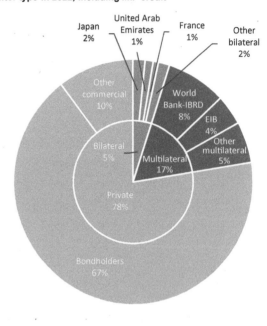

Summary External Debt Data	2010	2018	2019	2020	2021	2022
Total external debt stocks	**316,657**	**425,779**	**414,618**	**429,422**	**437,507**	**458,699**
Long-term external debt stocks	**216,379**	**332,135**	**317,298**	**316,531**	**311,528**	**303,125**
Public and publicly guaranteed debt from:	93,299	123,360	128,885	138,043	139,215	140,057
Official creditors	26,941	34,841	34,632	35,015	32,554	31,506
Multilateral	19,932	28,576	27,133	27,963	25,720	24,579
of which: World Bank	11,605	11,685	11,362	11,925	11,179	11,262
Bilateral	7,009	6,265	7,499	7,053	6,834	6,927
Private creditors	66,358	88,519	94,253	103,028	106,661	108,551
Bondholders	45,774	78,306	83,806	89,850	91,612	94,094
Commercial banks and others	20,584	10,212	10,446	13,178	15,049	14,457
Private nonguaranteed debt from:	123,080	208,775	188,413	178,488	172,313	163,068
Bondholders	6,202	38,894	36,115	34,660	34,011	27,241
Commercial banks and others	116,878	169,881	152,298	143,828	138,302	135,827
Use of IMF credit and SDR allocations	**7,277**	**1,490**	**1,481**	**1,543**	**7,749**	**7,368**
IMF credit	5,627	0	0	0	0	0
SDR allocations	1,650	1,490	1,481	1,543	7,749	7,368
Short-term external debt stocks	**93,001**	**92,154**	**95,839**	**111,349**	**118,231**	**148,206**
Disbursements, long-term	**48,834**	**69,893**	**60,814**	**59,797**	**56,326**	**50,762**
Public and publicly guaranteed sector	14,795	17,169	19,145	18,128	20,636	18,704
Private sector not guaranteed	34,039	52,725	41,669	41,669	35,690	32,059
Principal repayments, long-term	**45,504**	**67,995**	**69,245**	**68,780**	**56,166**	**51,493**
Public and publicly guaranteed sector	6,028	10,843	12,932	12,476	15,986	15,078
Private sector not guaranteed	39,476	57,152	56,313	56,303	40,179	36,414
Interest payments, long-term	**8,869**	**11,538**	**12,673**	**12,767**	**11,866**	**11,755**
Public and publicly guaranteed sector	4,693	4,891	5,544	5,743	6,064	6,318
Private sector not guaranteed	4,177	6,647	7,129	7,024	5,802	5,437

TURKMENISTAN

(US$ million, unless otherwise indicated)

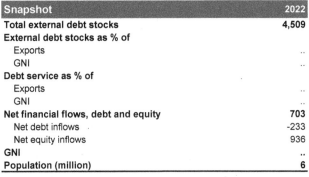

Snapshot	2022
Total external debt stocks	4,509
External debt stocks as % of	
Exports	..
GNI	..
Debt service as % of	
Exports	..
GNI	..
Net financial flows, debt and equity	703
Net debt inflows	-233
Net equity inflows	936
GNI	..
Population (million)	6

Figure 2 Average terms on new debt commitments from official and private creditors

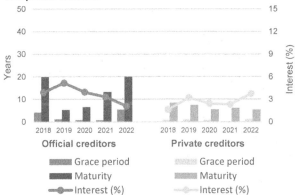

Figure 1 Public and publicly guaranteed debt, by creditor and creditor type in 2022, including IMF credit

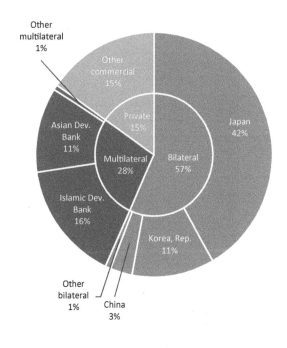

Summary External Debt Data	2010	2018	2019	2020	2021	2022
Total external debt stocks	1,682	8,160	6,516	5,636	4,851	4,509
Long-term external debt stocks	1,520	7,757	6,419	5,394	4,433	4,012
Public and publicly guaranteed debt from:	1,513	7,722	6,376	5,342	4,386	3,987
Official creditors	1,513	7,356	5,875	4,726	3,778	3,373
Multilateral	96	432	471	673	805	1,110
of which: World Bank	11	..	..	..	15	20
Bilateral	1,417	6,924	5,404	4,053	2,973	2,263
Private creditors	0	367	501	616	608	614
Bondholders	0	..	..	..	..	..
Commercial banks and others	0	367	501	616	608	614
Private nonguaranteed debt from:	7	35	43	51	47	25
Bondholders	..	..	..	..	..	..
Commercial banks and others	7	35	43	51	47	25
Use of IMF credit and SDR allocations	108	97	97	101	418	397
IMF credit	0	0	0	0	0	0
SDR allocations	108	97	97	101	418	397
Short-term external debt stocks	54	306	0	142	0	100
Disbursements, long-term	1,051	1,095	518	747	552	610
Public and publicly guaranteed sector	1,044	1,089	498	729	540	610
Private sector not guaranteed	8	7	20	18	12	..
Principal repayments, long-term	148	1,460	1,804	1,850	1,447	943
Public and publicly guaranteed sector	135	1,437	1,793	1,839	1,423	919
Private sector not guaranteed	13	23	12	11	23	24
Interest payments, long-term	50	364	355	240	205	185
Public and publicly guaranteed sector	50	363	354	239	204	184
Private sector not guaranteed	0	1	1	1	1	0

UGANDA

(US$ million, unless otherwise indicated)

Snapshot	2022
Total external debt stocks	**20,715**
External debt stocks as % of	
Exports	341
GNI	46
Debt service as % of	
Exports	16
GNI	2
Net financial flows, debt and equity	**2,269**
Net debt inflows	964
Net equity inflows	1,304
GNI	**44,778**
Population (million)	**47**

Figure 1 **Public and publicly guaranteed debt, by creditor and creditor type in 2022, including IMF credit**

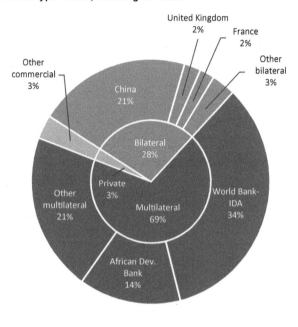

Figure 2 **Average terms on new debt commitments from official and private creditors**

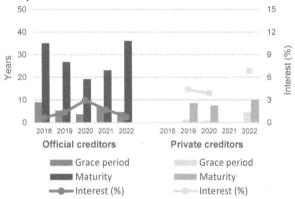

Summary External Debt Data	2010	2018	2019	2020	2021	2022
Total external debt stocks	**2,975**	**12,315**	**13,971**	**17,597**	**20,323**	**20,715**
Long-term external debt stocks	**2,673**	**11,566**	**12,780**	**15,637**	**17,066**	**17,459**
Public and publicly guaranteed debt from:	2,673	7,701	8,638	11,726	12,377	12,263
Official creditors	2,673	7,650	8,555	11,206	11,890	11,853
Multilateral	2,416	5,039	5,654	7,583	8,196	8,166
of which: World Bank	1,682	3,095	3,443	4,300	4,453	4,464
Bilateral	257	2,612	2,901	3,623	3,694	3,687
Private creditors	0	50	83	519	487	410
Bondholders	..	..	..	..	..	..
Commercial banks and others	..	50	83	519	487	410
Private nonguaranteed debt from:	..	3,865	4,142	3,911	4,690	5,197
Bondholders	..	..	..	..	..	..
Commercial banks and others	..	3,865	4,142	3,911	4,690	5,197
Use of IMF credit and SDR allocations	**275**	**241**	**239**	**769**	**1,484**	**1,532**
IMF credit	9	0	0	520	758	841
SDR allocations	267	241	239	249	726	691
Short-term external debt stocks	**26**	**509**	**952**	**1,191**	**1,772**	**1,724**
Disbursements, long-term	**489**	**1,167**	**1,411**	**2,851**	**2,132**	**1,367**
Public and publicly guaranteed sector	489	1,167	1,134	2,851	1,353	860
Private sector not guaranteed	..	..	277	..	778	507
Principal repayments, long-term	**40**	**422**	**166**	**402**	**339**	**474**
Public and publicly guaranteed sector	40	224	166	171	339	474
Private sector not guaranteed	..	199	..	231	..	..
Interest payments, long-term	**21**	**98**	**115**	**274**	**407**	**384**
Public and publicly guaranteed sector	21	98	115	149	280	218
Private sector not guaranteed	..	..	..	125	128	166

UKRAINE

(US$ million, unless otherwise indicated)

Snapshot	2022
Total external debt stocks	**139,595**
External debt stocks as % of	
Exports	199
GNI	83
Debt service as % of	
Exports	18
GNI	7
Net financial flows, debt and equity	**5,812**
Net debt inflows	5,035
Net equity inflows	777
GNI	**169,196**
Population (million)	**38**

Figure 2 Average terms on new debt commitments from official and private creditors

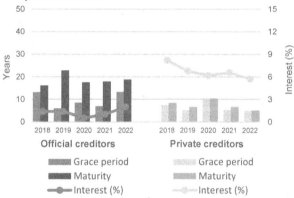

Figure 1 Public and publicly guaranteed debt, by creditor and creditor type in 2022, including IMF credit

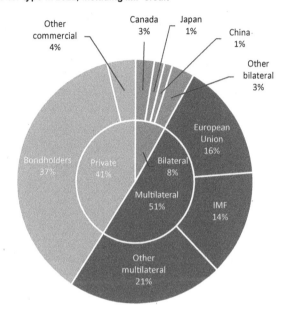

Summary External Debt Data	2010	2018	2019	2020	2021	2022
Total external debt stocks	**124,527**	**121,887**	**124,900**	**132,410**	**135,706**	**139,595**
Long-term external debt stocks	**81,001**	**88,200**	**91,546**	**96,180**	**98,933**	**109,732**
Public and publicly guaranteed debt from:	25,327	37,003	39,209	42,284	44,691	61,911
Official creditors	14,961	13,775	13,156	14,675	15,716	32,445
Multilateral	13,560	11,077	10,480	12,159	13,325	26,539
of which: World Bank	3,212	5,335	5,360	5,741	6,623	8,773
Bilateral	1,400	2,698	2,677	2,516	2,391	5,906
Private creditors	10,366	23,228	26,053	27,609	28,976	29,465
Bondholders	9,058	22,467	24,483	25,613	26,944	26,655
Commercial banks and others	1,308	761	1,569	1,996	2,031	2,810
Private nonguaranteed debt from:	55,674	51,197	52,337	53,897	54,241	47,822
Bondholders	4,313	4,519	5,635	5,294	4,833	4,654
Commercial banks and others	51,361	46,678	46,702	48,603	49,409	43,168
Use of IMF credit and SDR allocations	**16,262**	**12,997**	**11,328**	**12,824**	**14,505**	**14,434**
IMF credit	14,245	11,176	9,518	10,938	9,974	10,125
SDR allocations	2,017	1,821	1,811	1,886	4,531	4,309
Short-term external debt stocks	**27,264**	**20,690**	**22,025**	**23,406**	**22,268**	**15,429**
Disbursements, long-term	**32,240**	**9,172**	**11,203**	**16,500**	**12,820**	**19,049**
Public and publicly guaranteed sector	7,969	3,736	5,367	7,056	6,373	19,049
Private sector not guaranteed	24,272	5,437	5,836	9,444	6,447	..
Principal repayments, long-term	**22,885**	**8,921**	**8,350**	**12,445**	**8,992**	**7,528**
Public and publicly guaranteed sector	1,446	3,678	3,075	4,987	2,940	1,129
Private sector not guaranteed	21,439	5,243	5,275	7,458	6,052	6,399
Interest payments, long-term	**3,532**	**2,824**	**3,187**	**3,372**	**3,649**	**1,972**
Public and publicly guaranteed sector	594	1,479	1,699	1,893	2,126	1,268
Private sector not guaranteed	2,938	1,345	1,488	1,479	1,523	704

UZBEKISTAN

(US$ million, unless otherwise indicated)

Snapshot	2022
Total external debt stocks	**49,099**
External debt stocks as % of	
Exports	188
GNI	60
Debt service as % of	
Exports	28
GNI	9
Net financial flows, debt and equity	**10,460**
Net debt inflows	8,687
Net equity inflows	1,773
GNI	**81,289**
Population (million)	**36**

Figure 1 **Public and publicly guaranteed debt, by creditor and creditor type in 2022, including IMF credit**

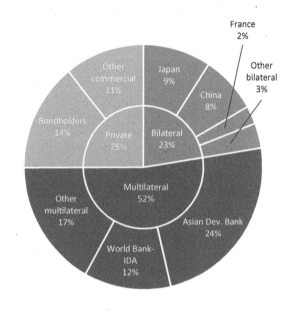

Figure 2 **Average terms on new debt commitments from official and private creditors**

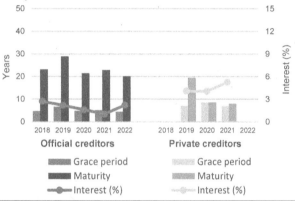

Summary External Debt Data	2010	2018	2019	2020	2021	2022
Total external debt stocks	**7,981**	**17,606**	**22,957**	**33,711**	**40,842**	**49,099**
Long-term external debt stocks	**7,154**	**16,343**	**21,921**	**30,560**	**35,786**	**41,505**
Public and publicly guaranteed debt from:	3,423	9,282	13,343	18,731	21,924	24,895
Official creditors	3,197	9,084	11,560	14,728	16,022	18,557
Multilateral	1,210	5,410	7,030	9,246	10,086	12,884
of which: World Bank	373	1,907	2,723	3,734	4,328	5,528
Bilateral	1,987	3,674	4,530	5,481	5,936	5,673
Private creditors	226	199	1,783	4,003	5,902	6,338
Bondholders	..	..	1,000	2,048	3,618	3,618
Commercial banks and others	226	199	783	1,955	2,284	2,720
Private nonguaranteed debt from:	3,730	7,061	8,579	11,829	13,862	16,610
Bondholders	..	..	300	600	900	900
Commercial banks and others	3,730	7,061	8,279	11,229	12,962	15,710
Use of IMF credit and SDR allocations	**405**	**365**	**363**	**775**	**1,493**	**1,420**
IMF credit	0	0	0	397	386	367
SDR allocations	405	365	363	378	1,107	1,053
Short-term external debt stocks	**423**	**897**	**673**	**2,376**	**3,562**	**6,175**
Disbursements, long-term	**1,191**	**2,834**	**7,331**	**9,359**	**10,379**	**11,996**
Public and publicly guaranteed sector	455	2,504	4,485	5,637	4,310	4,241
Private sector not guaranteed	736	330	2,846	3,722	6,069	7,755
Principal repayments, long-term	**493**	**691**	**1,950**	**2,363**	**3,689**	**5,904**
Public and publicly guaranteed sector	370	382	429	520	740	772
Private sector not guaranteed	123	309	1,521	1,842	2,950	5,132
Interest payments, long-term	**118**	**284**	**669**	**756**	**826**	**1,102**
Public and publicly guaranteed sector	63	144	257	303	350	482
Private sector not guaranteed	55	141	412	453	476	619

VANUATU

(US$ million, unless otherwise indicated)

Snapshot	2022
Total external debt stocks	**484.5**
External debt stocks as % of	
Exports	139.2
GNI	42.9
Debt service as % of	
Exports	6.8
GNI	2.1
Net financial flows, debt and equity	**26.0**
Net debt inflows	30.1
Net equity inflows	-4.1
GNI	**1,130.1**
Population (thousand)	**326.7**

Figure 1 Public and publicly guaranteed debt, by creditor and creditor type in 2022, including IMF credit

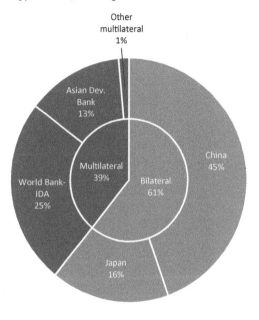

Figure 2 Average terms on new debt commitments from official and private creditors

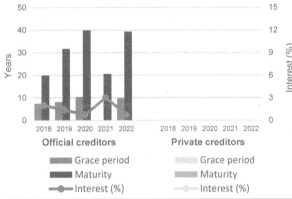

Summary External Debt Data	2010	2018	2019	2020	2021	2022
Total external debt stocks	**177.7**	**402.2**	**441.3**	**455.7**	**490.9**	**484.5**
Long-term external debt stocks	**102.6**	**313.8**	**362.0**	**382.8**	**388.0**	**395.0**
Public and publicly guaranteed debt from:	102.6	313.8	362.0	382.8	388.0	395.0
Official creditors	102.6	313.8	362.0	382.8	388.0	395.0
Multilateral	68.8	101.8	135.0	145.2	148.4	151.1
of which: World Bank	11.7	54.7	83.0	91.6	97.9	98.2
Bilateral	33.8	212.0	227.0	237.6	239.5	243.9
Private creditors	..	..	..	..	..	..
Bondholders	..	..	..	..	..	..
Commercial banks and others	..	..	..	..	..	..
Private nonguaranteed debt from:	..	..	..	..	..	..
Bondholders	..	..	..	..	..	..
Commercial banks and others	..	..	..	..	..	..
Use of IMF credit and SDR allocations	**25.1**	**43.3**	**37.2**	**34.4**	**63.0**	**57.7**
IMF credit	0.0	20.7	14.7	11.0	8.3	5.7
SDR allocations	25.1	22.6	22.5	23.4	54.7	52.0
Short-term external debt stocks	**50.0**	**45.1**	**42.1**	**38.4**	**39.9**	**31.8**
Disbursements, long-term	**3.3**	**46.4**	**55.0**	**10.7**	**25.5**	**55.4**
Public and publicly guaranteed sector	3.3	46.4	55.0	10.7	25.5	55.4
Private sector not guaranteed	..	..	..	..	..	..
Principal repayments, long-term	**3.6**	**12.0**	**4.7**	**10.0**	**12.5**	**14.9**
Public and publicly guaranteed sector	3.6	12.0	4.7	10.0	12.5	14.9
Private sector not guaranteed	..	..	..	..	..	..
Interest payments, long-term	**1.6**	**4.2**	**4.3**	**4.4**	**4.5**	**5.5**
Public and publicly guaranteed sector	1.6	4.2	4.3	4.4	4.5	5.5
Private sector not guaranteed	..	..	..	..	..	..

VIET NAM

(US$ million, unless otherwise indicated)

Snapshot	2022
Total external debt stocks	**146,589**
External debt stocks as % of	
Exports	38
GNI	38
Debt service as % of	
Exports	7
GNI	7
Net financial flows, debt and equity	**24,925**
Net debt inflows	9,905
Net equity inflows	15,020
GNI	**389,074**
Population (million)	**98**

Figure 1 Public and publicly guaranteed debt, by creditor and creditor type in 2022, including IMF credit

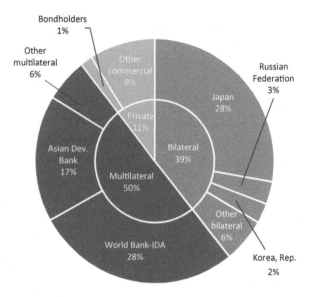

Figure 2 Average terms on new debt commitments from official and private creditors

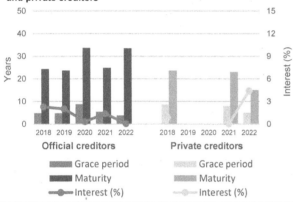

Summary External Debt Data	2010	2018	2019	2020	2021	2022
Total external debt stocks	**45,022**	**112,588**	**122,454**	**129,435**	**139,812**	**146,589**
Long-term external debt stocks	**37,560**	**92,566**	**97,621**	**102,378**	**104,592**	**106,545**
Public and publicly guaranteed debt from:	32,805	56,585	55,782	55,608	51,334	46,427
Official creditors	27,320	47,790	47,779	49,141	45,755	41,533
Multilateral	12,573	23,719	24,068	25,339	24,615	23,311
of which: World Bank	7,743	14,968	15,327	16,378	16,008	15,109
Bilateral	14,746	24,071	23,711	23,802	21,141	18,222
Private creditors	5,485	8,795	8,003	6,467	5,578	4,894
Bondholders	2,020	1,511	1,506	756	751	746
Commercial banks and others	3,465	7,284	6,497	5,711	4,827	4,148
Private nonguaranteed debt from:	4,755	35,980	41,839	46,771	53,258	60,118
Bondholders	..	35	1,014	1,094	1,444	1,769
Commercial banks and others	4,755	35,945	40,825	45,677	51,814	58,349
Use of IMF credit and SDR allocations	**529**	**438**	**435**	**453**	**1,987**	**1,890**
IMF credit	45	0	0	0	0	0
SDR allocations	485	438	435	453	1,987	1,890
Short-term external debt stocks	**6,932**	**19,585**	**24,397**	**26,604**	**33,233**	**38,154**
Disbursements, long-term	**6,965**	**20,775**	**18,624**	**17,323**	**23,264**	**28,471**
Public and publicly guaranteed sector	5,643	3,633	2,346	2,120	1,746	1,779
Private sector not guaranteed	1,322	17,143	16,278	15,202	21,518	26,692
Principal repayments, long-term	**1,055**	**15,225**	**13,607**	**14,386**	**18,777**	**23,488**
Public and publicly guaranteed sector	1,055	2,970	3,188	4,114	3,749	3,659
Private sector not guaranteed	..	12,255	10,420	10,273	15,028	19,829
Interest payments, long-term	**699**	**2,929**	**2,934**	**2,019**	**1,594**	**2,016**
Public and publicly guaranteed sector	554	1,163	1,256	994	755	738
Private sector not guaranteed	145	1,766	1,679	1,025	839	1,278

YEMEN, REPUBLIC OF

(US$ million, unless otherwise indicated)

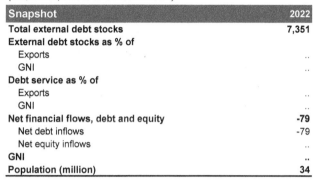

Snapshot	2022
Total external debt stocks	7,351
External debt stocks as % of	
Exports	..
GNI	..
Debt service as % of	
Exports	..
GNI	..
Net financial flows, debt and equity	**-79**
Net debt inflows	-79
Net equity inflows	..
GNI	..
Population (million)	**34**

Figure 1 Public and publicly guaranteed debt; by creditor and creditor type in 2022, including IMF credit

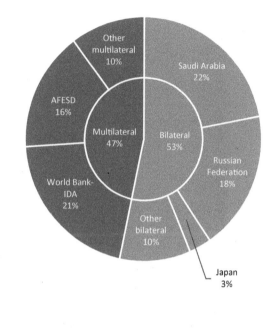

Figure 2 Average terms on new debt commitments from official and private creditors

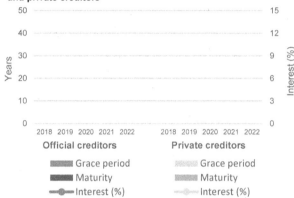

Summary External Debt Data	2010	2018	2019	2020	2021	2022
Total external debt stocks	**6,504**	**7,037**	**7,055**	**7,121**	**7,602**	**7,351**
Long-term external debt stocks	**5,945**	**6,205**	**6,188**	**6,251**	**6,108**	**5,896**
Public and publicly guaranteed debt from:	5,945	6,205	6,188	6,251	6,108	5,896
Official creditors	5,941	6,205	6,188	6,251	6,108	5,896
Multilateral	3,294	3,004	2,987	3,027	2,910	2,739
of which: World Bank	2,180	1,586	1,505	1,488	1,368	1,225
Bilateral	2,647	3,201	3,201	3,224	3,198	3,157
Private creditors	3	..	..	..	..	..
Bondholders	..	..	..	..	..	..
Commercial banks and others	3	..	..	..	..	..
Private nonguaranteed debt from:	..	..	..	..	..	..
Bondholders	..	..	..	..	..	..
Commercial banks and others	..	..	..	..	..	..
Use of IMF credit and SDR allocations	**436**	**469**	**440**	**410**	**1,021**	**956**
IMF credit	78	146	119	75	43	26
SDR allocations	358	323	321	335	978	930
Short-term external debt stocks	**124**	**362**	**427**	**460**	**473**	**499**
Disbursements, long-term	**297**	**19**	**66**	**38**	**13**	**9**
Public and publicly guaranteed sector	297	19	66	38	13	9
Private sector not guaranteed	..	..	..	..	..	..
Principal repayments, long-term	**155**	**71**	**72**	**75**	**80**	**78**
Public and publicly guaranteed sector	155	71	72	75	80	78
Private sector not guaranteed	..	..	..	..	..	..
Interest payments, long-term	**74**	**13**	**12**	**11**	**11**	**9**
Public and publicly guaranteed sector	74	13	12	11	11	9
Private sector not guaranteed	..	..	..	..	..	..

Note: Figure 2 shows no data values because the country did not have new commitments from 2018 to 2022.

ZAMBIA

(US$ million, unless otherwise indicated)

Snapshot	2022
Total external debt stocks	**28,701**
External debt stocks as % of	
Exports	230
GNI	102
Debt service as % of	
Exports	12
GNI	5
Net financial flows, debt and equity	**1,173**
Net debt inflows	666
Net equity inflows	506
GNI	**28,134**
Population (million)	**20**

Figure 2 Average terms on new debt commitments from official and private creditors

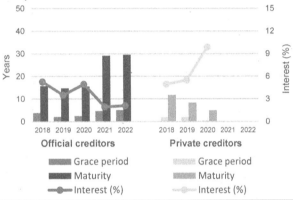

Figure 1 Public and publicly guaranteed debt, by creditor and creditor type in 2022, including IMF credit

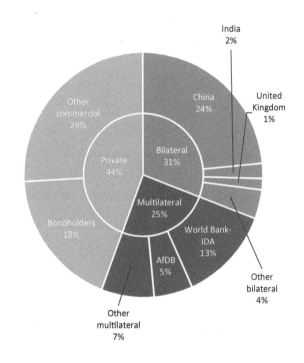

Summary External Debt Data	2010	2018	2019	2020	2021	2022
Total external debt stocks	**4,373**	**25,041**	**29,768**	**29,987**	**27,345**	**28,701**
Long-term external debt stocks	**2,106**	**23,704**	**28,261**	**28,577**	**23,987**	**24,027**
Public and publicly guaranteed debt from:	1,312	11,403	13,525	15,502	15,673	16,129
Official creditors	1,256	5,402	6,575	7,982	8,231	8,910
Multilateral	925	1,923	2,240	3,073	3,164	3,878
of which: World Bank	430	1,003	1,108	1,296	1,377	2,047
Bilateral	331	3,480	4,335	4,908	5,068	5,032
Private creditors	56	6,001	6,951	7,521	7,442	7,219
Bondholders	..	3,000	3,000	3,000	3,000	3,000
Commercial banks and others	56	3,001	3,951	4,521	4,442	4,219
Private nonguaranteed debt from:	794	12,301	14,736	13,074	8,313	7,899
Bondholders	..	..	..	..	..	..
Commercial banks and others	794	12,301	14,736	13,074	8,313	7,899
Use of IMF credit and SDR allocations	**1,117**	**715**	**667**	**678**	**1,969**	**2,058**
IMF credit	395	62	18	3	0	186
SDR allocations	722	652	649	676	1,969	1,872
Short-term external debt stocks	**1,150**	**623**	**840**	**732**	**1,390**	**2,615**
Disbursements, long-term	**251**	**5,326**	**6,584**	**3,318**	**493**	**1,423**
Public and publicly guaranteed sector	224	1,898	2,713	2,175	493	993
Private sector not guaranteed	27	3,428	3,871	1,143	..	431
Principal repayments, long-term	**94**	**722**	**1,844**	**1,567**	**1,510**	**1,192**
Public and publicly guaranteed sector	54	337	567	383	281	347
Private sector not guaranteed	40	385	1,277	1,184	1,230	845
Interest payments, long-term	**31**	**593**	**848**	**479**	**247**	**221**
Public and publicly guaranteed sector	13	503	514	347	120	89
Private sector not guaranteed	18	91	334	132	127	132

ZIMBABWE

(US$ million, unless otherwise indicated)

Snapshot	2022
Total external debt stocks	13,767
External debt stocks as % of	
Exports	185
GNI	68
Debt service as % of	
Exports	5
GNI	2
Net financial flows, debt and equity	586
Net debt inflows	258
Net equity inflows	328
GNI	20,101
Population (million)	16

Figure 1 **Public and publicly guaranteed debt, by creditor and creditor type in 2022, including IMF credit**

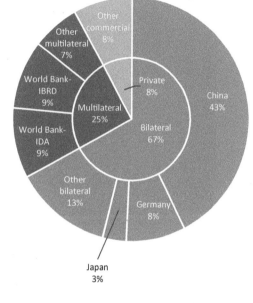

Figure 2 **Average terms on new debt commitments from official and private creditors**

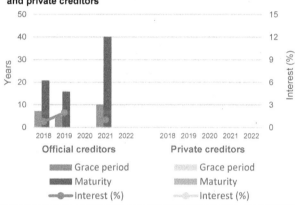

Summary External Debt Data	2010	2018	2019	2020	2021	2022
Total external debt stocks	6,763	12,655	12,286	12,784	13,751	13,767
Long-term external debt stocks	4,405	8,799	8,295	8,441	8,591	8,435
Public and publicly guaranteed debt from:	3,800	4,321	4,406	4,617	4,637	4,713
Official creditors	3,352	3,903	3,994	4,186	4,228	4,333
Multilateral	1,614	1,214	1,202	1,235	1,201	1,169
of which: World Bank	976	896	890	910	893	867
Bilateral	1,738	2,689	2,792	2,951	3,027	3,164
Private creditors	448	418	412	431	408	380
Bondholders	0	0	0	0	0	0
Commercial banks and others	448	418	412	431	408	380
Private nonguaranteed debt from:	605	4,478	3,889	3,825	3,954	3,722
Bondholders	..	..	..	..	..	..
Commercial banks and others	605	4,478	3,889	3,825	3,954	3,722
Use of IMF credit and SDR allocations	529	471	468	488	1,422	1,352
IMF credit	110	0	0	0	0	0
SDR allocations	419	471	468	488	1,422	1,352
Short-term external debt stocks	1,829	3,385	3,523	3,855	3,738	3,980
Disbursements, long-term	847	1,001	983	911	806	302
Public and publicly guaranteed sector	4	300	102	65	210	282
Private sector not guaranteed	843	700	881	845	596	20
Principal repayments, long-term	338	281	1,220	935	551	272
Public and publicly guaranteed sector	2	76	57	26	85	20
Private sector not guaranteed	336	205	1,163	910	466	252
Interest payments, long-term	32	254	313	22	29	44
Public and publicly guaranteed sector	14	14	13	17	25	12
Private sector not guaranteed	18	240	301	5	4	31

APPENDIX

Data Sources

The principal sources of information for the tables in *International Debt Report 2023* are from the International Debt Statistics database, which is based on reports to the World Bank through the World Bank's Debtor Reporting System (DRS) from member countries that have received either International Bank for Reconstruction and Development loans or International Development Association credits. The DRS has its origin in the World Bank's need to monitor and assess the financial position of its borrowers. Since 1951, borrowers have been required to provide statistics on their public external debt and private sector debt that benefit from a public guarantee. Reporting countries submit reports on the annual status, transactions, and terms of the long-term external debt of public agencies and that of private ones guaranteed by a public agency in the debtor country. The DRS maintains these records on a loan-by-loan basis. In 1973, coverage of the DRS was expanded to include private sector nonguaranteed borrowing; however, for this category of debt, data are provided by borrowers in aggregate rather than loan by loan.

Data submitted to the DRS are processed in the World Bank External Debt system, along with additional information received from the African Development Bank, the Asian Development Bank, the European Bank for Reconstruction and Development, the Inter-American Development Bank, the International Monetary Fund, and institutions of the World Bank Group (International Bank for Reconstruction and Development and International Development Association). The World Bank External Debt is an internal system of the World Bank. Among its outputs is the International Debt Statistics database, from which the tables in this publication and the online database are produced.

Data on exports and imports (on a balance of payments basis), international reserves, current account balances, foreign direct investment on equity, portfolio equity flows, and primary income on foreign direct investment are drawn mainly from the International Monetary Fund, supplemented by United Nations Conference on Trade and Development reports and country data. Balance of payments data are presented according to the sixth edition of the International Monetary Fund's *Balance of Payments Manual*. Official aid flows come from data collected and published by the Development Assistance Committee of the Organisation for Economic Co-operation and Development. Short-term external debt data are as reported by debtor countries or are estimates based on the Bank for International Settlements quarterly series of commercial banks' claims on low- and middle-income countries. For some countries, estimates were prepared by pooling creditor and debtor information. Data on the gross national income of most low- and middle-income countries are collected from national statistical organizations or central banks by visiting and resident World Bank missions.

Every effort has been made to ensure the accuracy and completeness of the external debt statistics. Coverage has been improved through the efforts of the reporting agencies and close collaboration between the World Bank and its partners, the Commonwealth Secretariat and United Nations Conference on Trade and Development, which provide debt recording and reporting systems across the globe, as well as through the work of the World Bank missions, which visit member countries to gather data and to provide technical assistance on debt issues. Nevertheless, quality and coverage vary among debtors and may also vary for the same debtor from year to year. Data on long-term external debt reported by member countries are checked against, and supplemented by, data from several other sources. Among these sources are the statements and reports of several regional development banks, government lending agencies, and official government websites.

Country Groups

Regional Groups

East Asia and Pacific

Cambodia (A)
China (P)
Fiji (A)
Indonesia (A)
Lao PDR (A)
Mongolia (A)
Myanmar (A)
Papua New Guinea (A)
Philippines (A)
Samoa (A)
Solomon Islands (A)
Thailand (A)
Timor-Leste (A)
Tonga (A)
Vanuatu (E)
Viet Nam (A)

Europe and Central Asia

Albania (A)
Armenia (A)
Azerbaijan (A)
Belarus (E)
Bosnia and Herzegovina[a] (A)
Bulgaria (A)
Georgia (A)
Kazakhstan (A)
Kosovo (A)
Kyrgyz Republic (A)
Moldova (A)
Montenegro (A)
North Macedonia (A)
Russian Federation (E)
Serbia[a,b] (A)

Tajikistan (A)
Türkiye (A)
Turkmenistan (A)
Ukraine (A)
Uzbekistan (A)

Latin America and the Caribbean[c]

Argentina (A)
Belize (A)
Bolivia (A)
Brazil (P)
Colombia (A)
Costa Rica (A)
Dominica (A)
Dominican Republic (A)
Ecuador (A)
El Salvador (A)
Grenada (A)
Guatemala (A)
Haiti (A)
Honduras (A)
Jamaica (A)
Mexico (A)
Nicaragua (A)
Paraguay (A)
Peru (A)
St. Lucia (A)
St. Vincent and the Grenadines (A)
Suriname (E)

Middle East and North Africa

Algeria (A)
Djibouti (A)

Egypt, Arab Rep. (A)
Iran, Islamic Rep. (E)
Iraq (A)
Jordan (A)
Lebanon (A)
Morocco (A)
Syrian Arab Republic (E)
Tunisia (A)
Yemen, Rep. (E)

South Asia

Afghanistan (E)
Bangladesh (A)
Bhutan (A)
India (A)
Maldives (A)
Nepal (A)
Pakistan (A)
Sri Lanka (A)

Sub-Saharan Africa

Angola (A)
Benin (A)
Botswana (A)
Burkina Faso (A)
Burundi (A)
Cabo Verde (A)
Cameroon (A)
Central African Republic (A)
Chad (P)
Comoros (A)
Congo, Dem. Rep. (A)
Congo, Rep. (A)
Côte d'Ivoire (A)

Eritrea (E)
Eswatini (A)
Ethiopia (A)
Gabon (A)
Gambia, The (A)
Ghana (A)
Guinea (E)
Guinea-Bissau (A)
Kenya (A)
Lesotho (A)
Liberia (A)
Madagascar (A)
Malawi (A)
Mali (A)
Mauritania (A)
Mauritius (A)
Mozambique (A)
Niger (A)
Nigeria (A)
Rwanda (A)
São Tomé and Príncipe (A)
Senegal (A)
Sierra Leone (A)
Somalia (A)
South Africa (A)
Sudan (E)
Tanzania (A)
Togo (A)
Uganda (A)
Zambia (A)
Zimbabwe (A)

Source: World Bank Debtor Reporting System.
Note: Letters in parentheses indicate Debtor Reporting System reporters' status: (A) as reported, (P) preliminary, and (E) estimated. The status "as reported" indicates that the country was fully current in its reporting under the Debtor Reporting System and that World Bank staff are satisfied that the reported data give an adequate and fair representation of the country's total public debt. "Preliminary" data are based on reported or collected information; however, because of incompleteness or other reasons, an element of staff estimation is included. "Estimated" data indicate that countries are not current in their reporting and that a significant element of staff estimation has been necessary in producing the data tables.
a. For Bosnia and Herzegovina, total debt before 1999, excluding International Bank for Reconstruction and Development and International Monetary Fund obligations and short-term debt, is included under Serbia.
b. Data before 2006 include Montenegro.
c. Guyana's data are reported and included in this report because the country is eligible for International Development Association resources. However, because it is classified as a high-income country, its data are excluded from the regional aggregates.

Income Groups

Low-income countries	*Middle-income countries*		
Afghanistan	Albania	Gabon	North Macedonia
Burkina Faso	Algeria	Georgia	Pakistan
Burundi	Angola	*Ghana*	Papua New Guinea
Central African Republic	Argentina	Grenada	Paraguay
Chad	Armenia	Guatemala	Peru
Congo, Dem. Rep.	Azerbaijan	*Guinea*	Philippines
Eritrea	*Bangladesh*	*Haiti*	Russian Federation
Ethiopia	Belarus	*Honduras*	*Samoa*
Gambia, The	Belize	India	*São Tomé and Príncipe*
Guinea-Bissau	*Benin*	Indonesia	*Senegal*
Liberia	*Bhutan*	Iran, Islamic Rep.	Serbia
Madagascar	Bolivia	Iraq	*Solomon Islands*
Malawi	Bosnia and Herzegovina	Jamaica	South Africa
Mali	Botswana	Jordan	*Sri Lanka*
Mozambique	Brazil	Kazakhstan	St. Lucia
Niger	Bulgaria	Kenya	St. Vincent and the Grenadines
Rwanda	Cabo Verde	*Kosovo*	Suriname
Sierra Leone	*Cambodia*	*Kyrgyz Republic*	*Tajikistan*
Somalia	Cameroon	*Lao PDR*	*Tanzania*
Sudan	China	Lebanon	Thailand
Syrian Arab Republic	Colombia	*Lesotho*	Timor-Leste
Togo	*Comoros*	*Maldives*	*Tonga*
Uganda	Congo, Rep.	*Mauritania*	Tunisia
Yemen, Rep.	Costa Rica	Mauritius	Türkiye
	Côte d'Ivoire	Mexico	Turkmenistan
	Djibouti	Moldova	Ukraine
	Dominica	Mongolia	Uzbekistan
	Dominican Republic	Montenegro	*Vanuatu*
	Ecuador	Morocco	Viet Nam
	Egypt, Arab Rep.	*Myanmar*	*Zambia*
	El Salvador	*Nepal*	Zimbabwe
	Eswatini	*Nicaragua*	
	Fiji	Nigeria	

Source: World Bank.
Note: Low-income countries are those with a GNI per capita of US$1,135 or less in 2022. Middle-income countries are those with a GNI per capita equal to or more than US$1,136 but equal to or less than US$13,845. Italicized countries are IDA-only countries as of July 1, 2023; IDA-only excludes blend and IBRD countries. Guyana is classified as a high-income country as of July 1, 2023, so it does not appear in this table or in the low- and middle-income countries' aggregates; however, as an IDA-only country, its data are included in this report. República Bolivariana de Venezuela is unclassified according to the World Bank FY2023 income classification owing to a lack of available data; thus, it is not included in this report or the International Debt Statistics database. FY = fiscal year; GNI = gross national income; IBRD = International Bank for Reconstruction and Development; IDA = International Development Association.

Glossary

This list provides general descriptions, not precise legal definitions, of the terms commonly used in this report. However, the descriptions include legal and policy elements relevant to how these terms are understood and applied in practice.

Arrears-to-debt ratio is the ratio of principal arrears and interest arrears to total debt stock.

Bilateral official creditors are official agencies that make loans on behalf of one government to another government or to public (and, in some cases, private) borrowers in another country.

Bonds are debt instruments issued by public and publicly guaranteed or private debtors with durations of one year or longer. Bonds usually give the holder the unconditional right to fixed money income or contractually determined, variable money income.

Central bank is a country's financial institution that exercises control over key aspects of the financial system. It carries out activities such as issuing currency, managing international reserves, transacting with the International Monetary Fund, and providing credit to deposit-taking corporations.

Commitment fees are fees that a lender receives in exchange for keeping the option for the borrower to draw upon the rest of the credit at the pre-agreed rate in the future. Although commitment fees generally are dwarfed by interest costs in the case of commercial credit, they can often be a substantial cost factor for certain project loans that are drawn down more slowly.

Commitments (of public and publicly guaranteed debt) constitute the total amount of new long-term loans to public sector borrowers or borrowers with a public sector guarantee extended by official and private lenders and for which contracts were signed in the year specified.

Common Framework for debt treatment beyond the Debt Service Suspension Initiative is an initiative launched in 2022 and endorsed by the Group of Twenty, designed to support, in a structural manner, low-income countries with unsustainable debt.

Concessional debt conveys information about the borrower's receipt of aid from official lenders at concessional terms as defined by the World Bank, that is, loans with an original grant element of 35 percent or more. Loans from major regional development banks—the African Development Bank, Asian Development Bank, and Inter-American Development Bank—are classified as concessional according to World Bank classification.

Debt buyback is the repurchase by a debtor of its own debt, either at a discount price or at par value. In the event of a buyback of long-term debt, the face value of the debt bought back will be recorded as a decline in stock outstanding of long-term debt, and the cash amount received by creditors will be recorded as a principal repayment.

Debt distress, as defined under the debt sustainability framework, is caused by unsustainable debt, wherein a country is unable to fulfill its financial obligations and debt restructuring is required.

Debt outstanding and disbursed is the value at year end of long-term external debt owed by public and publicly guaranteed debtors and private nonguaranteed debtors.

Debt portfolio analysis is the first step in debt analysis and forms the basis for both the design of debt strategy and debt sustainability analysis. It typically examines the nature, composition, and structure of an existing government debt portfolio, reviewing the past trends over a given period. The prerequisites for a meaningful debt portfolio analysis are sound, comprehensive data sets and relevant debt statistics.

Debt restructurings are revisions to debt service obligations agreed on by creditors and debtors. Such agreements change the amount and timing of future principal and interest payments. Debt restructuring is a complex process that requires the agreement of domestic and foreign creditors and involves burden sharing between different parties (for example, between residents and banks in most domestic restructurings).

Debt service is the sum of principal repayments and interest paid on total long-term debt (public and publicly guaranteed debt and private nonguaranteed debt).

Debt service to exports is the ratio of the sum of principal repayments and interest paid on total long-term debt (public and publicly guaranteed debt and private nonguaranteed debt) to the value of exports of goods and services and receipts of primary income from abroad.

Debt stock-flow reconciliation is the process of explaining the change in the stock position in a period with the comprehensive recording of transactions and other economic flows that allows a full integration of economic flows and stock positions from one period to the next.

Debt sustainability is the condition under which a country (or its government) does not, in the future, need to default or renegotiate or restructure its debt, or make implausibly large policy adjustments.

Debt swap (conversion) is an exchange of debt—typically at a discount—for a nondebt claim (such as equity) or for counterpart funds that can be used to finance a particular project or policy. In essence, public sector debt is extinguished and a nondebt liability created in a debt conversion.

Debt transparency results in readily available data on public debt, allowing governments to make informed decisions about macroeconomic policy and debt sustainability.

Disbursements are drawings during the year specified on loan commitments contracted by the borrower.

Domestic revenue mobilization is the process through which countries raise and spend their own funds to provide for their populations.

ESG investing is defined as the consideration of environmental, social, and governance (ESG) factors alongside financial factors in the investment decision-making process.

External debt flows are debt-related transactions during the year specified. They include disbursements, principal repayments, and interest payments.

External debt stocks comprise public and publicly guaranteed long-term external debt, private nonguaranteed long-term external debt, use of International Monetary Fund credit and special drawing rights allocation, and short-term external debt.

External debt stocks to exports is the ratio of outstanding external debt to the value of exports of goods and services and receipts of primary income from abroad.

External debt stocks to GNI is the ratio of outstanding external debt to gross national income (GNI).

Fiscal sustainability refers to the future implications of current fiscal policies and, more precisely, to the question of whether the government can continue to pursue its set of budgetary policies without endangering its solvency.

Foreign direct investment refers to direct investment equity flows in the reporting economy. It is the sum of equity capital, reinvestment earnings, and other capital. Direct investment is a category of cross-border investment associated with a resident in one economy having control or a significant degree of influence on the management of an enterprise that is resident in another economy. Ownership of 10 percent or more of the ordinary shares or voting stock is the criterion for determining the existence of a direct investment relationship.

Government sector debt consists of all external debt obligations of all levels of the government and its departments, branches, agencies, foundations, institutes, nonmarket and nonprofit institutions controlled by the government, and other publicly controlled organizations engaging in nonmarket activities.

Grace period is the time between the date on which a loan is committed and the date on which the first principal payment is due. The information presented in the International Debt Statistics database is the average grace period on all public and publicly guaranteed debt committed during the specified period.

Grants are legally binding commitments that obligate a specific value of funds available for disbursement for which there is no payment requirement. They include debt forgiveness grants and grants from bilateral and multilateral agencies (such as the International Development Association).

Green bonds are bonds that finance green projects and provide investors with regular or fixed income payments.

Green investments refer to the allocation of financial resources to projects or companies that focus on sustainable practices, environmentally friendly technologies, and the conservation of natural resources.

Gross national income is the sum of value added by all resident producers, plus any product taxes (less subsidies) not included in the valuation of output, plus net receipts of primary income compensation of employees and property income from abroad. Yearly average exchange rates are used to convert gross national income from local currency to US dollars.

IDA-eligible countries are the countries that are eligible to receive International Development Association (IDA) resources. Eligibility for IDA support depends on a country's relative poverty, defined as gross national income per capita below an established threshold, which is updated annually.

Imports of goods, services, and primary income constitute the total value of goods and services imported and income payable to nonresidents.

Interest arrears are due and payable immediately and are therefore regarded as short-term obligations. Thus, an increase in interest arrears on long-term debt will be recorded as an increase in short-term debt. Interest in arrears on the use of International Monetary Fund credit is also considered to be part of short-term external debt.

Interest payments are the amounts of interest paid in foreign currency, goods, or services in the year specified.

Interest rate is the interest rate applicable to a loan commitment as specified in the loan contract. The information presented in the International Debt Statistics database is the average interest on all public and publicly guaranteed debt committed during the specified period.

International reserves constitute the sum of a country's monetary authority's holdings of special drawing rights, its reserve position in the International Monetary Fund, its holdings of foreign exchange, and its holdings of gold (valued at year-end London prices).

Lender of last resort is an institution, often a multilateral creditor or a country's central bank, that offers loans to banks or other eligible institutions that are experiencing financial difficulty or are considered highly risky or near collapse. Loans from such lenders can happen in periods of financial turmoil, when banks may have doubts about lending to each other and depositors may suddenly seek to withdraw their money from their bank account.

Long-term external debt is debt that has an original or extended maturity of more than one year and that is owed to nonresidents by residents of an economy and is repayable in currency, goods, or services.

Maturity is the date on which the final principal repayment on a loan is due. It is the sum of the grace and repayment periods. The information presented in the International Debt Statistics database is the average maturity on all public and publicly guaranteed debt committed during the specified period.

Monetary policy is used by central banks to manage economic fluctuations and achieve price stability, with low and stable inflation. Central banks conduct monetary policy by adjusting the supply of money, usually through buying or selling securities in the open market. When central banks lower interest rates, monetary policy is easing. When they raise interest rates, monetary policy is tightening.

Multilateral official creditors are official agencies owned or governed by more than one country that provide loan financing. They include international financial institutions such as the World Bank, regional development banks, and other intergovernmental agencies.

Multilateral to external debt stock is the ratio of the stock of debt owed to multilateral creditors to total external debt.

Net debt flow is gross disbursements less principal payments.

Nonconcessional debt refers to loans with a market-based interest rate and substantially less generous terms than concessional loans.

Official creditors are governments or other bilateral public entities (such as export-import agencies or development agencies) and multilateral financial institutions (such as the World Bank and regional development banks).

Paris Club is an informal group of official creditors whose role is to find coordinated and sustainable solutions to the payment difficulties experienced by debtor countries. Paris Club creditors provide appropriate debt treatment as debtor countries undertake reforms to stabilize and restore their macroeconomic and financial situations.

Portfolio equity is the category of international investment that refers to portfolio equity inflows and covers investment in equity securities. Equity securities include shares, stocks, participation, or similar documents (such as US depositary receipts) that usually denote ownership of equity.

Present value of debt outstanding is the nominal value of all future debt service obligations on existing debt discounted at prevailing market rates of interest. The interest rates used in this calculation are the Commercial Interest Reference Rates for each relevant currency compiled and published by the Organisation for Economic Co-operation and Development.

Primary income on FDI (foreign direct investment) are payments of direct investment income (debit side), which consist of income on equity (dividends, branch profits, and reinvested earnings) and income on the intercompany debt (interest).

Principal repayments are the amounts of principal (amortization) paid in currency, goods, or services in the year specified with respect to long-term external debt.

Private creditors are bondholders, commercial banks, and other trade-related lenders.

Private nonguaranteed debt is debt owed by private sector borrowers to external creditors on loans that do not benefit from a public sector guarantee by the debtor country.

Public and publicly guaranteed debt comprises public debt (an external obligation of a public debtor, such as the general government or agency, the central bank, a political subdivision or agency, or an autonomous public body) and publicly guaranteed external debt (an external obligation of a private debtor that is guaranteed for repayment by a public entity).

Public debt is an external obligation of a public debtor, including all levels of government, the central bank, state-owned enterprises, public corporations, development banks, and any other autonomous public bodies of government.

Renegotiated loan is a loan that is modified by the lender before its full repayment. Debt renegotiation is therefore the process of paying a debt over a longer period than originally agreed or paying back less than the original debt. Its primary purpose is to make it easier for the borrower to sustain timely payments as well as ensure that the lender is eventually paid.

Repurchase agreement/loan is a transaction in which the borrower temporarily lends a security to the lender for cash with an agreement to buy it back in the future at a predetermined price. Ownership of the security does not change hands in a repurchase transaction. For this reason, these agreements are treated as collateralized loans.

SDR allocations are reserve-related liabilities, distributed to member countries in proportion to their quota shares at the International Monetary Fund. The SDR (special drawing rights) allocations are included in the gross external debt position and classified as long-term, special drawing rights.

Short-term external debt has an original maturity of one year or less. Available data permit no distinctions among public, publicly guaranteed, and private nonguaranteed short-term external debt.

Sovereign credit ratings indicate the capacity and willingness of rated governments to repay commercial debt obligations in full and on time.

Sukuk bonds, also known as Islamic bonds, are investment certificates issued by Islamic financial institutions to obtain funding. A distinguishing feature of Sukuk is that the holders are entitled to share revenues generated by the Sukuk assets and are entitled to a share of the proceeds of the realization of Sukuk assets.

Syndicated loan is a type of loan that is granted by a group of lenders to a single borrower. The lenders work together to provide a large sum of money to the borrower, which the borrower then uses for a specific purpose such as financing a major project or refinancing existing debt.

Use of IMF credit denotes members' drawings on the International Monetary Fund (IMF) other than amounts drawn against the country's reserve tranche position. Use of IMF credit includes purchases and drawings under Stand-By, Extended, Structural Adjustment, Enhanced Structural Adjustment, and Systemic Transformation Facility Arrangements as well as trust fund loans.